About The Author

Ian Wishart is an award-winning journalist and author, with a 29 year career in radio, television and magazines, a #1 talk radio show and five #1 bestselling books to his credit. Together with his wife Heidi, they edit and publish the news magazine *Investigate*.

Dedicated to the memory of Chris Arepa
& Cru Omeka
20 March 2006 - 18 June 2006

"I am the Alpha and the Omega, the First and the Last,
the Beginning and the End"
— REV. 22:13

BREAKING
SILENCE

THE KAHUI CASE

Ian Wishart

HOWLING AT THE MOON PUBLISHING LTD

First edition published 2011
Howling At The Moon Publishing Ltd
PO Box 188, Kaukapakapa
Auckland 0843, NEW ZEALAND

www.howlingatthemoon.com
email: editorial@investigatemagazine.com
Copyright © Ian Wishart 2011
Copyright © Howling At The Moon Publishing Ltd, 2011

ISBN 978-0-9876573-0-5

Typeset in Adobe Garamond Pro and Folio
Cover concept: Ian Wishart, Heidi Wishart, Bozidar Jokanovic
Book Design: Bozidar Jokanovic
Cover image: Ian Wishart
Interview transcription: Melissa Wishart

To get another copy of this book airmailed to you anywhere in the world, or to purchase a fully text-searchable digital edition, visit our website:
WWW.HOWLINGATTHEMOON.COM

Contents

Introduction

What you are about to read has been described as the most controversial book ever published in New Zealand.

It wasn't supposed to be. But news sent to the book trade of the future release of *Breaking Silence* was leaked to the news media by an over-eager bookshop in late June. Within 48 hours, a Facebook community page had been 'liked' by nearly 50,000 people, demanding that bookshops ban this book from their shelves or face a consumer boycott of their entire stores, not just the book.

No one had seen it. No one knew for sure, or even had a good guess, precisely what was in it. It was the biggest, swiftest overreaction to a book that had not even been printed yet, in the history of New Zealand. Opposition leader Phil Goff and Police Minister Judith Collins both waded in on boycotting the book, even though neither of them had read it.

Across New Zealand, and then via social networks into Australia, the US and Europe, people were talking, arguing even, about the merits of banning a book none of them had read. Ironically, the answers many of the boycotters professed to want are in these pages.

It must be a world first in literature, the ultimate example of judging a book by its cover, because there was nothing else to judge it by. Now, that's changed. As you turn the pages a story will unfold. Some of you will be wondering "who" murdered the Kahui twins, and that is indeed a question we attempt to address by the end of the book. But the "who" is specific to this case only. If we are to learn anything about child abuse, the real question is "why?"

And the next question after that is, how do we recognise and intervene more successfully and sensitively before things have gone too far?

That's the journey I want this book to take you on, because the "why" is common to so many child abuse cases. Everyone thinks they know why child abuse happens, and everyone thinks it happens in someone else's family situation.

And if you believe this book has nothing to offer, consider the argument that went down at the Coronial investigation into the deaths of Chris and Cru Kahui.

Chris Kahui's lawyer Chris Wilkinson-Smith tried to argue strongly at the recent inquest that Macsyna King's childhood, upbringing and background is fundamental to deciding whether she is, or is not, someone likely to have harmed the twins. He wanted the right to ask her questions about her past.

Coroner Evans said those issues might well be relevant and important to the bigger picture, but the narrow rules of the Coroner's Act prevent him from taking the investigation in that direction.

"It may have some relevance...but I am not empowered to have regard to what has gone on in the past with Ms King. This is not a criminal prosecution, it is an inquiry which is required to be carried out in accordance with the strict legislative parameters that I am enjoined to have regard to."

Readers of *Breaking Silence* are in the box seat to discover what lawyers, investigators, judicial officials and social workers have been desperate to do but can't: Macsyna King's story in her own words.

Walk in Macsyna King's shoes for a while, live her life as it unfolds in these pages, and ponder the choices she made that could have gone either way. King lays bare the darkest depths of her life, and in doing so shows the chilling reality of existence in many New Zealand homes. She tells a story that is personal, yet generic. There are thousands of houses around this country where similar stories exist right now. You may be living in one yourself, you may recognise your life in these pages. You might seek help from one of the agencies listed at the back of this book.

Many of you probably think you'd heard all about the Kahui case that you need to know. You've made that judgement based on news reports in the papers and on TV and radio. As I said in an *NZ Herald* Q&A, I can't criticise my fellow journalists on this story - the complexities and nuances of it have been too difficult to cover in a 600 word news article or 90 second TV news story.

As journalists we hit what we think are the main points and leave readers largely to guess the bits between the lines. The Kahui story has suffered because of that - a huge mythology has built around this case based on early Chinese whispers leaked from within the police or hospitals, or from various family factions, and frequently wrong.

While most of those errors were long ago corrected at trial, many people and particularly many Facebookers were trying to argue with me about the case using information that was five years out of date. This book will fix that. We should not still be having those arguments, because they are a barrier to understanding the case.

On that note, a couple of acknowledgments to Justice Venning who presided in the High Court criminal trial of Chris Kahui, and to Coroner Garry Evans who presided over the inquest, for making available the transcripts of evidence I requested, and to an un-named forensic doctor for providing a specialist's perspective.

This book is not intended to supplant the Coroner's report. Where it offers fresh evidence that evidence may or may not be relevant to the Inquest. Where I came across a conflict of evidence, I alerted Counsel Assisting the Coroner as I believed it was my duty to do. The weight attached to that is properly a matter for the Coroner.

There are two strands to *Breaking Silence*. One is Macsyna's narrative that begins the story. It is autobiographical in nature, and reflects her life seen through her eyes. As the story moves into the Kahui phase a different perspective emerges – mine as investigative journalist. Macsyna's becomes one voice among many as evidential lines are tested, and the threads of a depositions hearing, a double murder trial and latterly an inquest are compared then woven together.

Coroner Evans had one final piece of advice for Chris Kahui's lawyer after ruling that Macsyna King's past was out of bounds:

"Now, you may cross-examine, of course, Mr Wilkinson-Smith, as you may but if I find that any of the questions fall outside my purview then, of course, I will have to tell you so. Now, carry on, if you would..."

And so, this story dedicated to the memory of two boys who became symbols of the child abuse debate, Chris and Cru, begins.

CHAPTER ONE

Alpha

Wairoa. Say the name and it conjures up different emotions for different people. For some, it's the small East Coast township with the lazy blue river winding through it to the sea, where the sunrise hits the beach before practically anywhere else on earth. For others, Wairoa is the place where the Black Power holds one riverbank, and the Mongrel Mob rules the other, a place where people have been shot in driveby's whilst filling their car with petrol at a service station.

In recent times there's been a big drop in crime as the town licks its gang problem, but for 19 year old Faith Tahuri in 1976, it was the town where a pretty girl looking helpless on the roadside with car trouble could get the attention of a passer-by like Mac Mehaka King. Whether you'd want King's attention is a different matter. A gang associate with a long criminal history, Mac was twice the girl's age – old enough to be her father. Throw in his glass eye – a replacement for one lost to a softball-bat beating – and he wasn't exactly Brad Pitt. Nonetheless, Mac held some basic charms that a small-town girl might find appealing – a stranger, hailing from the big smoke – Auckland far to the north – and quite obviously a bad boy.

Mac eyed the damsel up and down, taking in her own charms in one sweeping instant. Something of a backyard mechanic, as most kiwi males were in the seventies, he quickly had her motor running.

"I'm going to a 21st. Wanna come?"

Somewhere in a darkened bedroom in a Wairoa gang house, with the disco beats blaring from the record player in the lounge, Mac found Faith that night. Hope, on the other hand, was about to abandon Faith…

My story begins in the small East Coast settlement of Wairoa. The story, as my Mum told it, is that she met my father in Wairoa.

Faith Tahuri was her name, although everyone called her 'Missy'. Part Ngati Kahungunu and part Tuhoe – a daughter of the Mist. Dad was Ngapuhi. Pig headed, would cut off his nose to spite his face. They went to a party, where Mum and Dad got together and conceived me.

Mac returned to Auckland after the party, and Faith continued living in Wairoa with my great-grandmother. She rings him around about six months later and says, "ah, look, I'm pregnant." And he does turn up eventually, but, I'm told, when he did I was almost ready to come into the world.

He turned up on the doorstep where Mum was living. "Righty-o, I'll do the right thing by you". He had driven all the way down from Auckland, and decided to take her back there to have the baby even though she'd begun having labour pains. So he picked my mum up and together they began the long roadtrip back to Auckland. Towards the end of the journey she yelled out, "I'm going to have the baby! I can feel the baby coming!", so instead of going to his home first, Mac drove her straight to Middlemore Hospital. It was the funniest thing.

So I was born on 22nd of February 1977 at Middlemore Hospital. They named me Macsyna Pono King. Macsyna after my dad Mac, Pono as the Maori word for my mother's name, Faith, and King. They got married just a short time after the birth, to make it all legitimate.

Mum and Dad took me home, and it was the first time Mum had actually seen his house. He lived in Mangere, had his own home at 19 Harania Avenue. He'd been previously married and separated at the time of meeting my mum. They celebrated the birth and the marriage with a huge party – it was the first time his family had ever met Mum. And he had a big family. My father was the youngest in his family, and there's something like 15 years between him and his next oldest brother, and there's 12 of them in total.

Dad never knew his own dad, though. Apparently after he was conceived, his own father died three months or so before he was born.

Early in their marriage, it was clear Mac's basic instincts weren't changing. He continued to get into trouble with the law, often for violent crime flowing from his drinking. Twenty-year-old Faith often took to the bottle too, leaving baby Macsyna in the hands of nine-year-old sister Fiona – the oldest girl of Mac's three children from his first marriage. Macsyna has only fleeting memories of her earliest years…

One of my earliest memories was being three or four years old, and Uncle Joe died. He was child number seven in the line of the King children, so he was an older brother to my father. Uncle Joe was deeply religious, a really big-as guy but he was known for having a big heart. I remember his tangi at Taheke, which is a tiny settlement in Northland, on the road between Opononi and Kaikohe. My father had a red XY Falcon station wagon and we actually carried my uncle's body up to Taheke, and the only reason I remember it is because my father drove, my oldest half-brother was in front, my second oldest half-sister Denise was in between, and I was sitting on her lap and behind me was my Uncle Joe's coffin. It was as wide as the station wagon and really deep because he was a big man, and I remember the road just winding away in front of us and the car just eating it up on that trip as we took Joe to his resting place.

After my birth in 1977, my sister Emily came along in 1979, Stuart was born in 1981 and my baby sister Ellen arrived in 1983, so there was a two year gap between each of us.

Dad was in and out of work during this time. He seemed to have a job and hold it down for a couple of months or so and then drop out of it. He worked at Hellaby's meat processing – I think they still make corned beef – it was one of the main works before AFFCO freezing works came along. So he worked at Hellaby's and he also worked at Pacific Steel which is about ten minutes down the road from Harania Ave where he lived and where I grew up.

Dad also did curb laying and excavation work because his oldest brother was in that business, he had excavating machinery and started out learning with one of the big contractors. They bulldozed and laid roads and bricks and my father had those many skills that I know of. And he just seemed to go in and out of jobs. But for the most part he was – that I learnt later – on a sickness benefit and collecting any family benefit dollars that he earned from myself and my three siblings.

Although he'd been in and out of prison, around the home Dad did not tolerate drugs. Cannabis was never allowed in the house, even at parties. The only thing he'd light is a hangi, or a cigarette, and he was really violent and staunch about that. Drinking, yes, plenty of drinking. Tuesday or Wednesday nights and Fridays and Saturdays.

When people get drunk, they go two ways. You can get the happy drunk, or the violent drunk. Dad was both. When he was drunk, he was kinder to me. However, when he was drunk he was more violent towards my mum and my older half-brothers and sisters. But to me and my youngers, when he was drunk, he was kinder. I still don't figure that out, don't want to even bother trying but that's just how he was.

> If you believe the stories told by Mac King's side of the family, Faith was a terrible mother "who once left all of [her children] in an Onehunga bus-stop, telling them to wait, but never came back."[1] That's the version that the news media carried, but that's not the last time a young Macsyna saw her mother – the truth is far more gruesome...

One night, after Dad had got drunk, I remember waking up in the darkness to sounds from my mum. I could hear a kind of gurgling coming from their room, which was right next to mine and I slept up against their bedroom wall.

I woke up in a bit of a panic, like when you're in a deep sleep and get shocked out of it, and all I could hear was this gurgling and spittling sound coming from my mother. She's asking for help, crying out help in a really strange voice. I get up, get out of my bunk bed and walk out of the bedroom, walk just around the corner to my mum's bedroom and find my mum pinned underneath my dad. He was lying on top of her naked, he's obviously had – now that I'm an adult I understand that he must have had his way sexually. I don't know to what extent but in any case they're naked and my mum's pinned under my dad and her eye, cause she was quite young and beautiful compared to my dad, she was twenty years younger than him. But she looked horrible.

She's bruised, she's got blood coming out of the corner of her mouth and her nose is just swollen and like a chopped off golf ball. She'd been badly beaten before my father passed out having sex with her. She's naked, and only her head and her left arm and shoulder

---

1 "Macsyna's World", NZ Herald, May 24 2008

are sticking out from under my father, because he was three times her size and they're on their bed. So I go to my mum and help her wriggle herself out of my dad, and then she asks me to get her the phone on the side table.

Dad was just snoring his ass off, he was totally out to it and he reeked of alcohol.

Mum rings a taxi and grabs a nightgown to cover her nakedness, then she finds another blanket and puts me in it and waits out the front of the house for the taxi to get there.

I don't know why – but Mum didn't wake up the other children and bring them with us. Ellen would have been only a baby, but she left her behind along with Ems and Stuart. There were just the two of us – Faith and me – standing out in the cold darkness on the roadside, waiting silently.

The taxi driver turns up. He's an Islander, and he takes one look at my mum and just opens the back door of the car, picks her up and lifts her in there. Then he just lifts me up, closes my mum's door, walks around the back, puts me right beside my mum in the back seat and he just takes us straight to the hospital. My mum hasn't even spoken to him. All she did was pick up the phone and ask for a taxi to 19 Harania Ave in Mangere. The driver figured out just by looking at Mum that she needed medical attention. When we got to hospital the nurses were already there to meet us. They still wore those funny hat things and the matron still wore that star thingy and watch on the other pinny. White shoes and white uniform, hat and white cardigan over her shoulders, that's what I remember of her. Anyway they take mum into the hospital and I can't really recall how long we were there.

After a while a nurse comes out. "You know your mum's really, really hurt, really badly, but we're going to take care of her, and we're really lucky that we got her here when we did."

The nurse just comforts me, and I remember she gave me a drink – Just Juice – and read me a story. I think I fell asleep in her arms or whatever cause I was asleep on her lap with a pillow under my head, just outside my mum's room and I wake up to all this noise. My old man's in the ward and he's going at the matron and she's going "no I'm not letting you through the doors." He's pushing her around, he's just swearing his head off at her, "Get the eff out of my way, that's my f***ing wife," and "that's my daughter, I don't care what you do to my wife but that's my daughter and she's coming with me." And all that sort of stuff.

It's all going down, and I'm standing up on the seat and I'm freaking out like crazy. I just ran into my mum's room and grabbed her hand and just screamed at Mum, "Please don't let me go, don't let me go with him, I don't want to go, I want to stay with you." But it wasn't to be, it wasn't to be.

My father came storming in behind me and made so much of a deal. He had two male orderlies on his arms, along with matron and three nurses, and the police were on their way. We could hear the sirens but my dad was in a rage and just not stopping, and all these people were just getting smashed about in the ward like rag-dolls. Some nurses were trying to protect me as my father tried to grab me, but I just flew out of their arms and ran back out of my mum's room and screamed to them, "Nah, just please, just stop – I'll just go with my dad and it'll stop."

He just picked me up, walked out and I just cried my eyes out, and the matron just stood in horror, watching as my dad's storming out like a giant wreaking havoc. Because back in the day they had big double doors something like every five metres, and he just swung through them like they were matchwood, with me under his arm. I remember they were green. Green with speckles of white up the wall halfway and a little beading halfway up the wall and then one painted colour, that's what I remember the ward looking like.

That was the last time that I would see Mum for years, really. She never went back to Dad after she came out of hospital. Mum and I went to the hospital; Dad and I went home. Mum never ever came back home with us after that.

The only words he ever spoke of her after that, he once told me, "She had the voice of an angel, talented-as with her hands, heart of gold, but a stubborn little bitch" – that's what he said about Mum.

She was beautiful, and he loved my mum. I really believe he truly loved my mum. When he talked of her – and it was only a few times – there was always a look on his face, in his eyes, of hurt, despair, loss. Like when you go to a tangi, you say farewell to someone you love or knew very well but it's just their time to pass. My dad, whenever he talked of my mother, he always had that look in his eye. He always seemed to really regret not being with my mum any longer.

It's weird, because I know he beat her to a pulp when he was with her. I've spoken to many family members and all that. Those that were on my dad's side that hated my mum, as well as those who loved my mum and hated my dad. The one thing they agreed on was that Dad was really brutal with my mum. She was really gullible, full of heart and meant well, but never really made good decisions. Dad, always headstrong and never really thought of the consequences, like a bull at a gate. Those are the memories that I have.

When we got back to the house from the hospital, the three youngest were waiting for us. They'd all been left alone together when Dad came out to the hospital. As best I can remember, I was six when all this happened, but I hadn't started school. Dad kept me back to help look after baby Ellen. I fed and nursed Ellen from a really young age.

I started school at Favona Primary later that year as I recall, but it wasn't easy. Dad left supervision of the three younger kids to me. If the younger kids were out of sight they were out of mind. If they cried louder than he liked it he would come in and check on me. If I was cooking and they were crying because they were hungry and waiting, he'd be a bit lenient. If they were crying because I was doing nothing or hadn't given a shit – or he *thought* I didn't give a shit – I'd get a hiding. So it would just depend on his mood and what sort of situation it was when he walked in.

Depending on the offence, Dad would hit me with a belt, a jug cord, the end of a hammer, a strap, gumboots, steel-capped boots, and he sometimes punched me closed-fisted.

A slap on the ears was good, compared with the other options. I'd get one of those just because he asked me to grab something and I was too slow, and he might just lightly backhand me or open hand slap my ear, but not too hard. But if I wasn't there when he called, I'd get a mean-as slap on the ears, "You f***ing open your ears, you f***ing listen to me! I don't care what time it is, I don't care if you were asleep. You f***ing answer me and you f***ing wake up!" That was my dad's way.

His meanest slap had a particular technique that made it devastating. If you hold your palm in front of you and then slightly cup your hand, so that it forms a little bit of a cup like you're going to catch water with it, then put that over your ear, that's how he'd slap our ears and I swear we would be deaf for like a couple of hours, the ringing would just last in our ears. They were pretty severe.

CHAPTER TWO

The Chicken Plucker

So I was balancing my home responsibilities with starting school, and my attendance at primary school was really poor. I'd spend weeks at home and go to school for another couple of weeks and then I'd be off school again for about a month.

As a result of all the disruption, I was well behind the other kids. Swimming, music and sports activities were not a problem, but reading and maths were definitely the worst subjects for me because I just had no idea. I had absolutely no idea. I don't know how I winged it I just know that I never got it, I never understood it, it always confused me.

I was teased heaps and always picked on. There weren't many people who'd play with me at lunchtime. I didn't have a lot of friends. Part of the problem was my family was poor. I always wore the same clothes to school and the other children would laugh at me.

To get the full sense of just how bad this was, I was going to Favona School in Mangere. This wasn't Remuera. It's not like the other kids were rolling in money. It's just that the King family was rolling in less of it than anyone else.

I was always being pushed over by the cool kids, so I just tried to avoid them. I found that if I stayed a distance from them and took my time dawdling to school, then I wouldn't get teased on the way there. So I suppose I ducked, dived and avoided as hard as I could and that would make my day bearable.

They say South Auckland kids grow up tough, but I discovered that I actually cried quite easily. I cried if I was teased, I cried if I was angry, I cried if I couldn't get anything. I remember one time I cried so hard, I was in Favona Primary School and my teacher was growling me for not listening, and I started crying so much that I weed my pants in class. I pissed my pants in class. Oh man, I just ran home. And I think I didn't go to school for like two months after that! By that time everybody had gotten over teasing me and they weren't allowed to tease me.

There were a few girls who treated me kindly. Rayna Jacobs, Melissa Te Moananui and Karmen Turu come to mind, but that's probably it. They were just nice girls, and they never ever teased me. They didn't have any problems being my friends, whenever I could catch up with them, or I was allowed to play with them. Because generally Dad wouldn't let me play with my friends, we weren't allowed to go and play at parks or any of that sort of thing. He just didn't like us going anywhere without him. "Can we go play down at the park, Dad?" "No." "Can I go over next door and play with my friends?" "No." It was just no. Just stay home.

Now that I'm older, I wonder if it was because Dad was lonely. He didn't like to be alone. This refusal to let us kids out of the house had nothing to do with chores, because the house was always spotless. We were not permitted to leave it filthy or dirty or chores undone. We had to do our chores before we went to school and he didn't care if we were late. So it wasn't to do extra chores and it wasn't really to help him with anything in regards to his personal health. He had asthma. Really really bad, but he managed that with his inhaler and his Prednisone steroids medication.

By the time I was seven I could cook three course meals. Emily could make a pita bread, a flat bread and boil eggs and make toast and do hot cups of tea. Emily would have beenb five, and Stuart and Ellen three and one. We had to always put them near us so that they wouldn't cry and get hit, while Emily and I did the chores. The babies just sat there watching us and learning from what we did.

Dad had a couple of gardens that were about 15 metres long, rose gardens. They were weeded every day and we'd have to always do the dishes, cook our own meals, do the washing, sweep the floors, then mop them, do the edges of the lawn and I had to mow the lawns. We kids had to stack the firewood. Sometimes Dad would buy chicken for dinner, and I had to prepare it. This was no super-market chicken – these ones would still be crowing as Dad walked down the driveway with them. I don't know if you've ever seen a chicken plucked but I was given the job from the age of six.

First, you have to chop the head off, and then wait until they stopped flopping around on the ground, and then dunk them in this big 44 gallon drum of hot boiling water, and then pull them out of the water and onto a trailer and start plucking the chicken. So we did things like that.

We'd get visits from the Truant Officers when we didn't go to school. "You need to be in school!", they'd warn me. And then Dad comes out there to the driveway. He'd go out the back door and he'd be cursing and swearing at them, "What the eff are you doing? Get the hell out of my property!" If they didn't back out of the gate as he was walking to them like that, and they, unfortunately for them, let him get close enough, he would clout them over the head. He'd punch them, he'd attack them.

My teachers would come sometimes, and they'd stay at the gate because they knew what sort of man he was. Dad would whack our bums at school in front of the whole entire school and he would never ever care, and that would be because we never came home early. He told us to leave school at one o'clock and we'd explain, "Well, we can't just leave, we have to have a note", and he'd go "No, I'm your boss, you don't need no note from anybody. And you just walk out of your class at one o'clock". As if we could do that at five, six or seven years' old! So we'd get a beating in front of the school at 3pm when the bell rang, and no one did anything about it.

So sometimes even my teachers would come to the gate. They'd dare not come up the driveway. And they'd plead with Dad, "Look, please can we just talk to you? Max is a really good student, we'd like to keep her learning." And he'd just attack. And they'd leave. But they never ever, nobody ever went further than that. They stopped coming, after a while. But they would never ever call the police to help them. That never ever came.

The front gate should have had a sign hanging off it, "Beware of the Dad".

He refused to pay for school exercise books or stationery, so one time I stole some money from the petty cash jar for me, my brother and sister, and I knew he would know because he counted every penny. Dad would write the total on a piece of paper and stick it to the jar, and every time he took money out, he'd count it out again and re-total. But I was just sick of us not having anything for school and it was the beginning of the year so we were getting our books for the first time. I didn't care about the theft from the cash jar. I really didn't care. I knew that I was going to wear it. And I did. And I wasn't allowed to go to school for two weeks, but still it was worth it. I'd been to school for about three years, and every year, not even a pencil. Every year we'd get a letter sent home with the list of stationery, and every year my father would go down and say to Ron Bacon, the Principal, "Don't F –ing tell me I've got to pay for this, this is free education. You get my name off that bill and don't you ever send me one again."

When they realised what they were dealing with, the school gave us pencils and books anyway.

Living at Harania Ave, I quickly learned to become afraid of the dark. Often I'd hear my father beating up my aunties and my uncles who were partying with him and it went wrong over one silly thing and he'd get offended. We weren't allowed to turn the lights on or anything, we had to just stay in the darkness.

They were getting dragged by the hair out the driveway at the end of the day and he'd have a sledgehammer in his hand sometimes. He'd attack their cars. We've seen him smash back windscreens, front windscreens, side panels of the old mudguards on those old, solid cars, my uncle had a Kingswood. That got wasted. Those were some real upsetting things that were going on at night and I was a young child and would see it and hear it. The police never came. Everyone was too scared of my dad to call police.

With Mum gone, other women started to show up. I remember a Jane, a Tilly, and maybe three he didn't introduce to us. Jane was blonde with blue eyes, she was beautiful. Then he met a lady named Mary who became a stepmum to us for a while, moved in with us. She was a widow herself and had five children that I met – one girl and four boys – who all came and lived in the house as well. We had a three bedroom house.

When they started their relationship there was drinking every second or third night. If she was sober, she was the kindest person you could meet, a good heart and very compassionate. But when drunk, a real bitch, a true bitch. Dad, on the other hand, was a dickhead, a real bastard to me when he was sober, but when he got pissed he became good, careful and kind-hearted. I never ever got a hiding once, when my dad was drunk.

Looking back now, I actually preferred it when Dad was drinking, in all honesty. Because it was a time for me to relax. I didn't have to be on edge, I didn't have to be listening out just in case Dad called me and I missed it. I didn't have to worry about falling off to sleep and then him calling me, and not hearing him. When he drank, he never tried to call out to us or catch me out. When he got drunk I didn't have to be so on guard, on key, listening out for it.

Mary's personality, on the other hand, would change horribly when she was drunk. She was a real egg. She'd say to me, "F***en hell Mac, always got to worry about Number One, eh?"

Dad would hear her and go "what?", and she'd start yelling at him, "Whenever you want something you call out to your daughter". He called me 'papa'. It doesn't just mean dad but it's also a term of endearment. He never told me why he called me that but I understand, now. He called me papa for sentimental value. She'd go off if he yelled that out to me. Sometimes he'd call out to me when they'd been on the piss for six hours or so, "Come out here, say good night to everybody, give us a kiss, I love you, lock the house up and go to bed".

If he said that when Mary was drunk she'd go off her face, man. She'd call Dad an idiot, she'd accuse him of having an eye for his own daughter. "Why do you ask your daughter to come and say goodnight to you? Do you want her to kiss you like I can't kiss you? Why don't you kiss me?", and those are the sorts of things she would say. At the time I didn't really get it, but now I think about her words I think what a drunken idiot. I have compassion for her, because she was obviously too drunk to know what she was saying, but I was only 8 or 9 and it made me feel stink and it rarked my dad up. He'd end up giving her a crack, and they'd end up on pretty bad terms for a good week or so.

To me it seemed she was picking fights.

Once you got close to my father, once you got in the gate, he would trust you implicitly. He'd let you see his children, he'd talk freely as he normally talked and wouldn't put up a mask or try to act good in front of people. Once he trusted you, you could see him for all that he was and all that he did, and he never tried to hide it.

Mary knew how to set him off. She knew his triggers and his weak points and his sore points, and depending on what kind of mood she was in and how drunk she was, she'd push him.

But it wasn't only Mac that Mary was pushing. She saw the child Macsyna as a threat, and seized the opportunity to stick the knife in, as a manner of speaking, one night after the ten year old had been given a hiding…

I was in my first year of intermediate school, attending Arahanga Intermediate in Mangere. One night my father went out and left me and Emily and our two younger siblings at home with Mary. And I was crying, I was crying in my bedroom because dad had just given me a bit of a hiding. I can't remember what for now, but I was in my room, crying and holding onto my pillow, and Mary walks in.

"I think you should run away. I think what you should do is take whatever you need to take, and keep warm and run away. Otherwise this is the life that you're going to live for the rest of your life."

I didn't even get along with her, and I knew she didn't like me, but when she said that I thought about it for maybe five minutes, then stood up from my bed – I shared the room with my sister Emily and we had those old iron bunks that belong in the army. I grabbed a jumper and a skirt, chucked them in a bag and got on my bike and I did – I ran away.

Outside it was dark, and stormy to boot. The young girl, sobbing, pedalled as hard as she could down Harania Ave and onto the main road. She didn't know where she was going and frankly didn't care. Her mother had evidently abandoned her, now the man who called her 'papa' had beaten her once too often, and her stepmother had told her to go and never come back. She didn't stop until the rain grew too heavy to bike through. By now she'd travelled a good three kilometres. Up ahead was what looked like the entrance to a school, maybe she could shelter there…

CHAPTER THREE

The Runaway

The sign on the gate said Viscount Primary school, and as I rode my bike into the grounds I could see a big old covered doorway with those vacuum-like door hinge things. My clothes were soaked so I hung them on the hinges. Took my wet jacket off and hung it on the door hinge and just sat down and huddled into the corner of the doorway, because it was really cold and windy. I must have been there for only 20 minutes or so, and nearly dozing off to sleep, when a security guard doing his rounds found me. He seemed really worried for me.

"What are you doing here?"

"Oh, I'm just stopping because of the rain and I don't want to get wet."

He looked at me doubtfully. "Well, I can give you a ride home."

"Nah, I'm not allowed rides home from strangers."

And he goes, "Well actually, you look like you've run away from home." And I started crying, I just started bawling my eyes out. "I think what we should do is, how about you just come inside, we'll turn on all the lights and we'll just get you out of the rain."

He was really kind to me. He rang a lady who did his housekeeping for him five days a week, and her name was Kay. It was dark, I think it was like seven o'clock or something. Kay came straight to the school in her own car and they had a quiet conversation before she came over to me.

"Look," she said, "I work for Manny who's a really trusting and loving man, and if he says that he will help take care of you for the night he will. But I'll stay with you if you feel safer." So she did. And he took me home. When the three of us were having breakfast the next morning, Manny ran through some ideas.

"Well, look. I think what we need to do is ring Social Welfare and let them know that I've found you and we need to tell the Police just in case your father's out looking for you or already been down to the police station. That's the best thing to do."

I just lost it then and screamed and cried. "No, no, my dad will find out and he'll find me and he'll just take me home!"

Manny tried to reassure me. "No, look, if we tell the police, and we talk to your father it'll be-"

"You don't know him!" I screamed. "He doesn't care about the police, he will just take me in front of them, he's taken me from the hospital before when I was a little kid and I saw my mum beaten, and he just won't care!"

They could see I was totally panicking, and came up with a Plan B. They took me instead to a safe house in Grey Lynn. There were a whole bunch of really lovely people there who eventually contacted Social Welfare and the Police, and instead of being sent home I was placed in foster care in a girls' home in Westmere. And for the first time in a long time, I began to thrive at school.

Macsyna King spent a year and a bit at Pasadena Intermediate school, completing the last part of Form 1 and the whole of Form 2. What she didn't realise was that her long-lost mother was living just around the corner in Ponsonby. And unbeknownst to Macsyna, things were happening behind the scenes.

At the end of my final year at Pasadena Intermediate, my foster parents had managed to find and make contact with my mum, who turned out to be living in Ponsonby. One day, after my first term at Auckland Girls' Grammar, my foster parents came in and sat down across the table from me. "Look, we'd like to reintegrate you to live with your mum, how do you feel about it?"

To be honest, I didn't know what to think. I was a little bit apprehensive, I didn't want to let go of all my privileges of being able to be schooled, be provided with just simple things, things that girls need; underwear, clothing, safety, security, and knowing that you're not going to be abused in any sort of way. I was a little bit reluctant to give that up and go and live with my mum, just in case. I'd already lived with my dad, and Mum had left so early in my life I'd forgotten what she was like.

"How do you feel about your dad, then?" my foster parents asked. I told them straight: "I'm bloody shit-scared of him and I'd never want to let him get close to me, he'd trick everybody around me." We talked around the issue for a while, and they steered it back to Mum. "Well, I really feel sorry for my mum, and I care for my mum and I miss her sort of sometimes".

"Well if you had the opportunity to have visits with her do you think you'd like to meet her?" I said "yes" automatically, despite my reservations. I don't think I even really thought about it. "Ok," they said, what about arranging a visit from her next weekend?" And so that's what they did.

I remember I was anxious as. I was scared. I was worried about what Mum thought, worried that she might not accept me. I wondered if she wanted to talk, I wondered what she wanted to talk about. Thought about what I'd like to ask her and how I was going to do that and if she would retaliate or show signs of being angry or threatening towards me if I asked her the questions I really wanted answers to.

And then she walked into the room. As soon as I saw her face I recognised mum's face, I knew her straight away. She still looked quite young. And then I saw the gap where her teeth used to be – they'd all been smacked out of her mouth – and her face had taken, like, a shrunken in look around her mouth, probably because her teeth weren't there but, yeah, I looked at those and remembered. I knew why my mum was missing her teeth, and despite that, to me she still looked quite beautiful.

Mum was dressed in work jeans and work boots and a long sleeved collared shirt with a jacket on, one of the old school zipped-front vest jackets. She was pulling her driver's gloves off her hands as she came into the room.

She'd seen me from outside, and had begun to cry, all the way from her truck, up the driveway, up the steps and down to the hallway. She was weeping and she just picked me up and hugged me and hugged me, she didn't really talk much for a while. Those tears kept flowing probably for ten straight minutes while she just hugged me and cradled me and cuddled me and played with my hair. Every so often she'd hold me at arm's length just to get a good look at me, then she'd pull me close again and squeeze me into her chest.

My mind was going crazy. "I can't believe she's here," I was thinking. "Far out, she looks so different. Those teeth look bad. Geez

I'm glad to see her. I'm pissed off that she left me for all these years and I had to do this. Too bad, she's here now." There were a million thoughts firing off all at once. Shock. Pain. Happiness – I was really happy to see Mum again. While the whole thing was overwhelming, it wasn't a traumatic one.

It was the first of what became many visits, but apart from some general conversations about how Faith had first met Macsyna's father, the 11 year old found a gaping hole remained in the area where she really wanted some answers: what had happened at the hospital, why had she left her children with Mac…

I did try sometimes to talk to my mum about that but she was very adamant, she would not be speaking about what happened to her in the past, she just would not have it. She told me her new partner – also named Mack – didn't like her talking about her past. "That's in the past and that's where it belongs," Mack would say. He was even older than my Dad, something like 22 years older than my Mum. He had white hair, was only about 5'2" and really skinny, with thin, chicken-like lips that kind of turned up – looked like a Maori Scrooge McDuck, really.

So my inquiries about her life during our years apart were pretty much shut down. And I didn't like that, I was like, "What? That's not fair, I want to know, and you know Mum – I went through all of this too, just like you!"

"Yes I know," she would say, "but never mind, just shush, it'll be alright." She just batted it all away basically and ignored what I had to say. A brush-off without actually brushing you off.

Within weeks, the weekend visits turned into full custody. Macsyna was finally back with her birth mother, who drove to the foster home in a truck from work to pick up her daughter. The family lived at 72 O'Neill Street Ponsonby, and quickly slipped into routines…

I carried on at Auckland Girls' once I moved in with Mum. She and her partner, Mack, would get up each morning and leave for work no later than 6.30, and they would always leave enough money for my bus fare to school. Two dollars to catch the bus to school and catch the bus home. If I walked, well, I walked.

During that course of time my sister, Emily, born just a couple of years after me, came to live with us as well. I hadn't seen Ems since the night of the storm when I ran away from home, a year and a half earlier.

It had been gutting to leave her behind. We'd shared bunks, we were mates and sisters. Leaving Emily behind that night was like choosing whether you leave your grandmother to die or your mother to die. As a kid it was that sort of a compromise. Those were the stakes, that was my shot at the title and those were what the odds were. It was really gutting to leave the younger ones behind because in many ways I had shielded them from the worst of Dad's violence. Here were these little kids trying to do tasks for adults, you set them for adults and you're trying to get a five or six year old to do it. You know, it used to make my heart bleed, the little ones would be told to do jobs and get hit for getting it wrong but of course they're going to get it wrong! That's an adult's task that a kid's been made to do. So in running away I knew – probably not as eloquently as I do now but I had an understanding of what might face the other kids and that's why I found it really, really hard. But on the other hand, I was only ten back then, and getting regularly bashed.

So when I saw Emily again after a year and a half, it was really emotional. Mum hadn't told me she was coming, and I remember I'd just moped home slowly after school one hot afternoon, half dragging my bag on the ground, and as I finally came toward the front door I could hear giggling inside the house, and it sounded like a young kid, or one of those cartoon character giggles. There was a bag in the doorway and suddenly Emily's face appears down the hallway. We both just leapt in the air and squealed. We hugged and kissed, and I think we totally forgot about Mum and her partner. I was crying, Emily cried. It was an awesome reunion.

Emily later told me how things had worsened after I left. I'd pretty much mothered the youngers while I was there, taking care of their day to day needs, cooking, cleaning, making beds and all of that. Emily had to take over my role.

The reunion was about to be overshadowed, almost as soon as it happened. Faith Tahuri's new man did not appreciate tangible evidence of Faith's past life interfering with his. As Macsyna tells it, Mack wanted the girls sent down to live with Faith's whanau in far-away Wairoa. It might take a village to raise a child, but Macsyna could be forgiven for wondering why the villagers all seemed so hostile to children...

I was just finishing up my third form year at Auckland Girls' Grammar. With Emily now home with us, Mum pulled another surprise and we soon had Stuart and Ellen joining us in the Ponsonby house as well. The next thing we know we're all on a bus heading down to Wairoa to meet some guy named "Uncle Kori" who I'd only ever spoken to on the phone, and it wasn't even a tangi. Mum wanted us to meet her side of the family, but I later found out her partner Mack had been putting the hard word to "get rid of the kids".

We lived down in Wairoa for three months that summer with Mum, spent Christmas and New Year's there. Then, sometime around March, because it was way after my birthday on February 22nd, Mack suddenly turned up in his car. He was with us for a few days, then one afternoon Mum gives us all a kiss and says she's heading off to the pub for a drink.

"Won't be long, I love you."

"Yeah, sweet as, Mum. Love you too, see you. See you when you get back."

I never saw my mother alive again, after that.

As they watched the car disappear down the dusty rural driveway in the late afternoon sun of an Indian summer, the chorus of late season cicadas soon drowned out the engine notes receding in the distance. Little did the children know that Faith had abandoned them again. She wasn't coming back, the car was on its way to Auckland.

They left at six, and in March it's still daylight at six. I woke up in the middle of the night – I'm not sure why – but it was two or three in the morning and there was still no car in the driveway. I knew the pub closed at 11pm, but presumed Mum had gone to a party. That's okay, I remember thinking, I'll just check on the kids. So I walk around the house, and the other three are all fast asleep. I made sure the doors were all locked, but I left the back-door light on. That way, if Mum came home in the dark I could see her from my window. Then I climbed back into bed, snuggled under the blanket and drifted back off to sleep.

By nine I'm awake, but there's still no car and no mum. So I just woke all the little ones and we went to feed the animals, tend to the pigs, go and move the cow into the other paddock and check on the sheep, and of course feed the ducks. Then Emily and I made the kids some breakfast, and we went for a swim. It's lunch when we finally get back to the house, but Mum's still not home and I'm thinking "ooh. Hang on. Nobody's here!"

My heart started sinking, my head started wandering all over the show, and I remember thinking "f***, what if Mum's run away?" I knew what running away was, because I'd done it myself to my father. Now it was starting to look that way for me, and I started really freaking out. So I took the three younger ones for a walk to the neighbour's, about six paddocks across from where we were, to the left. There was a woman standing there in a patch of sunlight as we arrived.

"Kia ora! You're the Tahuri children eh?"

We nodded, and she seemed to sense something was wrong. "You alright?"

"Not really," I told her. "Mum's not back yet, I was just wondering if you know Uncle Kori's number and if you can give him a ring and ask him to come out to the ranch please." So she did. Her name was Materoa Smith, she still lives there to this day.

Uncle Kori, who adopted me and who I've called "Dad" ever since, came out to the farm – it was probably four o'clock by the time he arrived. He goes "Oh, hello, how are you kids?"

"I'm alright Uncle, but Mum went out last night, her and Mack, they left about six o'clock and I'm just freaking out cause I don't know where they are."

He looked us up and down. "Oh, ok. Well have you kids got enough kai here or whatever, you alright?" We nodded. We were alright. "What do you want to do," he asked? "Do you want to stay here for the night and want me to come back tomorrow and check on you, or do you want to come home with me?"

We knew how to pluck chickens. There were sheep in the fields and food in the larder. "We'll stay," I piped up. Uncle Kori arranged to return and check on us in a couple of days, which would be Monday.

"Still no mum?" he asked, apparently surprised, when he pulled into the driveway Monday morning. They called a big family hui among the whole Tahuri clan, got in touch with CYFS, and we all got sorted by way of a big whanau hui and a big kai. The plan was agreed that each of us kids would be whangai'd out to live with different relatives around Wairoa. My new parents would be Uncle Kori and Aunty Grace.

I would lie awake at nights at the end of that summer, wondering where my mother was, wondering why she had deserted us again. It was a major bummer. For so much of my life, ever since I was carried screaming from the hospital ward, I'd longed for her, pined for her, wondered how she was, how things would be.

To go from that to having it for such a short while – less than a year – and then it's gone again. Man, it's like 'was that real or did I just dream part of it and then some of it… I don't know.' It just seemed like a bit of a whirlwind that breezed through my life, made me smile for a short season. Geez, it really picked up my self esteem and all of that sort of stuff. Then it was gone again. It was an upheaval and then a major let down.

Actually, I think it was at that point that I decided "Oh, stuff you, man, I hate you, both of you. Irresponsible, stupid, selfish people." I got sick of the crying and hurting over them. What was the point of hurting over them when they'd already decided that that was it? Our fate as children had already been decided before Mum kissed us goodbye and turned the ignition key, and she never discussed her plan with us.

What should I do? Carry on crying or harden myself up? I chose the latter. I didn't have to cry, and I did my best to shut them out and I was pretty successful for about ten years at least. When I next saw my mother, they were placing her in her grave.

Faith Tahuri had returned to Auckland with her partner Mack. Later that year Emily was sent back to Auckland to live with Faith, but Macsyna stayed with the couple she now called "Dad and Mum" – Uncle Kori and Aunty Grace in Wairoa. Two years later, at the age of 15, a phone call shattered the early morning peace in King's new home…

CHAPTER FOUR

Teenage Hopes

We got word that my birth mum (Faith) had passed away at the Ponsonby address. But nobody knew where Emily was. She had run away from home earlier, and none of us had heard from my mum either for months. Emily had only been gone for a couple of days, but in that time Mum died in suspicious circumstances, supposedly from drinking poison – I think it might have been diesel fuel, they said.

Emily's only spoken of this incident once and she refuses to do it again, but I remember it. She had no idea that Mum had died. She'd run away, and mum's body was held in Auckland for one whole day and halfway through the night before it was cleared, but then we had to wait for the next day before we could organise a vehicle to go all the way to Auckland, pick it up from the hospital morgue and come back.

We were all trying to find Emily, who was aged 12 at the time, and a girl whose foster home I had stayed in at Surrey Crescent when I first ran away from home recognised Emily, and had heard we were looking for her. Eventually she got a message through, and Emily finally made it down to us the day after Mum's body had already arrived for the tangi in Wairoa.

She was devastated, my sister. When I saw her I just got up off the marae – you're supposed to stay there and I know tradition – but I just couldn't leave my sister at the entrance. I ran to her and we just cried. "I ran away from home because Mack was sexually abusing me, I didn't know Mum had died," she sobbed to me. Apparently the abuse had begun the previous year.

He was forcing himself almost to the point of sexual intercourse, and my sister would be screaming at the top of her lungs for my mother to do something, and nothing came of it. At the end it was always the neighbours, my sister said. She deliberately left her window open, where they lived on O'Neill Street, and the neighbour, without fail, would come over and knock on the door and go "is everything alright there?" as soon as she heard anything. She was a vigilant old bird. Emily just had to keep finding ways to get my mum's attention.

I couldn't believe what Emily was telling me, and was just beside myself. "Did you tell her?", I asked, and she goes, "I told her and I cried, and she did nothing, she said nothing and she just went into shock. Mum just sat at the table, smoking cigarette after cigarette and having coffee, and wouldn't speak. Just yes and no, just vaguely replying."

Emily went on strike at her school, telling the counsellor she would not leave the school grounds unless her mother agreed to pick her up and take them to live somewhere else. Faith finally broke off from Mack, got a one bedroom flat in Epsom and moved in with Emily there. Mum even did a study course.

For a while they were happy, then one day Emily came home from school and found Mack sitting in the flat with her mother. "I just lost it," she told me, "and ran screaming and crying down the road to the park, and just kept running till I was sure Mack couldn't chase me."

Emily was gone for two days. But within hours of Mack finding Faith, Faith was dead, supposedly from drinking diesel fuel. Macsyna King doesn't believe it was a suicide, despite what the coroner later ruled based on Mack's evidence. Faith Tahuri's family did not have the money to pursue an investigation, and police were not interested. While the coroner's verdict lay in the future, Mack surprised Macsyna by turning up at the tangi as well…

On the day that we buried her, he rolled in the gates and I hit the roof. I got in heaps of trouble. I played up hard out, I was going 'what happened to my mum that died?'. I just wouldn't stop screaming until he got out of there. "He's not welcome here. He's done it." And I just flat out accused him actually. It was horrible.

With the death of my mother, Emily stayed in Wairoa with

whanau. Although we all lived in different homes, we all ended up at Wairoa College, which is where I met the father of my first children, Kevin.

It was an unusual way to meet someone: I gave him a hiding. He was walking home and on his way to his house past the Wairoa touch fields, everybody used them, and he was on his way home and I was running to catch a long ball, and I didn't bother to look to see where I was running to. I just had my eye on the ball and kept running and didn't look and I just collided with this tree.

It must've been hilarious but I didn't find it funny, and then all I heard was "ahahaha", and he was just rolling on the ground, pissing himself with laughter. His books were all over the ground, his bag was on the ground. I just got so wild, I forgot what I was doing, walked over there and booted him while he was on the ground. He just carried on laughing! As he carried on laughing I got more frustrated, but the more I kicked him the more he laughed. I just ended up laughing myself.

That was that. Went home. The next day, he saw me at school. "Hey, you're that girl that hit the tree!" So I kicked him again. I just wouldn't talk to him. I carried on like that for about two years. "I don't even like you…" But he persisted. "Hey! How's the tree going?" That sort of thing. I was like "Up yours." And then he just came out with it one day. "You know what, I really, really like you, I don't know why cause you're such a b.i.t.c.h. but I like you and I'd like to go out with you."

I'm just "Good luck. My brother's at home and you'll have to go and meet my Dad (Uncle Kori)," That's what I said. He turned up the next day, knocked on the door and I hadn't even agreed I would be his girlfriend! He knocked on the door and said "Hi, I'm Kevin, I like Max and I had to come and meet you." I just froze, I didn't know what to say.

We were high school sweethearts the rest of the way through college. Dad used to suspect we were in a sexual relationship, because of the time I spent at Kevin's house, but we didn't. I didn't dare. Sexual education had just started becoming a part of our schooling. It was still one of those subjects, we just used to crack up at the proper names for the body parts and all that. Overall we were just pretty immature and all these words were just new to us. I didn't want to disappoint my father either. But I used to go home with

Kevin at lunchtime and help him do chores on his one and a half acre section. We'd clean house, do the washing, everything, during school lunch hours.

One day Uncle Kori asks me, "What do you and Kevin do at lunchtime?" And I said, "we talk, and clean up and do things." And he just gave me the "Oh, don't hand me that carry-on, I know what you's are doing, you're doing exactly what I was doing at 15." I refused to argue the point with him. If he believed it he believed it.

Honestly, I was too scared to have sex. It happened that Kevin also was a bit scared as well. If his Uncle found us in a compromising position he would have splattered Kevin, he was one of those no-nonsense men. A smack was just something that you got if you weren't there on time for him, pretty much.

During all this time, despite what people might think, I was studying hard. I passed School Certificate in five subjects, and attained Sixth Form Certificate in five subjects, which as I recall were Science – Human Biology, Maths, English, Music and PE as well in my sixth form year. I can only go from memory because the police took all my family documents when they seized the twins' cot and other items from the house, and they still hold most of my records and family photos. To top it all off at college though, I passed my University Entrance as well.

I had my heart set on training as a pilot, but then found my vision wasn't the best, so my second option was training to be a Physical Education teacher.

It wasn't until the end of high school that I lost my virginity. Kevin had got himself a job down in the Hawke's Bay, so we ended up living together in Napier in 1994 while I studied at polytech. That's where I fell pregnant with my eldest son, Sean [children's names changed]. Kevin wanted his son named after his brothers, and I didn't, so I told him, "No, stuff it, I'll choose one." And I did. He was born in July 1995 when I was 18 and a half.

Although it wasn't a "planned" pregnancy, in the sense that we purposely sat down and decided to have a baby, we also knew that in having unprotected sex we might well get pregnant. So we knew what could happen. When I found out I was pregnant I remember thinking, "Wow, I've got life growing inside of me and here's my chance to have that little somebody".

It was a big moment. I always said that if I had children, I would never do to my children what my parents did to me. I would give them everything that I could. And let them eat lollies; I was sure that I was going to buy them lollies and I would always buy their stationery and they'd always have clothes. And I couldn't wait. He was going to be my own little special little someone.

Sean's dad was a different kettle of fish. By the time I got pregnant, Kevin and I had been living together for three to four months. I realised that I had to help him to learn how to take care of himself in regard to things like personal hygiene and cooking.

I knew I had to ring Dad (Uncle Kori) and tell him. "See Dad? I told you I wasn't sleeping with him then. I'm pregnant!" I wasn't sure how I was going to do it. I worried about telling Dad because it mattered to me if it mattered to him. I wanted it to be okay by him that I was pregnant. I didn't want him to be down-hearted or disheartened. So for me telling Dad, it was a bit, 'man, I'm scared!'

Telling Mum (again, these are my Aunty and Uncle, I call them my parents) telling Mum was going to be a breeze, I knew it. She'd go "Oh, bloody hell." And "you've done it now so, yep. Good on you. Good job." That's how she talked. So funnily enough, Mum was the one who did all the growling when it came to me, but I never worried about telling her. It was Dad. I guess in writing this now I realise that my fathers have been the ones in my life whose opinions I wanted. I cared what they thought. If they thought it was ok, or if they were 'nah.' It mattered to me.

I didn't consider Kevin's feelings, now that I think about it. We both knew the consequences to our actions, unprotected, but for me I saw it as a definite joint act that we had taken together, a joint responsibility. I just assumed that he would fall into the responsible role, even to the point where I thought he would just do what I'd seen my Uncle Kori do. "You've got children now, your job is to provide." Well, if not that, work towards it.

If there's a lesson in this, maybe it's too much emphasis on *sex* education in schools and not enough emphasis on *parenting* responsibilities. Maybe if we were taught more about the realities of parenthood and having to provide, we'd be more careful about what we did. Kids today get lessons in flavoured condoms, but not so much emphasis on what happens if the condom fails.

So here I was, studying at polytech and pregnant with Sean, working part time at Valentines Restaurant in Napier. It was pretty tough trying to juggle study and work commitments with the demands of pregnancy as well. I knew we needed time to prepare the home, myself and Kevin for baby's arrival, as well as getting a cot, clothes and all that sort of stuff.

Kevin and I were living in a one bedroom apartment, which had suited us really, really well. It was affordable, but it was starting to look grim as time progressed. Kevin did not want to do anything. He wanted to stay home, play video games. That would be about it really. He would clean if I asked him to. But I would always have to ask him, he didn't volunteer.

He wasn't well trained at all despite my crash course when we moved in together. All I did was nag, "Babe, how can you sit in this mess? If you clean up, everything around you, I don't expect you to have my dinner cooked or anything, but if you cleaned up around you, that would be nice. How can you just do nothing?"

I was working and bringing in the family income. I was also studying. He was doing nothing. I was always in his face about it. His response was a grunt and up goes the volume, on continues the game. It was frustrating. Much as it annoyed me, I kept telling myself that I'd chosen him as much as he'd chosen me. Our son was on the way and I did not want it to be a failed relationship at 18. I didn't. I really, really didn't.

In the final few weeks of the pregnancy Kevin manned up and found a forestry job, which enabled us to move into a two-bedroom flat at Maraenui in Napier just a few days before I gave birth. He was at work in the forest when I went into labour. Mum (Aunty Grace) was with me though. Mum had moved to Hastings to 'find' herself. She'd been pregnant since she was 15, given birth to six children of her own as well as helping raise me, so she'd taken some time off and moved to Hastings.

I woke up one morning, I just said "Mum, I feel like I need the loo, but it's not." She goes "Yep, baby's going to come." I panicked. "What? *Now?*", and I started to hyperventilate. Mum's trying to reassure me, "Oh, calm down, calm down, it's alright. Go and have a shower."

It hurt. Man it hurt, and I told Mum I couldn't handle the pain. "No, you can, you just think you can't," she said. "It's sore, but you've got to do it while you feel that, cause it'll help birth the baby really, really easily."

"I feel like I'm dying!"

I did that for like four hours. Finally she'd had enough of my whingeing. They rushed me to Hastings hospital, because Napier's was closed, drove me up to the hospital in her neighbour's mini. And I could barely fit. Got out, and my mother goes to the nurse, "hey, my girl's going to have a baby, can you just put her somewhere? She thinks that I'm telling her to do something and being cruel. Tell her!"

"Tell her what?" asked the nurse.

"I told her to walk around while she's in pain, but she thinks I'm just doing it to be mean, but can you tell her that's what she needs to do?"

The nurse just stifles this laugh and goes "She's giving you sound advice." And so she turns the stern nurse voice on and says "You've got to walk."

"I don't want to! I'm not going to!" And I just sat down in the hall and started crying. All these other babies in the ward started crying, about ten babies that were in the ward started crying and the senior nurse comes out and goes: "Well now you've upset ten children, so now you've upset me. So I'm going to pick you up myself."

"No, no, I'll walk. I'm sorry!"

And she goes: "You know, all these mothers have just gone through what you're going through, you're not the only one. Welcome to childbirth."

Twenty minutes later I had my son. They didn't offer me an epidural, well, they did, but Mum told them, "No, she doesn't need it."

"Oh, well we can give her some pain relief and some gas."

"No, she doesn't need it."

"Maybe it'll deter you," Mum told me. "You're the brainiest out of all the kids and now you're pregnant. Now look. Your brothers are older than you and yet you're having a baby first."

So that was Sean's birth. Golly, when he was born and I held him in my arms, I could not believe. I just could not, I just ogled over him and just sat there in awe of him and watched his chest rise. He woke up and cried and the nurse goes "You can feed him."

"Oh no, I'm fine, I'll just watch him."

"No, no, you've got to feed him."

I'd had plenty of experience looking after children – my own youngest sister and brother up in Auckland when I was still living with my birth Dad, and I'd gained more experience as a teenager after moving to Wairoa to live with Mum Grace and Dad Kori, who'd always had children in their home. We older teenagers would always help them babysit the kids they were looking after.

"We don't want to babysit," we'd complain.

"Too bad. Learn. We can't teach you when you're older and you're going to have the baby, so you'll learn now."

So here I was with a newborn, but I'd had all the training. I knew about bottles, I knew about breastfeeding, I knew how to change them, bath them, everything. And give them Pamol, check for temperature. We even knew how to lower a baby's temperature if they were feverish and what to do. Mum was really clear about it.

Her advice was to strip them down, get them onto a cool flannel blanket if you can, make sure the room isn't freezing, close all the windows off, no draft. Strip them out of their clothes and get a damp flannel and wipe them down. Feet, under the arms, in the pulses, round the neck – not the head – and then get a dry flannel and dry them off. Sit them up and give them water in a bottle. Hold it in their mouth if you have to, even if just to get a couple of sucks down into them. Then just soothe them and console them.

Grandad's advice, though, was more old-fashioned. "No, you run a cold bath, no hot water, just a cold bath and you just dunk them in. Pick them up, hold them, wait three seconds, dunk them in again. Pick them up, hold them out for three seconds, you do that three times. Then you wrap them up in the towel and you put them in their clothes and wrap them up in blankets again."

Sean was about two hours old when Kevin finally comes into the maternity room, and he's still in his forestry gear. Dirt, twigs, leaves. I don't know how he made it past the nurses. He comes in and he just sits down and goes "Hi!"

"Our son's over there."

"Yeah."

It was like "You can stand up and go and look at him."

"Oh."

I think I can remember Kevin just gawking at the baby and going "Whaa, I helped make him." He was awed as much as I was, and floored.

Our new home was warm. It was clean and professionally painted. I didn't really like the area but it was a sure thing that had come up. We needed it. By the time that we got in there I had everything sorted for the baby. Clothes, cots, bassinets, carry cots. A lot of them were gifted. Good old family. Clothes, nappies, treasures. A couple of my cousins, they had real thoughtful gifts. They had maternity pads and breast pads and breastfeeding pumps. I hadn't seen them at work before, but I soon learnt.

Kevin's job was a real financial boost to us as a couple, and he seemed really proud of actually landing a job and being able to sustain it. His boss, Rex McPhee, even gave Kevin a present to celebrate Sean's birth – a new pair of pruning loppers. "Congratulations," he said.

Macsyna fell into the role of mother with gusto. Her de-facto husband Kevin was gainfully employed, and she balanced motherhood and housework with resuming tertiary study at EIT for a Diploma of Sport and Recreation. The family was able to afford a better house in a better area, shifting to Marewa in Napier and the comparative luxury of three bedrooms. Then, 19 year old Macsyna King discovered she was pregnant again, and was forced to come to the rescue of her 16 year old sister Emily…

CHAPTER FIVE

Imploding Family

Emily had been adopted out to Mum's brother, Uncle Fred* and his wife, Aunty Cecilie* [*names changed]. Around the third quarter of 1996 Emily came to live with me when I was five, six months pregnant. Ems had been kicked out of home. When I asked her why, she burst into tears, and it turned out Emily had accidentally come across Aunty Cecilie's deepest, darkest secret.

Emily had been going through a tough patch in her relationship with her new mum, Cecilie, and Cecilie's sister Milly* had tried to comfort Emily, who was only 16, by sending her a letter.

"The letter," explained Emily, "read that I should take heart in the fact that I'm a good person and try not to be too angry that Aunty Cecilie is mean towards me, or that the other kids leave me out. 'Aunty Cecilie is not a saint by any means. She is the reason that my first husband and I split up', said Milly's letter."

I couldn't believe it. Aunty Cecilie and scandal? She's one of those hard-nosed ladies. Black is black, white is white. You get home at five. One minute past five, and you've got a boot up the ass coming for you. She was one of those ladies. A no nonsense woman. So when I heard it I was like "Eh? No way! Not Aunty-"

"Yes, Aunty Cecilie."

After reading about Cecilie's long-ago affair, thereby skewering her holier-than-thou stance over Emily at the time, Emily folded the letter up and put it away in her bedroom. Sadly, Cecilie's young daughter Hinemoa* found the letter while looking for something in Emily's room, read it and took it to her mother.

Poor Emily was at a prizegiving ceremony at the school, Wairoa College, while all this is going down. She has no idea what's unfolding back home. Aunty reads the letter that her own sister wrote to Emily, and breaks down in tears in front of her youngest daughter. Uncle Fred, he'd never ever been told, he did not know his wife had been having an affair. It was like a nuclear explosion going off in the house, a throat-ripping controversial letter no one else was ever supposed to read.

First of all, Uncle Fred and Aunty Cecilie had this major fight.

"When the bloody hell did you sleep with him? If you slept with him when Milly was married to him, I was married to you!" So he found out that she was unfaithful. Aunty Cecilie was just after blood. She was seething at the teeth, and packed all of my sister's gear in a sheet and bundled them up, threw them in a van, drove around to our house, Kori's house, and threw her belongings on the front lawn and cried on my mother's shoulder.

"You've got to take this girl before I murder her, she's this and she's that and I don't want her in my house." Mum said ok, and consoled her, then drove her home because Cecilie had lost it, and rang Dad to come and pick her up from Cecilie and Fred's house. When Dad arrived to drive Mum home she and Cecilie explained what had happened. "Oh that bloody girl, she's interfered in Fred and Cecilie's marriage."

"How?"

And Cecilie goes, "She bloody told Fred that I slept with Milly's husband." Dad goes "Well you did, I was there. But how did Emily know?" She goes, "She didn't, my sister wrote her a letter. I don't want that girl living in my house ever again. I don't even want to see her again."

And my Dad's like "How the hell, what's wrong with you?" he just walked out of there in disgust actually. Mum was going, "Get back here, she needs our help!"

"No, no!" yelled Dad. "She needs help alright, but she doesn't need that sort of help! She did it! Not the girl! But she's angry at the girl because now Fred's found out. I knew. Heaps of other people knew Cecilie had done that."

So this supposedly good intentioned letter, meant only to lift my sister's spirits and give her a bit of heart, ended up being a family timebomb, it created some tension. Dad rings me that same afternoon and he goes "Darling, I'm bringing your sister Emily down to you."

When he put Emily on the phone she was just crying her little heart out. She'd been brought up as one of Fred and Cecilie's daughters for four years since our birth mother had died.

She was heartbroken, she just did not understand. The timing was severely unfortunate. That prizegiving ceremony she was attending that afternoon at college was her own: she had literally just been awarded a $5,500 scholarship to study design in the South Island – it was a scholarship for promising young fashion designers and she had won it. They were going to pay for her school and board for six months and allow her to come home every second weekend. So while she's up on stage in front of the whole school getting this prize, back at home her belongings are being thrown out and she's being evicted from the only home that's been safe for her. She was very diligent as a student, very bright, and this was just gut-wrenching.

Man, I believe it broke her spirit a little more, if you can say that. She'd had a hard life anyway. It sort of had just got to a place where she was not being abused, still feeling a little bit left out, really in need of love. Not really getting what she wanted, but safe nonetheless. She wasn't getting hit, she wasn't being beaten. So her needs were provided for. Then all of a sudden, because of this letter, her home was taken away from her.

It was rejection, third time round. The first was our birth mum being taken to hospital and not coming back. The second was when Mum went to the pub that summer evening in Wairoa and never came home to us. Now this was Emily's third blow. I know I can relate to being kicked and having your spirit knocked out of you.

So Emily turned up on my doorstep, tells me what's going on and what's gone on for her. I listened to her. In the meantime, we got her enrolled at high school in Napier.

The scholarship did not go ahead. The details had to be confirmed within a week, and Emily was just so shattered that she didn't want to go away, she wanted to stay with me, and I could not bring myself to push her to do it. My parents, when they brought her to Napier, asked her themselves, "You know, if you want to still do it, we do have your Uncle Frank that lives down there, and if you did want to do it we could send you down there to him." But she was just done. Broken. And done living with aunties and uncles no more. Seen it. Done it. Unreliable. Wasn't willing to part from me again.

So Emily stayed in Napier, finishing her college education at Colenso High. After school, she would help Macsyna with chores around the house as they prepared for the birth of Macsyna's second child, daughter Narelle in January 1997. At 12lb 10oz she was a big baby…

Yeah. Big baby. My father was at her birth. And Kevin. At the time Narelle came along, Kevin wasn't working. It ended up being a job that he would have had to be away from us for two months and back for two months. I was young, a new mum, wasn't keen. Kevin was starting to learn that it was hard work. I guess he would've done it if I'd have pushed him to. But he said he didn't want to. So that was that. By now I'd accepted that I would have to be the breadwinner in the family, and I kept up my physiology studies at EIT.

Sean at the time was 19 months old and had begun a Kohanga reo run by members of my distant family. They were awesome to Sean, and they were good to me too.

When it came to Narelle's birth, it was a family event. Emily was there, my brother Stuart was there, aunties, Mum (Aunty Grace), some of my whanau brothers. Kevin was there, even Dad was there at the birth. Every time I had contractions Dad was like, "I just got to go outside and get some fresh air." You'd think he was a smoker, but he wasn't, and I knew he was just making excuses for not being there during contractions – he wanted to leave me with some dignity, not physically watch Narelle being born.

Kevin had gone outside for a smoke and just as he walked in the midwife was going, "OK, now push!". So I start pushing and I'm just aware of Kevin's eyes going wide as saucers – that's all I can remember seeing and then suddenly he was on the ground, out cold.

Just then Dad walks back in and he sees the sheets up and the midwife doing the business, and he's like, "Oh, bloody hell." Then he sees Kevin unconscious on the ground and says "Oh, *bloody* hell!" So Dad legs it out to the corridor of the hospital, grabs a sheet of some kind, lays it out on the ground next to Kevin and yells out to my brother, "Quick, grab his legs!" They roll him onto the sheet, tie it up, like a two man tie on the end, top and bottom and drag him out into the hallway to recover. "Bloody going to sleep in there while my Moko's being born, bloody . . ." Dad's cursing under his breath. My sister Emily just thinks it's a clown show, she just cracks up laughing. Meanwhile it feels like my hips are going to split, so

I wasn't quite as amused at the time. Mum still wouldn't let the doctors give me pain relief.

Narelle was born in ten minutes, after a three hour labour. Despite her size, I had a better time with Narelle. I'd learnt from Sean's birth and this time I'd taken pregnancy tablets with all the essential vitamins and minerals throughout my pregnancy. I drank water during the birthing process and I felt fine. Narelle was just so placid. She came out hungry. She didn't cry, she just looked around and hugged and tried to eat my hand, then my arm, so I fed her. And the nurse is going "No, no, don't feed her."

"Sorry mate, she's hungry."

So I fed her and then a doctor – because I had a midwife and a doctor with Narelle – comes in and he goes, "We've found something that we think might be a problem, but we're going to need you to not feed her and we're going to have to bottle feed her some liquid." The liquid was a dye. They did some more tests, then told me I could feed her again. When they came back an hour later it was not good news.

"Your daughter only has one kidney." They'd missed it in the ultrasound scans, and couldn't explain why they'd missed it. "But she'll be fine. As long as she stays healthy she'll be able to live a good and full, pretty much a healthy life. She may have to adjust her diet according to her body and what she needs, but she will be fine."

I didn't know what to say. I still don't. I still don't know how I actually feel about that. I know that I care about it and that I worry for her now as she gets older. I'm aware of the importance of the kidneys, I know its job and I know its function. I know what dialysis is and I know the reason they need it and I'm wondering about that now. But as a young mum, I don't suppose I focused so much on that. I'm not completely happy that she might not be doing right by her body. Her diet may not be right. On the other hand she has not been in my care for a long time, so what am I to do about that? Apart from let her Aunty know, who raises her in Australia with my parents where they've been for the last ten years or so.

I was not a smoker or a drinker while pregnant. With any of my children, twins included. Fitness was always a priority. At the time I was studying, and I knew the importance of maintaining a healthy body. Being pregnant doesn't mean you can't exercise, and things like walking short distances are still good. Seated stretches were absolutely safe and fine. Reflexology you have to be careful with because it can trigger early birth, those sorts of things. So I made it a point to know what I could and could not do in pregnancy. While Mum (Aunty Grace) had given me a lot of insight about childcare – feeding and winding babies for example – she hadn't really discussed fitness in pregnancy or what happens to a woman's body.

I was already studying human physiology, so what I had learned I put into practice. At school I was always sport-minded and fit, active. I maintained walking right up until I gave birth really. I would still walk to the shop. I would walk to the supermarket for exercise, then catch a taxi back once I had the week's groceries bagged. I really, really saw the benefits of it when having Narelle, a child of 12 pounds, 10 ounces, and I needed no stitches. While it wasn't by choice, and I can't take the credit for not having pain relief, I think it actually benefited me, because I had no sedatives in the system and was quickly able to walk and shower myself.

Narelle was born, wrapped and dressed, and after about 20 minutes Dad popped his head through the swing doors to my room and announced "Kevin's alright, I'm out here watching him."

"Oh good one Dad. An adult knocked out really needs supervision."

But Kevin's comatose state in the delivery suite was being matched by his attitude at home. In the months leading up to the birth, the presence of sister Emily meant Macsyna could continue working at Valentines restaurant to bring income into the family, while Emily helped with household chores after school and looking after toddler Sean. Kevin, unemployed, became addicted to video games on the TV. When Emily left in the new year to begin a food preparation course in Auckland, suddenly a gaping hole in the household opened up: with Macsyna studying in the day and working nights, and Kevin playing video games, who was looking after the children?

CHAPTER SIX

My Demon Drink

Emily left in early 1997. We'd been contacted by Robert, my birth father Mac's oldest son – our oldest half-brother. Robert explained that Mac had passed away and we hadn't known, because Mac's first family and his second family – us – had lost contact after we'd ended up in Mum Faith's care.

It was an emotional re-union, and when Robert heard Emily was going to be studying in Auckland he said she could stay with him while she studied. "Yeah, come and live with me."

And we were like, "really?" Emily and I. "Do you think I should go?" Ems asked me. "I don't want to sit around not doing anything and I don't want to end up like Kevin. I don't want to stop school-ing, but also I just don't want to leave you, Max. So I don't know what to do."

I looked at her and inside my stomach was churning. I remember thinking, you know, 'crap, if I don't do or say something that's going to help her to go now and make the most of her life, then I'm not going to let her go ever.' That's because, quite frankly, she wasn't just my sister but my companion, and a help to me with my children. More help than their father ever was. As selfish as that is, as I think about it, that was me being selfish, but I knew to do something for her. She'd just been majorly bummed the year previous with being booted out of home and missing her opportunity to take a scholar-ship and I just couldn't see that happen to her again. In a sense I guess my maternal instincts kicked in. I'd almost raised my younger brothers and sisters on my own for a while before I ran away from the beatings. I was their one constant carer for them throughout their lives. Here was my chance to either help her and make her go, push her if I had to, or she could stay there and help me.

If you love something, set it free, they say. So I told her to go to her room and pack what she needed, not everything, just what she needed. And go with our brother, "If it doesn't work out you can come home," I told her. "If you don't take the chance you will never know what you might have missed."

Emily became very upset. "No! I don't want to go! I don't want to leave you!". But I just told her straight: "Get out. Get out or I'll throw you out." And it came to that. It broke my heart to say it but it was necessary. It wasn't so much a sad thing, it was just really hard to do, particularly to her – mainly because Aunty had just told her to get out of her house. What's big sister going to do, tell her to get out? But I had to. It took her like two hours to leave, but leave they did and she went up to Auckland.

My sister came back for weekends every few weeks or so. She was doing really well, had learnt some awesome skills, acquired her awesome set of Victorinox chef's knives and was building up her collection of pots and pans. She looked really vibrant and she was really happy in those early visits. It sounded like things were really going well for her.

For me, on the other hand, the house without Emily turned into a nightmare. What I'm about to say about Kevin, you need to understand, is describing Kevin as he once was. He's not the same Kevin now, he's a good father now, but back when we first had our children he was the most useless father known to man.

Narelle was three months old and by this time I'd started work again because we needed the money. Kevin was still unemployed, but he was just getting worse. He'd stay up till like four, five in the morning playing video games. I'd leave Narelle beside him to look after while I worked or shopped for groceries, and when I came back she would be drenched. She's been given a bottle but it was all down the side of her face. The baby is lying right next to him crying, and he's just gaming. Those small little things, they used to just drive me nuts. She was such a good little child, she hardly ever cried. Hungry, wet. That was it. She was one of those sorts of children, Sean's needs were a bit different, he didn't care where he was, but he had to be able to see and hear everybody. He didn't care if he didn't have things. He was one of those babies who had to see and hear everything. So if I would go and do shopping, or go to work, it was really bad, I would dread leaving the children with Kevin.

I really started to miss my sister because I knew I could trust her to look after the kids. Get their dinner ready, follow my routine – dinner at this time, they go to bed at this time. I don't care what the excuse is, with kids you don't break routines, and Emily would always sustain it for me.

Kevin, on the other hand, I don't know how to say it. This is not an attack on him as a person, but his understanding that he needed to do these things for the kids. Don't ignore them, don't feed her lying down. Narelle has only one kidney, so I'm always mindful of that. What could we possibly do? The best we could. And what was that? Feed her properly, wind her properly and change her properly. Give her attention and love. Short times if that's all you can give, at least that. But do it, nonetheless, do it. We helped make her, she is our responsibility, and that's what we should do. But every day was a constant fight to make Kevin understand that this was his job as a father, as much as it was mine as a mother. And I was the one working and studying to support the household.

He wasn't willing to work, and I had no power to force that. But he had to help me out somehow. Getting him to step up as a parent was always a fight. I had to jump up and down, scream or fight with him to make him do it. As I said, the kids could be lying right next to him and he wouldn't move. Kevin never hit them or screamed at them, but he just didn't know that he needed to take care of them. Spending 14 hours on gaming and only four minutes to make a bottle and hold the bottle in her mouth, without even bothering to change her, is just not good enough.

This clash over parenting and housework started to make us really fight, really argue, to the point where Kevin was starting to swear at me. I was swearing back. My language was never any better than his, probably worse in fact.

"Don't bloody well tell me what to do."

"Well actually I need to, cause it's not happening. And at the end of the day when they're sick, when they're down, when they need real care, I've got to do it. But you are not helping and I need you to do it."

"Nah, stuff you." Some days Kevin would just grunt, "Meh, can't be bothered."

You can see where this is heading – a huge resentment building towards what I regarded as his irresponsibility and failure to man up and help out. Sometimes I would actually turn the power off to the house, physically remove the fuse from the switchboard so he could not plug in the video game. Just to make him do something. Kevin would reluctantly do it because he knew that I would not give back his gaming controls or put the fuse back in until he pulled finger. And that's how it was.

So I guess over those three months after Emily had gone I started to resent coming back to the house where everything was upside down, Sean would be in a nappy so soggy it was disgusting. He'd be cold, with a snotty nose, after wandering up the stairs and all over the house all day on his own, half-clothed.

I was starting to dislike Kevin, and it frightened me. He'd been my childhood sweetheart so there was a real internal conflict for me. Kids. Relationship. Myself. Of the three, which one is causing me the most pain? Even then, I knew, his reluctance to want to become involved was causing me pain. Kevin wasn't abusive towards me or the children physically, but in regards to his behaviour he neglected us and it did have a major effect on me.

I know now that only I can make myself feel things, that the power to control how you respond to pressures is within you. Was I falling out of love with him, was our relationship dead? These were things going through my head. I could feel things changing, but had this growing awareness that Kevin wasn't going to change, not for me.

I didn't have a network of friends in Napier. My immediate whanau were my family and focus, Kevin and the kids. My children were my world, I loved watching them grow. They were only little, two and newborn, but I just thought they were the most beautiful children in the world, the best looking kids in the world and I was really, really proud of them. But my relationship was falling apart.

Some people would have walked at that stage, gone and applied for the DPB, and become stay-at-home solo mums. I didn't want that. I wanted my education, I wanted to provide for my family, and I didn't want to admit to myself that I was a failure in relationships like my mother. I wanted so much to break the cycle.

Unfortunately, I couldn't escape the increasingly depressing thoughts I had about Kevin. 'Shit. I've chosen somebody who has this habit about them, and it's in them, and I don't know how to change that so that it helps me and him and our family. Try as I might, I'm not able to do it.'

Maybe if guidance counselling was more available, maybe if we learned more about choosing the right partner and sharing common goals, maybe things could change. I don't know. I kept telling myself I'd made my bed and I had to lie in it, that for better or worse I'd chosen to have babies with Kevin and he with me. Yet the more I thought about it the more I knew it was a lost cause, and I did actually begin to contemplate leaving him and bringing up the kids with the help of my parents supporting me.

It was enough to make someone turn to drink, and I did. Contrary to public speculation, I didn't begin my life as a party animal. I wasn't a drinker and only had my first drink when we were over at Kevin's family home one time. "Try drinking this," they said, offering me some spirits I think. "I don't drink," I told them. "Well, have a cigarette then."

"I don't smoke."

"Well, try a beer."

I relented. "Ok, I'll try a beer." So I went inside and got myself a glass and poured some icecubes into it. I didn't realise you don't put ice in beer, I thought it was like Coca Cola. So I poured myself a beer on the ice and took a mouthful. Yuk! I just choked and cried, the beer came flying out my nose in this kind of reverse snort. They thought it was hilarious. I didn't know how to drink beer, man. They all laughed, and I just thought, "Stuff you! I don't like the taste of it anyway so stick your beer."

So when they first invited me to after-work drinkies at Valentines once a week, I wasn't fussed. I didn't drink, and I didn't like drinking. My work colleagues though could see I was getting sadder and thought I could do with the social time.

It was just my luck that Valentines was across the road from my house and two doors down. So I could literally see my home from work, and the same again for Kevin, he could always see me. So these drinks after work started happening and I just thought 'Yeah, I'll give it a go.' It would last for an hour. And we'd just have quiet drinks. Clean down the restaurant, put all the chairs up and go into the back office room and just have a few quiet drinks. I whined, talk about the day's work, then off everybody went. So I started attending those. It started off one night a week, then two nights a week, then three nights a week. Then I thought, 'heck, I'm starting to enjoy this.' Without realising it, instead of coming home and being annoyed at

Kevin, I'd be so happy, I'd come home and just clean and take care of the kids and fix up when he didn't do anything. I did it unknowingly. I didn't realise what I was setting myself up for. I just felt some relief through these after-work drinks. I wasn't so focused on Kevin being lazy and not doing anything at home while I was working.

This carried on for about two months with my colleagues, and pretty soon it grew to "Come out on Fridays!" And I'd never ever been out to town in Napier and at that time I think I was 20. They were like "woah, let's go out."

"Nah, I can't, I've got kids at home."

"With their Dad?"

"Yep."

"Oh, just come out for an hour."

So I did. Started going out for an hour. That would happen once a week at the weekends and then the second week would roll around, it got to two hours. I started to really look forward to these weekends. 'It's going to be the weekend soon. I want to go out. Have some mean time out.' And in the meantime at home, I would overlook Kevin's neglect and tell myself 'the kids are ok because they're with their dad.' The drinks left me so chilled that I wasn't on Kevin's case so much and I was doing all the housework without moaning.

Finally, though, Kevin lifted his nose up from the video games and began to wonder why I was coming home later and later. "Where are you after work all this time?"

"Oh I'm at work, Kevin, after work drinks."

"Well, why? You should be home with me."

"Well I don't want to come home looking at you on the game. I come home to that every day. Before I go to work, which is three quarters of the day, that's all I see you doing. I don't want to come home to that again, I'm going to do this, this one little thing for myself, I'm going to have drinks with my friends."

He's like "Well, what about the kids?"

"What about you do something with the kids? Because I have done and you have done jack and I'm sick of it. Not sick of our kids, but sick of you doing nothing. I'd like you to do more. And seeing as you think you don't need to, I might just leave you to do it. And so you bloody should."

It was a detrimental attitude, and I know it. It resurfaced later when Chris Kahui developed a similar pattern of behaviour with the twins. But I see now that this choice I made was the beginning of the end for Kevin's and my relationship, because Kevin began to resent me. We stopped sleeping together – I would not engage in sexual relations with him anymore, I refused. I did not want him to touch me.

People at work were always telling me stories of how their husbands were working two jobs in order to provide, while they themselves were working the job at Valentines just to make ends meet. I began measuring Kevin against everyone else's husbands. When Kevin actually began stepping up and making an effort, it was too late. In my head our relationship was dead. "Max, can we go out for dinner sometime?" he'd ask.

"Nah, I don't want to go out for dinner with you."

He'd look at me with sad eyes. "You used to want to." And he's right, I did. We would always go, once a week, out somewhere to the park and then Mcdonald's with the kids, doing something together. Us. Me and him and the kids. We'd go down to Marine Parade and play in the ponds, the rock pools and I'd have to push him to get off the couch and do it but I put the effort in during those early days. But as my resentment of him had grown, I'd stopped pushing, I'd given up on him. He was right, I used to want to go out as a family, now I'd lost the energy.

"Stick, it. Stuff you. You didn't want to do it before but now you do? Well I'm sorry, but it's a bit too late. I just need to pretty much carry on." That was my attitude and my poisonous way of thinking.

"Where are you going?" Kevin would ask as I walked out the door. And I'd be like, "None of your business, really." And I really was rude, stink towards him. For me it was 'oh, he doesn't care so it doesn't matter if I do it. You did it, so I'll do it.' So that was my stink attitude and thinking towards it. So I would just go and leave him with the kids. After work, weekends, or one night a week or something. He'd just stay home and play games.

And the kids fell between the cracks. I stopped being so pedantic with their clothing. All the children's clothing was done in a hot wash cycle with Napisan. I'd always dissolve the washing powder first. I used to care. But now, with my eye on the booze or the partying, I'd start doing it fast, just chuck it all in, going all together, chuck it in the dryer, fold it all away and didn't really care. So I went from washing all their clothes, on their own and separate, to just washing them with anything. I'd just cook all the meals, plate it, cover it, leave it in the microwave, just heat and go. I wasn't really putting that same nurture, that same care and touch into their food, into their needs.

I'd still take Sean and Narelle with me if I was home during the day and going somewhere, but at some point I stopped caring about the smaller things that I used to do for them. Play dumb games, funny games, games that used to make them crack up, I stopped doing them. And I did it without realising it. I'd stop leaving funny little notes and funny little toys for Sean to crawl under the table and he'd find it stuck to the chair. I stopped doing all those little things, and I didn't even realise I had stopped it, I was so wrapped up in my new-found "freedom" at the age of 20.

My priorities had once been the kids, then the home, and Kevin, and then me. Now I'd moved myself from the bottom of the list to the top. It was all about me, then the kids, then the home and the priorities there and then Kevin. Did I realise I'd done this? No, I was blinded by the joy to come and the fun to be had. I was working to live, but live for me instead of live for my kids. I thought only of making sure that financially I was able to see things through, paying the bills. I had stopped putting the energy into the tiny little things that make a difference, and the overall wellbeing of the kids. I really, really did. I was horrible to Kevin, by withdrawing my affections. I used to show him how much I loved him, and I'd play stupid jokes on him, like jumping out of the cupboard and going "RRRAAAR", or I'd wait under the bed cracking up, wait for him to walk past and grab his leg and freak him out. They might sound silly but the games that two people play, and the fun they have with each other, is really important. I just stopped doing all of that sort of thing.

I know that Kevin never really missed it or noticed it until I stopped doing it. And I never noticed it had slipped away at all. I kept telling myself that because I wasn't hurtful to the kids, and I wasn't lying to Kevin, that everything was ok. That nothing else mattered as long as I was the breadwinner, I was still Mum. I still wanted my word to be, my word, whatever I say, that's what goes in this house. In other words, I saw myself as a kind of matriarch: I was earning the money, I was working hard out, I deserved some me time – just like some men go play golf or rugby every weekend to wind down. I did not see anything wrong with my attitude or my growing taste for alcohol and parties.

When I was 18, starting out as a mum, my intentions were honest and simple. My wants were very small and my needs were always taken care of. I can say that despite all the hard things in my early life and up to the point where I was a new mum, I'd come to understand how to make a simple life and provide for my wants and needs. I'd beaten my background, made good despite it.

Now here I was with Narelle as well as Sean, and I was adding complexities. I figured I could have enjoyment, as well as have the kids, as well as study, as well as work, and have a relationship. And I kept telling myself I was a success at this, balancing them all despite the fact that I've lived the life that I've lived as a young girl. I thought that I was doing pretty good.

I was about to get a rude awakening, one that suddenly haunted me with memories of my drunk mother. It was mid 1997, Narelle would have been around five or six months old, just before Emily came back from Auckland to stay with me. I got drunk with some new friends, which I was quite stoked about, and was pissed off my face. I woke up sometime in the middle of the night after passing out and went 'shit, my kids. F***, I've been out all night! Oh no, are they alright? Oh no, I've left them with Kevin.'

I realise now, but only vaguely understood it then, that this was how my mum would have started the ball rolling with her way of life. She'd escaped the hum-drum of her life in Wairoa by partying hard, drinking, having so-called freedom. My path was beginning to look similar.

'Whaa, I've made friends. I'm the breadwinner, I have found something fun to do and enjoy it. And it's mine. And I like it and want to do it.' And a little bit further on from that, you like it so much you forget about the responsibilities. Yet it hadn't been so long before this that I was really together, responsible, accountable all the time. To slip that far in such a short space of time, I now realise, was to dance with my mother's demons.

I'm not making excuses. This book is not about excuses, it's about showing the journey so that if you are reading this and you come to these forks in the road, think about which path you will take. I quit. I quit too easily, I took the road of least resistance rather than put the effort into helping Kevin become a better father. I guess I quietly expected him to know how things went. You have children, you provide. When you have children together you share the responsibility. When he didn't shape up, I gave up and the kids suffered.

I can think of a few things that helped fuel my way of thinking at the time. I bloody deserved it, I told myself. 'I've had a shitty life as a kid, and nobody ever took the time out for me. And I finally found somebody who said they loved me.' You know, I started finding justification in life. In a sense I told myself that Kevin owes me for this. Why? Because I love him and he loves me, and we've made a solemn, sworn oath that we would love each other. And in love, you do these sorts of things. And not have to fight for it. It should be done willingly. I've just thought about all of this, I've thought this is the way it should be. I've never actually seen it in my previous life and childhood, before coming to Wairoa to live with my Aunty and Uncle, I'd never seen my birth parents do that. So where did I come up with this notion that this is how our relationship should be? Probably only in my daydreams and too much TV. Could I say that my expectations were born of things that I had seen in my own life? No they weren't. In fact, they were the exact opposite. My expectations did not match my reality.

In the end, our relationship came to a head and just collapsed. It was only 1997, Narelle was still less than a year old. Kevin said to me one night, "Max, I want to make our relationship work." He had been out looking for work – and he genuinely had been. And he said "Look, I'd like to spend some more time with you again." I was just not interested. I had truly started letting him go from the inside. And mentally I'd started telling myself 'get ready to leave him.'

I remember looking at him, this guy who'd watched me run into a tree, my childhood sweetheart. And I was so dead inside I just answered, "I don't want to work things out with you. I want it to be over. I've had enough."

CHAPTER SEVEN

A Parenting Fail

So Kevin went away, I never saw him for three days. When he came back three days later I had some friends around – men and women. He comes in and he truly, he deeply cried, and I believe it was genuine and he said "You know Max, I want you back in my life, and I want to make it work, I'll do everything I can to help you this time. Now I know what to do, and I miss you." He poured out his feelings and his thoughts to me. But I wasn't having a bar of it. I showed him no compassion. I wasn't harsh or rude, just cold. "Look, I'm sorry, I can't. I don't want to have you back in my life. I want to move on." So that was it. That was the finality of our relationship. I wasn't having him back, and he knew it.

Emily turned up briefly, telling me it had all turned to custard in Auckland with our other family.

It turns out that our half-brother Robert, who'd agreed to look after her, had been booted out of his house because he wasn't paying the rent – even though Emily had been paying board to him from her student allowance while she did her food preparation course at the Stamford Hotel. Kicked out of yet another home, Emily went to live with her half-sister Fiona, who was next in line after Robert on that side of Dad's family. Fiona was one of the sisters who were on TV one time, with the other sister Denise, giving an interview on *Campbell Live*.

So anyway, Emily went to live with Fiona and was paying her board of $120, which was pretty much all of her student benefit. She couldn't afford bus fare as a result, and had to sometimes walk or hitchhike from South Auckland into the city each day where she worked at the Stamford.

She had no money, and never smoked, didn't drink. And if she did, it wasn't because she bought it, and I believe her. Because she showed me her bank statements when she came home, withdrawals $120 and given to the sister. Realising that she needed money, she started doing some paid night shift hours at the hotel, doing dishes and general service in the kitchen. They were just paying her kitchen rates but it was money to her, and it started working out for her.

When Fiona realised Emily was earning more money, Emily says Fiona began asking for more and more money for room and board. Our sister came in one day and said to Emily, "You're late giving me my board." And Emily goes "It's seven o'clock in the morning. I always have it to you by the end of the day."

"Yeah, well I need it now."

So Emily gets up, walks up to Manukau City, withdraws her money, gives her the $120, and her sister Fiona starts picking at her, going, "Who are all these men that are picking you up or dropping you off at night?"

"They work with me," said Emily. "That's the head chef, the other night."

Fiona didn't believe her. "Oh, whatever, I think you're doing something like prostituting."

Emily was angry. "Nah, these people just know for a fact that I walk from here all the way to downtown Auckland and back, and they just felt sorry for me and gave me a ride home."

"Bullshit," goes the sister. So Emily just found that she was going hard, doing what she should be doing and just getting kicked for it. She was starting to feel abused. And that was the last straw for her. She got the $120 anyhow that day at seven in the morning, walked back and Fiona goes "Nah, I want more than that. Now that you're doing what you're doing you can give me an extra hundred dollars."

"I don't even have that," Emily told our sister, but Fiona goes, "I don't care, you're making it somehow, and I need help. You're eating my children's food and you're living off me for nothing."

Emily snapped, showing Fiona the bank statements and emptying her pockets to show she only had a handful of coins left, and they had a blazing row about it. Fiona's partner Charles had to step in and tell our sister not to be so mean. "Hey, just leave her alone and that, cause she's trying to do right. She's got a job, she's not a no-hoper, she does whatever you ask her to and she pays her board, more than your other brothers and sisters, and you treat her like crap."

The intervention by Charles did not go down well. "Oh, what, is she sleeping with you too?" screamed Fiona. Here was poor Emily, again at the centre of another family conflict through no fault of her own. She just couldn't handle it. She went to work and she was working away and on a break one of the staff asked her "are you alright?" and she broke down and cried and said "no, I'm not. I live with my sister and she's so bloody cruel and she takes everything I have, and I don't know what to do, my only sister that I'm alright with, she lives down in the Hawke's Bay and that's just too far for me."

They said "Well, why don't you just get your own place?" And she did. Emily went flatting in central Auckland, much closer to her work, and she was earning enough money by then that she would bring gifts for the children when she came to visit us.

So Emily's visits I looked forward to, but my own life was falling apart now that Kevin had left. I carried on drinking for a short time – probably around three months – and it got pretty bad. I was starting to get so hungover that sometimes the kids, I'd wake up and they were all over me trying to wake me up, and my cousins or friends, whoever I had babysitting at the time, would be going "Hey, hey. Your kids need some more milk powder." So it got that bad. I was out of milk powder sometimes, out of Treasures sometimes. Dishes would be left in the sink overnight. Every fibre of the good mother I had once been was draining away.

The first month hadn't been so bad. My parents came through to Napier, and I rang them and explained, "Look, Mum, Kevin and I have broken up. I'm done with that life that I was living, I've got to do something more, it just isn't working. And I was unhappy as crap."

Mum was angry. "Oh bloody Hell, what did I tell you, you made your bed and you lie in it. Now what, it's just not good enough for you?" She gave me a right good talking to and told me exactly what she thought, she thought I'd quit before I'd actually given it a go, didn't accept my excuses about my lazy husband. She was always of the mind where, "five years of enduring something like that, you've given it a pretty good go for a young mum. You's were together young, but you weren't together that long once you'd had the children and what about them?

"That's a failed relationship, girl. Now your children are living in a broken family home just like you." It rang in my ears, it engaged in my brain, I felt stink at the time.

Mum took baby Narelle away from me. "I'll just have her for a time." But I knew that Mum wanted her to have her for their own, and raise her. And she came to me and she goes "Oh I'll just take this girl, just for a month or so."

I'd quit work by this stage, wasn't functioning anymore and couldn't get reliable babysitters to look after the kids, so I knew Mum was doing the right thing.

"Get yourself together," Mum told me. "Think about what you want to do. I'll come back and see you in a month. If things are still not cool with you I'll have this girl and that'll make it just a bit easier for you. You only need to care for you and Sean. Bit easier."

So yep, I was just keen. One less child that I needed to worry about and I thought 'ok, yeah, I'll try. I'll try get myself on track.' But I didn't, because the one remaining child I needed to stay sober for was going to Kevin's every weekend, leaving me with time on my hands and a craving to drown my sorrows.

During the week, Sean would be at Kohanga reo during the day, so I'd really only have him at nights. Kevin had moved back in with his mum so they took Sean at weekends, and me? I was left to my own devices.

I could drink in the weekend and I just could not resist the temptation. I kept making excuses, about how I was just getting over Kevin, 'Oh, I'm just getting it out of my system. Just get over being separated from Kevin, and the kids are safe, in a safe place, sweet. Just go out and explore the world now I'm not tied down. Here's my opportunity.'

So I'd live for the weekend. A week went real fast and a month came real fast. Next thing I know, my house is a mess, Kevin had brought Sean back in the middle of the night but my cousins were staying cause they'd travelled through from somewhere. So Kevin dropped Sean off at my house, but left him there with my cousins and I didn't even know – I was at the pub on the turps. Get home, fall asleep, wake up and Sean's crawling all over me and I'm asleep on the mattress, out on my balcony cause I just couldn't stop being sick. Suddenly, the doors open and my cousin goes "Oh, I just let your boy out to you, I've just given him breakfast and changed him."

"Thank you," I said groggily, and just as I was doing that my parents pay a surprise visit and see me in this absolute state, with Sean beside me.

"What the bloody hell's going on here?" They looked at the house and it was a mess, there were so many kids there. My cousin had six kids, aged from eight down to the newborn, and her partner was off and she was upstairs or something. I know now that my parents looked at me and could tell that I hadn't done anything, in fact, I'd just gotten worse.

Most of all, they could see I had continued to get drunk. I think my father saw it in my eyes, and he knew that I had now developed a strong taste for it, a strong desire, a strong *habit* for it. He just lost it with me, and deservedly so.

"You fool! I'm going to bloody well keep this girl, you're not getting her back until you get your shit together! What the bloody hell's going on with you?"

I just cried, I tried to make excuses. "Kevin's gone." They were just excuses, and in my hungover state I forgot my parents already knew Kevin had gone. Heck, I was the one who refused to take him back. I don't remember all the excuses I came up with that morning, but I do remember the genuine pain in my father's eyes. My father wasn't just disappointed. He was disgusted. Angry, but sad at the same time.

He goes, "You know you're a smart girl. You've never ever been without the ability, and you work hard. And this is what you make of your life? Just because you're heartbroken? Never mind you're heartbroken, what about your kids?"

I just wallowed in the 'woe is me' and 'I feel sorry for myself' mode, thinking and not saying much.

My mother goes, "Nah, I'm not leaving Narelle here with you. And now I'm taking this boy as well." And she did. So she took Sean and she took Narelle. "You're not getting them back until you snap out of your crap, you do something. Look at this bloody house!" They just gave it to me. Grabbed Sean, they didn't even bother grabbing clothes, they just bought him new clothes when they got him to their home.

The house was suddenly empty without my darling boy and girl. My life was empty, and my parents' harsh words were still ringing in my head. Something in me snapped.

"I can't have this anymore, can't have parties at my house," I told my friends. "I can't let you be over here having drinks before we go to town anymore, gotta get myself together because I want my children back."

I stopped just short of saying "Get the F out of my house," but they got the message. Those "friends" left and I never saw them again.

What did I learn from everything at that point? I learnt that I had become something that I didn't like; actually, I had become everything that I despised and said I wouldn't do and wouldn't be. But still, I remember trying to make more excuses for myself: 'it's ok, it's not so bad, you're not as bad as Mum and Dad were because you've realised it. And you're still young and you haven't been beaten, and you aren't in hospital and you weren't raped.' It's easy to keep measuring yourself against worst cases, and kidding yourself that you are still in control.

I did try. Got myself back together and I started cleaning up the place. I quit drinking so heavily. I think I still knew that I wanted to drink but I just didn't have the money to do it. And I had a major power bill to pay. The rent was also in arrears, so I had a bit of catching up and putting right to do.

In the meantime, Kevin turns up. "Where're the kids?"

"Oh, they're in Wairoa."

"Why?"

"Cause I wasn't doing too good, and my parents came and got them."

"See! You were bloody pissed again!" So he was on my case, and he was right. What he said was true. What he was saying to me was true. I just didn't like hearing it.

"You know what? Piss off."

And he goes "Yeah, I will!"

So I go out on my balcony to watch him drive away, and it was really funny because he walks up the next driveway. He'd moved in right next door to me with a girl we both went to school with, named Mary. I couldn't believe my eyes "What?, you've moved in with Mary, 'Fang Face' from school?"

He's like. "Yeah?"

"What's the matter with you Kevin, you went from this (I gestured towards my own body) to that!?"

I start giving him crap like a fishwife, and he's like in his driveway yelling back, "You know, you got a bloody cheek. I was down and I was out. I was in need of somebody for me. She was there, and now we get along, now I'm with her. So get over yourself!"

And I went "What? You don't tell me to get over myself!"

He goes, "Yeah, get over yourself."

I'm going, "You can't be living next door."

He goes, "Well I do. And I am!" And the door slammed behind him.

Two weeks. That's how long I lasted with my ex living next to me, and then I thought, 'nah, stuff this, this is just too weird, I've got to move out.' So I gave my notice. I didn't really have any animosity towards Mary, and I'd realised by now that I was truly over the need to have Kevin in my life. It was just weird. "Bro, you're like right next door man!"

During this two weeks, the weirdness increased, however. I'd begun to clean up my life. Instead of going to the pub I was going to the gym, and I picked up my tertiary studies again. It was while I was at the gym that I met Gerald, who was to become the father of my third child, Katie.

He claimed to have seen me at the pub drinking, but I didn't recognise him. We had lots of things in common – sports, strong with family, cleanliness (that was a big one). He had a good work ethic and was quite blunt and old fashioned. In fact, he was kind of like a 1970s Wairoa Maori who'd landed in the 1990s, still dressed like something from that 70s show, and he talked like I remembered from my childhood.

One day Gerald goes "Where do you live?", and I told him. "Oh, yep, I've seen you up there with your cousins. You's were dancing on the balcony. We saw you from the pub down below."

I'd lived there two years and hadn't even realised there was a pub down below. Anyway, one evening Gerald turns up on my doorstep looking sheepish.

"I went to the wrong house. Knocked next door and this guy answered the door. 'Oh, how's it bro? Sorry have I come to…. Are you Max's man?' And the guy tells me, "Nah, I'm her ex, she lives next door."

It was one of those awkward things. When Gerald found out Kevin and I had been together seven years and only broken up three months earlier, he kind of shuffled on his feet. "I think I'm just going to take off with my mate and I'll see you later."

Despite the shaky start, we ended up spending more and more time together, and one day he just moved in. In the early days, I'd stopped going to the pubs as much because I was trying to stay clean and Gerald wasn't a heavy drinker, which helped. Mum, who'd seen a change in me, brought Sean and eventually Narelle back.

But my natural mother's ghosts came haunting me. It's easy these days to slip in and out of a relationship. Too easy. You can end up with the wrong person, and that can have lifelong consequences. Gerald and I were good friends, but we shouldn't have been lovers. Lacking any direction in life, we just exist. What was a successful relationship? I didn't really know, I didn't have too many examples from my childhood to work with. Gerald and I would go out to the pub maybe once a fortnight, and when we did I felt the old temptations come back, plus some new ones.

He took me to meet his family. His mother was a bad influence on me, she introduced me to cannabis. I'd never touched the stuff as a child. My birth father wouldn't allow it in his house, said it was for "losers". Gerald's mum was a lovely old dear and always good to me. She'd raised all her children herself. Gerald's father, her husband, he was just a really cruel man towards her. He just bashed the crap out of her every night. Whenever he had piss in him he bashed the crap out of her. Sober, sweet as. So she'd come from that sort of lifestyle so she had an appreciation for what it was to be a single mum. And not just be a single mum for a short time. She had been a single mum for over, I think Joshua was ten or eleven, at the time. 11 years at that point, she'd been alone. Imagine my surprise when she hands me a joint.

CHAPTER EIGHT

Lust

No sooner had I battled my alcohol addiction, than I started having a taste of weed. I'd just have a smoke of weed and I would be absolutely obliterated. Couldn't move. Stoned as crap and could not move. Couldn't drive. Couldn't speak hardly. I was 21 and discovering I wasn't very good at smoking weed. I wanted this quick release from my life, and I turned back to alcohol. The cycle was beginning again. By the time the weekend came around I wanted to drink. I would do whatever it took, favours, I'd be really nice to Gerald, cook his favourite meals so that he and I could go out and go get a drink. All this time the kids were with me.

My life was sliding out of control again, and this time, for the first time in my life, I was unfaithful. I'd never cheated on Kevin, but I did on Gerald. It was 1998, and I remember Gerald and I met up with some old school friends of mine from Wairoa. Gerald had a rugby do he wanted to attend, so we went our separate ways that evening. "I want to hang out with my mates," I told him.

Later in the evening as we partied, this dude just turned me around and kissed me. I didn't do anything, I just stood there, shocked. But that was the start of it. I was getting male attention, and it blew me away. It was innocent enough, I even told Gerald about the kiss. He was disappointed. "Yeah, that's why I say to you, don't you go out with me. There are some guys that'll just do that. They don't care about you, they just want what they want. They just want some ass. They want some goodness and whatever you're willing to give, they're happy. And if they can just take it quickly and get out of there without a slap in the face they'll do it. So you've got to watch out for it."

His words fell on deaf ears. On my journey of self destruction the train had stopped at Booze station, Weed station and now it was taking me to a new kind of destination entirely. Soon after, I found myself really, really close dancing. I kissed this guy back. I just lost control and didn't really care about Gerald's feelings, I just cared only for myself. It felt good, and again, I never thought about the consequences. 'I'm with a partner. If it was me in those shoes, I'd be kicking that girl's head in and then wasting him with my mouth or something.' Where was the Macsyna who had carefully laid out the nursery for Sean and Narelle, played games with giggling babies, and washed their little clothes in Napisan with love and care? Where was the girl who'd promised her babies she would never be like her mother? She was gone, and in her place was a hollow, self-centred husk of a woman who knew she was once again failing and didn't know how to pull out of the spiral.

When Gerald and I would go out, I'd see men eyeing me up, and I'd fantasise about what might happen if Gerald wasn't there. A bit of booze, a bit of Dutch courage, and my inhibitions – few as they'd become – dropped away entirely.

I'd sleep overnight at parties, which led to sex with an old schoolfriend of Gerald's. It was despicable of me, and I regret it to this day. I did not realise that it was going to be my undoing. This man had me by the short and curlies, threatening to tell Gerald if I didn't give him sex on demand. "Every time I come and pick you up, you're going to give it to me."

"No, I'm going to tell Gerald what I've done," I said.

That didn't faze him. "He'll smash you," he told me. "He'll beat the crap out of you. You've seen him beat whatshisname up just for looking at you, he'll waste you. Especially cause he knows that you slept with me."

I was in shock. So I let that carry on for about a month before I chopped it off and I went "You know what? I don't give a flying f***, I'm going to tell him. And I will tell him today."

So I did and Gerald hit the roof. He slapped my face. It was hard enough to hurt, but nowhere near the force that he could have inflicted. I told him what I'd done and he wanted to know details so I told him. "Got pissed as after the pub, went to his sister's house, went to sleep on the couch. He started kissing me, I never stopped him and I carried it on. And we ended up having sex together there on the couch."

Gerald went on a rampage and he would have at the time, obliterated the guy, but I think his friend realised I was serious about telling Gerald and he skipped town for a while. "You stay the f*** home," snapped Gerald at me. "We're moving in with my mother so she can keep an eye on you."

I tried to tell him we should break up. "I think what you should do is just let me go like I said earlier. I don't want to hurt you but I like all these things and I know you don't like it. I think I should leave. And I think we should separate, we're no good." He honestly begged me not to give up. He cried, just said he'd do whatever I needed.

It was a wake-up call. Gerald had been nothing but a good friend and a good person towards me. I knew that he wanted to do right by me and for me to do right by him. He never had any high expectations of me, far from it actually, he was willing to be the provider for me and my children. Yet I was the one who was unhappy with that funnily enough. I was toxic. I'd started this habit of drinking and going out, I'd started mucking around on him with his own best mate. From a woman who'd once craved a solid relationship with a solid foundation, all I could do was destroy them. Where do you go to learn about good relationships? Who are the role models I could take inspiration from? In an ideal world we as children learn how relationships work by watching our parents. That's the big picture view, but the little picture view is that at the end of the day it is still my responsibility. Did I have the tools and the strength within me to make the choices I should have? How strong was my character when it mattered?

Throughout my relationship with Gerald, I would have bouts of just outright crying. I'd just weep and I wouldn't know why. If the world wanted to beat me up they could take a card and stand in line, I was already beating up on myself big time. Again, I resolved to try and put the old ways behind me.

About six months after this, in early 1999 I discovered I was pregnant. It wasn't something Gerald or I had intended, and on this occasion it happened despite me being on the pill. After Narelle was born I'd made damn sure I was taking precautions, and I took the pill religiously for two years without a hitch. But in early 1999 I'd had to take a course of antibiotics, and the doctors later explained to me that antibiotics can weaken the pill's effectiveness. I stopped drinking, smoking and partying, and took the pregnancy tablets again, but I couldn't shake the darkness. When I gave birth to our beautiful daughter Katie on Father's Day, in September 1999, I loved my little girl but I absolutely hated myself and my life. I remember looking at her, knowing my relationship with her father was so wrong. What could I offer this tiny baby looking up at me from her cot?

Everything was black, but the news kept getting blacker. Soon after she was born the doctors told me they believed I had a possible cancerous cyst on my ovaries. I couldn't handle it, and fell into my "poor me" syndrome. One of the first things I did was ring Kevin.

"Kev, I need you to come and pick up our children and I need you to raise them." Sean and Narelle were four and two at this point. He asked me why, I just said "I've just had some results and they ain't the best and I ain't in the best frame of mind, so I need you to take our kids."

People say that when you can't cope, you should reach out. I knew I couldn't trust myself, and I knew the best place for Sean and Narelle was out of my care. Kevin and I had once made a pact that he would get first option on looking after our children, rather than my parents – who I knew would have taken care of them at the drop of a hat. I didn't even know whether I was going to live, and if I was going to die it was better to get them settled with their dad now.

Anyway, Kevin didn't believe me at first. "You f-ing b, I know what you're up to, you just want to go out partying." And I go, "Yeah, I do, but that isn't why. I need you to come and get them cause I'm not doing right by them. That and I'm scared, I need you to care for the kids. I'm going through something real bad here and I've got these tests back." And he couldn't hear me. Of course he's entitled to be upset and all of that. But he just wouldn't listen. I just kept saying to him, "You and I made that pact – now's your time to choose, because I can ring my parents if you say no."

He was silent for a moment. "Remember that?", I prompted.

"Yep."

"Well, now's that time."

He hissed and he fumed for a bit, and then told me he'd need to discuss it with his partner Mary – who is still his partner today. They agreed to take Sean and Narelle by the end of 1999, giving them three months to get ready. "I still think this is bullshit," he told me in that final phone call.

"Oh, I don't really care about that right now bro, I just need to know that the kids are going to be sweet. Once I piss off to go and start dealing with this, I need to know that they're sweet, and I need you to do that."

It was a big ask. Kevin had failed as a father when we were together, but I'd hit rock bottom, or so I thought. The kids needed some stability.

I told Gerald my news, and that Kevin was going to take over looking after the older two at the end of the year. Then I fell into a deep, dark hole.

Katie was only a month old, but I wanted to kill myself and even took a lame shot at it. I'd been experiencing headaches, migraines and wooziness now and again. As I looked at the paracetamol packet it occurred to me I could overmedicate and maybe kill off the cause of my headaches – me. So I got a big script of paracetamol, about a hundred or so tablets, and over a couple of hours I managed to swallow 50 tablets. I figured it would at least be a painless way to go. It wasn't quite what I expected. Death by panadol began with a feeling of light-headed wooziness. I couldn't see things straight, they seemed to be on a tilt. Then my vision was crossing and going up and down, blurred vision. Gerald found me in this confused state and hauled me off to the hospital.

"What seems to be the problem?" the doctor asked, "there's nothing obviously wrong with the blood pressure and temperature checks the nurses have done." With that much paracetamol, I'd have been highly surprised to hear I was running a mild fever.

"Oh, I know what's wrong with me, I've taken like 50 paracetamol."

And they were like "What? Why?"

"Because I've screwed up my life. I'm with this guy, just had a baby. Found out there might be something majorly wrong with me and I'm freaking out. I've done some stupid things. I don't think I can take it back and I thought that this was the easy way out of it."

They referred me to somebody from victim support, who in turn gave me an appointment for counselling.

When I went home the next day, Gerald had taken control. "The kids have gone to Kohanga. Mum's going to take care of the kids for a couple of days while you recover. I'm going to go to work." He got me to drive him to work, and I was supposed to pick him up at the end of the day. But I didn't. I went visiting friends and ended up drowning my self-pity in a bottle. I started avoiding Gerald, taking advantage of his Mum babysitting – I'd just disappear for a day or two and get hammered.

It was stupid of me, and it was wrong, and I'm sorry. I was blowing the rent money from Gerald's job on booze. I'd get the basics done, get the kids sorted, food and supplies, but then I'd disappear again. This went on for nearly a month as I tried to deal with this blackness in my soul. Gerald would shake me when I came home, he was furious.

I remember Gerald telling me that if I left him I would never get Katie. "You're not doing this to my daughter!" And he was right. I had no one to blame but me. Everyone has issues in their lives. It's how we handle those issues that matters. I wasn't handling them well.

At the time though, I couldn't see his point of view. I was too busy wanting to feel sorry for myself. But at the same time something was different: 'Yeah, yeah, poor you. But you might be getting just what you deserve.' I've got the worries of the children. I'm doing all these stupid things and I don't want to. Gerald's a good dude but I've met him at the wrong time of my life. So I know all of this, now what to do? The hospital was still putting me through tests for this ovarian cyst, and they'd told me they'd detected cancerous cells – made me drink some kind of strange liquid for their tests. I was playing up hard, and ended up in the Women's Refuge three times leading up to Christmas, 1999. The loneliness, the guilt and the stupidity – all three things were colliding in my head and my conscience just wouldn't let me rest. I'd repeatedly tried to pull myself back up off the floor and do right, but I kept on slipping short.

So I did what my mother did. I ran away. Kevin had promised to pick up the kids so I rang him. Narelle and Sean were at home with me and Gerald, and I told Gerald that Kevin would be around at 5pm to pick them up. I even put the two men on the phone together to make the arrangements. When Gerald hung up, I said casually, "I'm just going to go to my interview for my course. To attain my position in the class."

He assumed I meant the local EIT, where I'd been studying up till now. I didn't tell him I was heading down to Massey University at Palmerston North to enrol for the third year of my diploma, and that I wasn't coming home. Ever. The bus rolled out of town that afternoon, and I was on it. I'd rung Gerald's mother's place and explained I'd left a letter for him, apologising for everything I'd done wrong. I'd told the kids goodbye, and that I loved them and that their Dad would be looking after them for a while.

Kevin, in that first test of responsibility, was an epic fail. I didn't know it but despite promising to pick the kids up at five that afternoon from Gerald, Kevin didn't turn up. In fact I think Gerald kept them for two weeks and ended up driving Sean and Narelle up to my mum and dad at Wairoa. He explained what was happening. Mum and Dad were just really grateful to him and felt really sorry for him at the same time too. They apologised on my behalf for my stupidity. It took Dad and Mum a few days after that fact even to get a hold of Kevin and tell him to come and get the kids, or they would keep them. Kevin finally showed up, but that's how long it took.

Christmas in Palmerston North came and went, alone. I'd found low-rent accommodation, and begun my diploma year at the University. A couple of months into my studies, I finally plucked up the courage to phone Gerald back in Napier and thank him for continuing to look after the kids when Kevin had failed to turn up.

"I'm sorry, for how things went. I'm sorry that I've hurt you. I've been such a bitch, then mucked around on you and then left you. Thanks for looking after my kids. You could have not cared, or phoned CYFS, but you didn't. You did good by them and that was good for me even though you got the short end of the stick."

His answer surprised me. "Yeah, but I don't care. I love you and I want you to come back."

"I can't come back to you, I can't commit to you until I know that I'm not going to do any of that crap that I was doing before."

"I understand that," he said, "Yep, that's good enough for me. Just try it and see."

So I agreed to return to Napier for a weekend visit, and paid off some of the bills I'd run up before I left him. He couldn't stop talking.

"Man, I want to marry you. This is how much I care for you. I'm stuffed. I can't think of other women, I tried and I couldn't do it. I even had them falling all over me and one of my mates shouted me three chicks at once and I couldn't do it Max, I could only think of you, so I know that I love you and I know that it's you that I want to be with so please would you give me a go? And even if you give me a go and you still feel the same way then I'll let you go on your way. My only terms are that you just be faithful to me. I know you've got stuff to work through and you've had a shitty life. Your parents told me all the things that you've had to go through and I didn't even know."

That came as a nasty shock. I'd never discussed my past and I felt intruded upon, defensive. To me, my upbringing was something to be ashamed of, not shared with everybody. No-one needed to know what had happened to me, and I had gone to great lengths to hide that from people. I didn't want to be a leper and felt sorry for. I wanted people to like me and care for me on the basis of who I am, not because they felt sorry for me.

So I was annoyed, but didn't let it fester. We had dinner, saw his parents, stayed with a friend, I didn't stay at his house, it was just too wrong to sleep with him when I hadn't sorted my life out. I wasn't ready to commit.

When I returned to Palmerston North it was back to full time study. I was a 23 year old with three children to my name, back at Massey University studying, trying to get my life back on track. I'd met a couple of men at the time and had a couple of one night stands, and I happened to mention this to Gerald at one point – in the interests of being utterly honest. He was none pleased, pissed off as, but said he would still wait for me.

As Queen's Birthday weekend, 2000, loomed, Gerald invited me to stay with him during the mid-year study break. He even bought the train tickets. But what awaited me was a shock.

I jumped on a train, came back and he got down on his knee and proposed marriage to me. I was asked to take a leap of faith and return back to be with Gerald on the understanding that I have to leave my past lifestyle behind me, no more boozing, no more carrying on, and that I would agree to make a real effort to try and make a life with him.

I knew it wouldn't quite be so easy, but I agreed to give it a try, on condition that we had some space, because he and Katie had been living with his mum – a lovely woman but she's the granny who kept giving me weed. Didn't judge me, gave me good support, but a little bit of a bad influence.

"Right," said Gerald, "I'll go get my own house. Me and Katie, I'll make sure that it's big enough and I'll take care of all the bills.

And you. You just come back here by me and get your head straight. Get back on track."

If I look at it objectively, it's all I had asked for. A man to stand up and be a father, to provide an income and a roof and share responsibilities, not just leave it all to me. And he loved me. The problem was I wasn't in love, and I didn't know whether I could give him what he really wanted in return. But I agreed to try.

It was OK for a little while, and then Hastings Hospital rang to give me a date for my operation on the cancer. This stupid fear had crippled me off and on for months, and it pushed me off my perch again. I imagined my hair falling out, I imagined all the things that cancer victims who I'd seen on TV documentaries go through. Of course, the reality was nothing like that, mine was a routine procedure, but I was feeling sorry for myself again, and slipped back into drinking.

I was shaken from my bad ways by a phone call from my youngest sister Ellen, up in Wairoa. She'd become a mother at 16, had tried to hang herself a little while later, lost custody of the boy to the father, and then attacked him quite viciously during an argument. She was no longer welcome up at Wairoa and had nowhere left to turn except her big sister.

Gerald was cool, he let me borrow his car and drive up to get her, and she stayed with us for several weeks. I had a near miss with an old male schoolfriend when we went out for drinks one night – stopped it before it went too far but again it was proof to me that I had not yet got my life in order. I wondered if I ever would.

The time for the operation was looming, but when they did a test to check the ovaries, they discovered I was pregnant again. I burst into tears in the doctor's surgery. It was the final straw. I couldn't stop crying. They were like, "Is this an unplanned pregnancy? Are you going to get in trouble or have you been raped?"

I just wept. All I can remember saying was, "I just can't have this child. I can't. I've got to have this procedure. I'm trying to regain this partner that I'm back with, his trust. I just about mucked around on him again, and my sister. . .." I was just an emotional wreck, and this poor nurse who worked at the doctor's in Napier, she got a counsellor in beside me and they organised an abortion over in Hastings that same day, even though there was a long waiting list. Gerald drove me there. I told him what was happening, I told him that I was pregnant. And that I was absolutely detrimental to this unborn child. "If I have this child, you know, I'm too irresponsible right now and I've got these stupid things going on with me, and I don't think it's the right thing, what do you think I should do?"

And he's like "Yeah, nah, I don't want any more kids."

In that short time, in what I now think was haste, I terminated a pregnancy. Some readers will probably be saying that was a great thing. Some readers will say it was a terrible thing. I say that to this day I still burn over that decision. I still burn quite badly about it actually.

From being in the doctor's office to going over to the hospital and having that abortion, the whole process took less than two hours. Counselling? Consoling, I think. They asked about my situation at home. Was I happy? Was I with a good partner or was this something that's the result of infidelity or something?

And I said, "No it wasn't, he's the father. I just don't know if I'm ready to put another child through this sort of life that I'm living right now. It's not right for me to do this, I don't deserve to be a mother again to a new baby. I don't know."

The nurses told me it might be for the best to terminate, with the other health issue already there, and they left me in a room to think about it for a few minutes while we waited for Gerald to arrive.

My regrets are huge. I know now what it takes to create life. How special it is. Some babies are born with deformities and abnormalities and inabilities and yet they'll still strive for whatever little bit of life they can, they still cling as hard as they can to it. And there I was at the time, young and full of myself, and a life is gone.

If I could have had some more knowledge about it, if I could have had the right tools, not just the right information but the right tools to really understand the choice I was making, maybe the outcome would have been different. You can hear things when people tell you, but actually learning them is another thing.

All I know is that I do dearly regret it and still have heaps of emotions about that decision I made then. I find a little bit of peace from time to time with that abortion, only when I start thinking back on track that what is done is done, and regardless of how I feel about it I must still live if that's my decision. If I still wish to live then I must live. Do I think I should be held accountable for having an abortion? Yes, I do. I took a life because it was inconvenient to me.

If I was able to share with people the emotional upheaval that it cost me, – the mental anguish – you cannot stop memories from recalling, you can't stop those things. And when those memories recall and they come about and they're fresh in your mind, you don't just get the memory of the action of lying there, waiting for this abortion to happen. You also at that same point have the understanding that however much information I got, it was my decision, nonetheless. And I cannot look at blaming other people, or the fact that there wasn't that much time to make the decision. It was my choice. Now I must live with it.

I can promise Mums or girls who read this, if you have an abortion you will remember it. For me, when the memories come, so do the emotions I felt at the moment it happened. The memories still come, and it's as fresh as if it happened yesterday, but I had done it more than ten years ago now. It doesn't hurt any less. I still live with it right now. I imagine myself walking around and there's this child that I could have mothered and nurtured. We may all have good reasons for what we do, but good reasons don't protect us from the realities of our actions. I remember. That is what I live with.

So not long after that abortion, I transferred my studies from Massey University back to EIT Hawkes Bay. Although I tried to continue with my tertiary studies, it just wasn't working. Secretly, I wanted to blame Gerald for not talking me out of the abortion, and my resentment for him grew every day. "Nah, I don't want any more kids" – it was all I had needed to hear to justify my own choices. It was my choice but I wanted someone else to blame. I began looking for a way to leave.

My opportunity came a week or so later, when I went to my brother Stuart's home in Hastings. I pulled Stuart aside, and explained that I was leaving Gerald. He's like, "Oh man, you just keep doing this."

"Yeah, but I've got to go. He just doesn't deserve this, but I'm starting to get angry and I hate him, I think it's all his fault." I was full of emotion. Full of heat and wind. But I just wanted to run. And I wanted to leave. And I felt like, if I ran, I told myself, if I ran, if I just didn't have to look at his face, then I wouldn't remember that I just had an abortion.

Stuart told me to come and see him that evening at the nightclub he DJ'd at in Hastings. When I got there, I ended up talking to a guy from the Waikato, Peha. He told me he was leaving town the next day, heading home, "anywhere but here", and he asked if I wanted to come. You already know what my answer was.

We ended up sleeping together that night on my brother's couch. I didn't know him. Met him that night. So got on the piss, went to sleep in my brother's lounge. I was woken up by a hell of a noise, and Gerald shouting. Turns out he'd txted Stuart and Stuart had said, "oh yeah, she's here" – even as he saw me snoring on the couch in the arms of Peha! So Gerald turned up and golly, man. He went off his face.

"What the Hell are you doing?" he yelled.

"I don't want to be with you man, I want to go, I've got to go."

He goes "Why? You were sweet just yesterday!"

"Well I'm not now, and I've got to go."

"You're not going anywhere. You're going to be with me and nobody else and that's it."

That was the first time I heard that from him. First time he'd ever tried to force me to do anything like that. And this guy Peha, poor dude, he tries to step in, he's like "Bro, just leave her alone, she doesn't want to be with you."

And Gerald just wasted him. They had a tussle on the ground and I went to go and run and call the police and he yelled out to my brother to grab me, "Just grab her bro, don't let her do this. This needs to be sorted. If she's going to leave, sweet, but she's not doing it like this."

So my brother did, he picked me up and he held me. And he's got me up in the air and I'm dangling and I'm screaming at my brother going "F*** man, let me go! I don't want to be with him, why are you helping him?"

And he's like "Because you've got to just do this. If you do want to get out you can, like he said, but you've got to do this properly."

He held me. So Gerald deals to Peha, then opens his car. Poor Peha's lying on the ground all beaten up. Well, sore anyway. Sore and scared and he's not keen to have a second go with Gerald. "Just put her in the car," he tells Stuart.

So he puts me in the car and holds the door closed so I can't get out and Gerald just gets in the car and he drives me home and he's furious. Slaps me around the head a couple of times. "Man, I just want to waste you. You've been sleeping around on me!"

"Yeah, I told you."

"So it's just the last straw, I just want to knock you out." He never did it. But he felt like it, that's how he talked.

Gerald was just beside himself. We got home and his younger brothers and sisters were all there, and they're all seething at me. Like "How can you do that to our brother?" You know, they were all really angry at me and rightly so.

The next morning, Gerald sat me down and said "Right, so, if you want to go, you can go. I'll let you go. You can go now but don't you ever come back. And don't you even try and take Katie."

He was still willing to forgive me, again, but he had this list of ultimatums and things I had to live up to. I'd failed all the way through so far so it was pretty easy to see I wasn't going to be meeting his expectations anytime soon. Really good guy, but a better friend than soulmate.

A couple of days later, I made my choice, but it was to have devastating consequences on all our lives.

CHAPTER NINE

Kidnapped

It dawned like any other day, and began with a familiar instruction from Gerald. "Right, can you drop me off at work?"

The three of us, including 18 month old Katie, jumped in the car and I drove him to the works at Whakatu, outside Napier. From there, I drove Katie to her Nan's – Gerald's mum. She thought I was off to study at EIT. I wasn't. Driving home, I grabbed a handful of clothes, not all of them, and swung past Stu's place.

"That fulla you was here with the other night, left a cellphone number for you," said Stu.

I sent a short txt to Peha, "Sorry for the trouble." Beep went the phone a few seconds later with his reply: "I still want to go to Huntly, are you keen?"

So we did. Peha had some money, and we drove up in Peha's brother's car.

Three, maybe four days later, Gerald came looking for me in Huntly. He knew I'd gone there – I presume Stuart told him. And I get this phone call. "Look, I just want to reconcile with you Max. I can't sleep, I can't eat, go to work. My boss is going 'You can have your job back anytime,' my mum can't get me to eat. I haven't eaten in four days, please just come and see me."

I kept saying no, but he insisted on seeing me and convinced me to let him take me to lunch one last time. He drove me to Hamilton, and wanted to take me shopping – insisted on it in fact. "I've never ever bought you anything all the time we were together, so choose anything you want at any shop, I'll buy it for you."

I just chose this, struth it was ugly, dress. It was the wrong size, didn't even like it. But I did it just to save time. I said "Look, I've done lunch with you. I'm sorry." And he goes "Nah, just spend the night with me. I'm sorry I can't let you go."

He wouldn't take no for an answer, and drove us to a motel room. "We had sex but I just, I couldn't, I wasn't into it. It just felt mindless and numb, and I just went through the motions to keep myself safe. None of this was in his character, and it was beginning to feel dangerous.

The next morning he tells me we're going back home, and we stop in Rotorua for gas. While Gerald was in paying, I just jumped into the driver's seat and took off with his car, leaving him stranded on the forecourt. I drove back to Peha's place in Huntly.

Unluckily, Peha and I were in the car that night and got stopped at a checkpoint for a random breath test. The test came out fine, but the status of the car, not so good.

"Well, well," said the officer, "this car has been reported stolen."

"Nah, it's mine. Well, it's my partner's and he let me use it. It's not stolen."

"Well he wants it back, so we're going to impound it."

I kicked up a stink but they took the car still, nonetheless. And the police took down my details. When they asked for my address in Huntly I gave them Peha's mother's house where we were staying. I'd only known Peha less than a week. I don't know how, but Gerald found my address. The only people who can have given it to him were the police.

Gerald hadn't wasted time at the Rotorua service station. He'd travelled straight back to Napier overnight and picked up our baby daughter Katie. What I didn't know was that he'd also picked up a sawn-off shotgun.

When police impounded his car, they rang him, and he was up in a flash. The next day, we got a knock at the door. "Is Max here?". Peha's family who answered the door said "yeah, hang on".

Poor people. They had no idea what they were in for, and to be frank neither did I. As I came around the corner I could see Gerald in the doorway holding a bag, and baby Katie. Our little girl recognised me with a big smile and toddled towards me. I picked her up to cuddle her.

"Yeah, you can have her," he snapped at me. "I don't want to be looking at her and reminded of you. I can't handle it."

I said "Ok then." Gerald said yeah, then mumbled something,

and suddenly his eyeline shoots up and he's eyeballing me. "Nah, actually, I changed my mind, you're coming with me."

"Nah, nah I'm not. Gerald, just go away. Get out of this house." I closed the door and it was then that we knew he had a gun because he wasted the front door with the butt of the sawn-off, and then he booted the rest of the door in. Peha, still licking his wounds from his last tangle with Gerald, comes running, "What the Hell's going on?". That's followed by pretty much the same comment from Peha's mum who'd been woken by the smashing of the front door.

"My ex is here," I screamed. "He just dropped off my baby and now he's got a gun and he's here to take us away!" I was freaking out as the door was being kicked in before my eyes. I grabbed Katie and dashed for the back door, running over to the neighbours, asking them to call 111. Next thing I know he's got the gun to Peha's mum's face, and meantime Peha's run out onto the front lawn and he's going "You need to come. You need to get your ass out here wherever you are Max, get out here now, he's going to kill my mother."

I was in the neighbour's house, begging them to let me use the phone. "Please I need to ring the police. My ex is here and he's got a gun. But he's got the lady next door by gunpoint. He's told me that he's going to kill me and my baby, I don't care about me but I can't let the baby die. Please help me!"

The neighbours just froze. They could see out the window as well as I could, and there's Gerald coming around the back of the house with the gun, barking "Get out here now!"

Katie was screaming in my arms as I came out of the house.

"Put her down," he snarled. "Put her down and let her come to me."

So I put her down, but she wouldn't let go of me. She just clung on and was screaming her face off. The neighbours were doing nothing, they were just in shock. They were like, absolutely in shock. Nobody even moved. I believe that none of them had even seen a gun before at that point. I couldn't leave Katie so distressed so I just picked her back up and went "I'm not putting her down bro, I'm not letting you do anything to her."

And he's like "I'm going to kill you."

And I'm like "Yeah. Probably, and I'd say that I deserve it. But right now you've just got to do something for this child. You can't do this in front of her. I'm the one that's done wrong, not her."

It made him think. So he jiggled the gun. "Get in the car."

"Nah." I don't know to this day why my automatic reaction when I'm challenged is to go , "Nah". I did it to my partners, I did it to the hospital people and the media when the twins died. And here I was going, "Nah" to a man with a sawn-off shotgun.

"Get in the car. Hurry up or I'll shoot you." I was hoping – I'd almost convinced myself – that if push came to shove Gerald wouldn't kill me. He had a good heart, or I thought he did. I had caused him so much heartache, and I could see this. So I decided to follow his instructions and see where it led.

His two-door Honda Prelude was parked out on the road, and we must have made a chilling sight as I was forced at gunpoint, still carrying our screaming daughter, to climb into the driver's seat while Gerald clambered into the rear. He's got the barrel at my neck. "Drive!" And he's lying down in the car in the back seat and he's got his face shielded with a jacket that also hides the gun from nosey motorists alongside.

"You f***ing bitch, I'm going to kill you, I'm sick of your shit. You've done all of this to me just to say you don't want me and I've gone through all of this pain and you don't even give a shit. So what have you got to say for yourself?"

What could I say to a clearly off-the-edge former partner with a gun to my neck? "I don't have anything to say to you that you don't already know. What I did was wrong. I already said sorry. I'd keep saying sorry but I know that that's not enough. It just makes you angry. It makes you want to question me more. I've already done this with you. I know what I've done is wrong but right now you're just so angry, nothing I say's going to be good enough. So I'm not going to talk."

We got as far as Ngaruawahia, and there's already some police road stops set up ahead of us, and two or three police cars travelling behind us. Flashing us. All this time I've got Katie in my lap to comfort her, and I've strapped her to me.

Gerald could see all this as well, just a wall of police cars across the highway, parked at angles to stop me coming past. One car had been positioned like an arrowhead to block off my lane of the road. Another car ten metres back blocked off the opposite side of the road. "I can't keep going, there's a police stop."

And he's like "Don't effing stop driving or I'm going to shoot you. Get on the phone to 111." And he goes "Drive around them, drive around them."

Once again, I give the wrong answer to the man with the gun. "Nah, I'm going to stop." And I go to slow the car down. As I did so Gerald lifts the gun from where it's been sitting on my neck and points it directly at our baby girl.

"Go on then, and I'll shoot her and it'll be all your fault and you'll never live with it."

So I just carried on driving. By that time I had a 111 operator for the police on line. "I'm driving a car and my ex-partner has a rifle pointed at me and I've got my daughter on my lap. There are police officers that know and are following us, but my partner's said to tell you's to stop following us or he's going to shoot my baby. So I need you's to stop following us."

Like something out of a bad movie, the emergency operator says, "I'm sorry caller, can you hold the line please?"

I know the time is ticking over, and in my head I'm going, 'Since bloody when does a 111 operator say can you hang on please? You ring up a KFC or something 'Oh, please hold,' or maybe, I don't know, a law firm and you'll get a 'please hold.' But not from 111.

So I get a 'please hold' and Gerald's like, "What are they doing, what are they doing?"

"I don't know, the operator just said to hold."

Gerald didn't believe me, and why the heck would he? I didn't believe it either. So he's just getting more and more agitated, and he orders me just to drive around the roadblock. "Keep driving, keep driving."

We get to the township Ngaruawahia and we see the pub there, and suddenly Gerald changes his mind. "Turn around! Head back up Pokeno way."

I don't know what anyone was making of this, but suddenly I'm pulling a U-ey in the middle of Ngaruawahia and heading back up the highway towards Auckland. There are police officers watching, and Gerald and I can both see a police helicopter above the car, and the 111 operator has finally returned from their lunch break, or whatever she was doing, and is asking what's happening?

"The same thing," I told her. "I'm still driving the vehicle. My daughter's still strapped to me in the front seat, there's still police cars operating now and now there's a helicopter and he's getting really irritated and he's getting angry and now he's cocked the gun and loaded the, I've just seen him put some cartridges in."

And she's like "Ok, can you just hold?"

She just kept doing it! Like "Man! These could be my last moments and you're saying please hold?"

And my daughter, by this time, she's just not happy. I can't recall where along the way we went but we started running out of gas. Gerald goes, "Tell the operator that they better not try anything. I need you to get the petrol pump."

Anyway, we get to this garage and this gas attendant is pretty much standing there with the gas pump in hand waiting, sees me, I just pop the fuel cover from inside the car. The attendant has obviously been told by police just to follow instructions. Opens it up and pumps the gas in and I'm like, I can't believe that this is going on. My bad movie experience just seemed to get worse – this was the scene where you want to be rescued but no one can get to you even though they are right there.

As the petrol's going in, suddenly the attendant is at the window bringing us supplies, unloading food in for the baby and drinks, cigarettes, a lighter. Everything police apparently thought we might need for a hostage ordeal.

And all the time, Gerald kept talking, half to himself and half to me. "Do you know how much you've hurt me? Do you? Talk!" I didn't reply. I just knew, somehow I knew that maybe it was better for us all if I kept my mouth shut, so I let him rant and rave, and sometimes he was in tears.

At one point the 111 operator had asked, "Where are you heading?", and I told her Gerald was taking me to one of his mother's properties, so it was kind of weird when Gerald had ordered me to take a turn near Pokeno and the operator comes back and says, "Ok, we've got some directions for you. You're going along the wrong road."

Gerald's going, "Gotta go find the house."

When we finally got there, it was obvious the police had beaten him to it. They'd cleared everybody out of the house, and left nothing sharp in the premises, and I mean nothing. There were no knives, spoons, there were no forks. There were no window latches or door handles on anything in the house, except for one pair of French doors where they'd left the lift-up latches in place, but that was about it. All the windows in the house had been lifted up and jammed open with screws. Only the doors could be closed but all the windows were made open. It was surreal.

I've got Katie. Gerald's got me mainly, in the crook of his arm. I don't remember which arm. But he's got me fairly solid in the crook of his arm, held tight to him and I've got Katie, and the rifle he's got close to our bodies but aimed at my head. He walks me inside and we can see these armed offenders officers all watching us, black combat gear, guns, scopes, binoculars, walkie talkies. Then Gerald yells out, "Don't try anything, I'll just kill her on the spot. And it'll be all your guys' fault." He shoves me into the lounge at gun point.

CHAPTER TEN

Speed Kills

So we made it inside the house, we get inside the house and he just goes on and talks more about how he felt. He's saying things to me like "I didn't even want to be with you, but then I felt stink cause you were such a cool person and you said that you wanted to give it a go. Then it was too late, I fell in love with you, started liking you and you didn't even give a shit. I tried and I tried and I tried to make a go of it but you just kept wrecking it."

"Yeah I know! I know it is, it's not fair on yourself for you to do this to me and you by forcing me to stay with you is no good. I'm the one who's no good, I do need heaps of help. I need counselling I think."

He didn't want to hear it. Every time I went to go and talk he'd just yell at me, "Shut up! Just shut up! Just f*** up, I don't want to hear from you!" and he truly meant it.

I still had 111 on the cellphone, but something in me snapped and when he was ordering me to tell the police something, I just went, "Nah". Again. I'd had enough of it, I really had. I just hung up the cellphone and threw it on the ground. "You f***ing bitch!" But immediately, the phone in the house rang. "Answer it," he orders me.

"This is the police. Are you ok?"

"Yes."

"Is your baby ok?"

"Yes."

"Have you been hurt yet?"

"No."

"Are you bleeding yet?"

"No."

"Do you have everything that you need for Katie?"

"No."

"What do you need?"

"Well we need proper food. She needs her formula." At that time we only had cold milk, flavoured milk. "She needs Treasures."

"Right, so what we're going to do is we're going to throw some things onto the back step."

So they did. It took about an hour, that whole thing. In getting it, Gerald held the gun to me while I carried Katie, same thing as when he walked us in, he held onto us with the gun. "Go outside, pick it up, go back in."

I changed the baby, got her bottle, settled her down, played with her. He kept us locked in the lounge, which was probably the north –facing wall. And anyhow, his mum ended up getting on the phone. The police talked to her and said "Your mum wants to talk to you."

He started crying when he heard his mum's voice. And then he just went "Nah" – ripped the phone out of the wall. Next thing I hear police speaking through a megaphone, and they were quite close. She said "Look, Gerald, we understand your frustration with Macsyna. You don't deserve to be treated this way. And she needs to be held accountable for it."

Immediately I'm thinking 'Oh, good one! You're just hanging me out to dry! I'm not even in safety yet and you're just encouraging him and fuelling his already intense anger!'

Now, I understand they were trying to get him to clearly focus his anger on me rather than Katie, but it sounded harsh at the time. "Well, It's Max that you're angry with. She's really done it now. So how about you let Katie go? She is the innocent one in this and I don't really think that she needs to be seeing anymore."

Gerald's listening to all this and he just goes, "Nah! Tell them no. Get your face up to the window and go 'Nah'."

The ordeal had begun at 7.30 in the morning, it was now approaching midday. Finally, we convinced Gerald to release Katie, and I took her to the door. This time, Gerald didn't come with us. I pushed her out the door and gave her to police. I could have kept running myself but I didn't. The cops were motioning me to run to them, but I turned around and walked back inside.

I just looked at Gerald and thought 'Nah. I've got to face the music.' After all that time I was scared as, but I was pretty sure that he wasn't going to do it. I still hoped. In the end, he came close maybe three times. And he goes "Just tell me that you love me."

I go "Can't do that. Can't do that. The most honest thing I've ever said to you, if I truly loved you I would have treated you better. I would have treasured you, given a damn about your feelings, not done any of this to you, but I didn't. So in truthfulness, I would be lying again if I was to say that I truly loved you. I want to love you, I have a love for the things that you do and I like the person that you are, but do I truly love you? I don't think so."

And he cried. He really, really cried. And he goes "Thanks. Least you told me. Just go."

I froze, the danger to me seemed to have gone but I sensed he might be about to do something stupid. Sure enough, he starts to speak again. "I'm going to get out. I can't live without you, I can't. So get out. I'm going to shoot myself, I'm not letting these bastards take me. I'm not going to jail. I've never done anything until now. Now that I know I've done this, now that I know I'm going to go to jail, I don't want to live anymore."

"You can't do this," I pleaded with him. "You can't wrap your life up in just me. I know I might have screwed up heaps of things but I'm not the only thing that can be good in your life. I'm actually far from it. There's somebody out there for you who wants just what you want and is going to be good to you. But right now you just can't take yourself out man."

"Ah f*** up," he says, "you don't really care. You just told me."

"No, I just said I don't love you as I should, but I do care. I don't think that you deserve to take yourself out and end your life. You're young, you still got plenty of time left. You're not going to be in jail for ten years or more. You've not killed me, not killed Katie. You threatened us. I was ratshit to you and I know why you're angry and I've told them that. And I'm sure that they'll be lenient, I'm sure."

"Ah f*** off."

"Nah! I'm not going to leave."

So he starts picking me up and trying to push me out the door, and I just refused. I did. I blocked the door as he was trying to shove me through it. "Bro, if you say that you're going to kill yourself and you really, really might, the least I can do is stop you from doing that. The least I can do."

I don't know how long that went on for, but he ended up giving me the gun, and I tossed it out the door to the police. Then I walked out, and a short time later Gerald came out with his hands in the air.

When I got outside, I was briefly re-united with baby Katie. While the hostage negotiation had been going on I had spoken to Gerald's mum on the phone. She had told me "I want to have Katie and I'm going to have her. If you don't agree, I'll have you for abandoning your children in my son's care. And I will win her anyway." I was in no position to look after Katie properly, my head was all messed up, and even though she had introduced me to smoking weed I wasn't going to win a court case. So once the police got us out of the situation Katie never ever came back into my care, I never ever saw her again for years after that.

Gerald, a 24 year old forklift driver from Napier, was in June 2001 charged with kidnapping, breaking and entering, unlawfully detaining and threatening to kill. He was sentenced to three years jail. His mother took over care of Katie, and Gerald became the child's caregiver after his release from prison. Macsyna's relationship with Peha didn't last long, and she drifted up State Highway One to South Auckland…

I'd begun working out in Takanini, and one day one of my work-mates, Donna, invited me to after work drinks nearby. We went to this place and it looked pretty good. Clean, tidy. There were spacies and pool tables and gambling machines and a bar. The bathroom had been nicely tiled. "What is this place?"

"Oh, it's the Highway 61 pad."

I was just wowed by it. People were freely smoking weed in there. One of the gang members, Johnny, was close to the head of the Highway 61, a dude called Link. Anyway, Johnny cornered Donna later and asked about me, "Where's your mate? Like her. Want her."

"You're not her type," Donna told him. "She don't need you in her life, she's just got herself back on track."

But Johnny wouldn't take no for an answer, and bribed Donna with LSD trips to give him my address. A few days later Johnny turns up at my house. "What are you up to? Want to go get some pizza? Go out on a date?"

I'd never ever had that said to me before. So anyway, one thing led to another and I dated Johnny. About the second month of knowing Johnny, I'd see him once a week, he's like "Do you want to try this stuff?"

"What is it?"

"It's just called Speed."

"Oh, ok. What do you do?"

"You just snort it up your nose."

"What does it do?" I never knew, didn't know anything about it, had never seen it before.

"Oh, it just gives you a little bit extra legs. You can stay awake longer at parties."

"Really?"

"Yeah."

"Oh ok, yeah."

Talk about hurt. I had a nasty reaction to snorting what I now realise was methamphetamine up my nose. I've got bad sinuses anyway. It just burned the crap out of my nose so bad, one eye wouldn't stop crying and I could taste it down the back of my throat. Started gagging on it. I just felt sick. I couldn't dry retch either. I felt sick. Spinny motion sick. It was just really dumb anyway.

It's fair to say I didn't like methamphetamines, and contrary to all the inaccurate media stories and innuendo from Chris's lawyers, I never tried speed again. I didn't have a meth "habit", and I didn't have a "P" habit. In fact, my time with Johnny was the first time I was ever aware of P, when I saw him appearing to smoke Speed in a pipe. "Didn't know you could burn Speed?"

Johnny's mate leans over to me. "That's not Speed. This is Crack, or what we call Crack. It's P, a solid kind of methamphetamine, don't you know what that is?"

No, I didn't know what it was and after snorting some of the stuff up my nose and feeling like crap, I had no urge to get acquainted with speed or P any further. Johnny, on the other hand, had a habit going. I tried to stay away from him when he was on it. He wasn't violent towards me, but once he started smoking 'fries', as they called it, it made him really horny and he just wanted to have a mass orgy. I didn't like the effect it had on him. "Bro, I don't share. Any other chick come up, touch you like how I do, I will waste her. And that's the same for you, you'd do the same, I know you would, so I'm not keen."

But Johnny carried on, and I just turned a blind eye pretty much. I knew what he was up to. Then it started getting messy because he started lying to me. One night I turned up at his house at a new subdivision in Manurewa. Went to grab my stuff, and told him he wasn't welcome at my house while he was on that Crack cause he was just all over the place – I couldn't get a decent conversation out of him. He'd be all frantic and pacing and grinding his teeth. Then he'd sit down and go, "sigh", and then do it all over again. And continue to do it. I didn't like it, I was just awkward and uneasy around him when he was under the influence of P.

It finally came to a head because while I was visiting I was adjusting an earring and it dropped into the bathroom rubbish bin. I reached in to retrieve it and found my hand brushing against a used condom.

He'd gone out a little earlier so I txted him. "Bro, you been mucking around on me?"

And he goes "I'm f***ing sick of your accusations, you bitch. You're always accusing me."

"Well," I told him, "I just dropped my butterfly in your rubbish bin and there was a used condom in there so that's not my mouth lying, that's you trying to tell me that you haven't done it but I've found evidence, so whatever."

He sent a sheepish, apologising txt back, but I let him have it and told him it was over.

Next thing I know, someone's knocking at the door of my own flat later in the day, and it's Johnny. From his face I can tell there's a bit of déjà vu about to take place. He grabbed me and drove me to the Highway 61 pad, telling me that's where I'd be staying.

"I don't want to stay."

And he goes "Too f***ing bad, you're staying here. And you're going to stay here and you're going to do as you're f***ing told or I'm going to punch your f***ing head in."

"Nah," I said. Thwack, went his hand across my face with a huge-as slap. He marched me to the back of the gang pad, and hidden at the back is a secret staircase that he had to reach up and pull down. He shoves me up the stairs into a kind of attic space, and locks the staircase back up from below. I was stuck there, with no way out. The attic at the Highway 61 pad became my prison for the next two weeks. Johnny stayed there with me, and if I showered he came and stood outside the shower door, or if we made food in the kitchen he'd be right beside me.

I only managed to escape when one day he brought his young

daughter up with him on one of his visits to me. He was drunk, or tired or stoned or all three, and he asked me to look after the little girl while he slept. So I let him pass out, and when he was asleep I found out from the child what her mum's name was and found it in Johnny's cellphone.

"Could you come to the pad and come and get your daughter please? Because I've been stuck here and I'm going to leave and I'm going to do it really soon, and I don't want to leave your daughter unattended."

Johnny's just out cold. She goes, "Ah f***, has he been on the fries again?"

"Yep."

After I ran away from the Highway 61 pad, the only address I knew in the local area that Johnny didn't know belonged to an old guy named Banjo Kahui.

Now, I'd met Banjo for the first time a few months earlier at the Clendon Tavern, purely by accident. A workmate had suggested a drink there, and she was running late so I had arrived first.

There were a few people in the pub. And Banjo, Chris Kahui's father was one of them. Hadn't met him at this stage. While I was waiting for my friend, this fight broke out. Well, I thought it was a fight. A kerfuffle. Then all I could hear was this strangled voice, Banjo's voice, quite groggy and froggy. He was like "Nah bro, nah bro, that's *my* beer!"

"Oh come on bro, just put it back."

There were two guys, one around about my age – mid to late 20s at the time – and the other I later found out was the guy's father. Anyway, one of them's got Banjo by the throat and the other one's holding him by the shoulders and they've pinned him to the wall. Both of them exceed him in height by at least a foot. And my first impressions are 'How can you pick on this poor old man? As rough as he looks, just get a life man! Leave him alone!'

So I went over and I just pushed my hands between them, "Just let him go man! What are you's doing?"

The bartender's caught wind of all this and goes, "Oh, no, that's Banjo! He always does that!"

I was going "I don't care! And obviously you don't care! Well I care enough to not let that happen to him."

It was what would go on once Banjo got started, he had this ability to wind people up, rub them up the wrong way. So this was one of those occasions but I didn't know. The older of the two men, he turns around and goes "Piss off little girl, this is none of your business."

"You piss off! If that was your grandfather would you stand there and watch it? You idiot! Get a life!"

And he goes "You get a life!"

We just started arguing, and he goes "What are you going to do?" And he pushed me, so I pushed him back, I didn't have any fear I guess. "I'm not scared of you bro. Then what? You're going to hit me? What a coward. What a pathetic fool. If you call yourself a man, you're a pathetic excuse for a man."

I just kept going at him. He backed off. They let go of Banjo and decided to turn their attention on me. "Who the F are you? This is our pub. You're a nobody, get out!"

"No, you're a nobody! This a public bar, it doesn't say 'this belongs to these two fools over here beating up some old man.'" It was just all on. In the meantime the bartender's over by the table and the security have come over and they're standing there having a good old chuckle. I'm still standing there all fired up and Banjo's just standing there making this sort of Billy-T cackling noise. Suddenly Atawhai, the girl I'd been waiting for, turns up and is horrified to see all this carry on. "Oh my gosh, Max, what are you doing?"

I was going "These eggs are picking on this old fulla and they were going to try and beat him up."

And she goes, "Oh no. He always does that, that's Banjo."

"Who cares if he always does that? You don't do that, he's an old man!"

They all started laughing at me. It was like the day I ran into the tree in front of Kevin, everyone was just pissing themselves. Banjo comes up to me.

"Girl, thank you. Thanks for that. I'd buy you a beer but I'm broke."

So Atawhai and I struck up this friendship with Banjo Kahui, and the pair of us would often meet Banjo down at the Clendon on a Tuesday or Wednesday when the pub was relatively quiet. It got to the point if we turned up there a bit late he'd go "Where were you girls? I was waiting for you. Got a party to go to!" He had this Bongo wagon van, and we would go to parties with him.

Sometimes we'd get taunted, Atawhai and I, "Which one of you's are dicking the old man?"

And we're just like "Oh both of us, idiot." None of it actually ever happened. There was nothing sexual between me and Banjo, or Banjo and Atawhai. Sure, he tried his luck, he propositioned us, but he never physically forced himself onto us aside from have an extra long hug and then slip his hand down our shoulder and we'd quickly grab his hand. But it was harmless. For me I'd call it harmless. I just never ever saw him as a threat I guess, he was an old man.

I was asked this by Chris Kahui's lawyer, Lorraine Smith, at the high court trial. The very first one. She point blank asked that question "Did you have any sexual relations with Banjo Kahui? Chris' father."

"No."

"Well did you *try* to have any?"

So she just went along that path. We didn't. I told her he was an old man. But I think it was just part of Lorraine trying to sow doubt about me in the minds of the jury, having a dig at my supposed sexual preferences and trying to hint that I was a sexual predator.

It was through Banjo, obviously, that I met Chris.

Banjo was a huge drinker, the whole house was, and he would invite us to his home where he'd be throwing this big party. There was lots of alcohol, but only this tiny transistor radio for sounds. Just then this teenager comes out of his room, and we're like, "Whoa, are there kids in this house?"

CHAPTER ELEVEN

The Childhood Of Chris Kahui

The inquest would later hear evidence that Chris Kahui had left high school at the end of third form. That was his highest level of education. Despite the law requiring all children to remain at school until at least 15 at the time, Kahui fell through the cracks, and ended up doing odd-jobs for his father for the next three years…

Chris was only 16 at this stage. I got to know him over the next couple of years. There was nothing sexual for a long time, but Chris was this quiet kid who would only talk if he trusted you, and he opened up to me. We'd had a similar background.

To understand the Kahui clan you first have to know the background. Chris' big sister Tracey is the result of a relationship between their mother Gwen and her first partner Herman. They had Herman Jnr and Tracey for sure that I know of. There's another sister Rachel but I never knew exactly where she fitted in.

Then on Banjo Kahui's side there were the children from his first relationship with Caroline. They had a Frank, a Charlene, a Tanya. Then Banjo hooked up with Gwen and they had William, Chris, Mona, Eva and Elvis. William is the oldest full brother to Chris, and he's gay and dresses as a female.

If you talk to Banjo and Gwen, they'll tell you their time as a family together was a happy party time. That's what they call it. "Everybody was always happy". But Chris, William and Mona have told me they found it bloody horrific.

The kids would often have no food for up to three days. Yet everyday their mum and dad would always come back rotten as skunks. They'd come back with takeaway food and hide it under their beds. And their kids would know that it was there, but their only hope of eating would be to wait for Banjo and Gwen to pass out. Then the kids would crawl in underneath the bed and raid the stash and feed themselves with what was left.

They always felt loved – or that's what they called it. Always. If Gwen was sober, she always attended to them, cooked for them. She was the gentler of the two. They did get smacks from her but she would be fair and firm, not outright bashing the kids, at least at first. This is what Chris and Mona told me. At first she was like that. But as they grew older, so they were coming up to just before primary and just going into primary, she became as shitty and angry and violent as Banjo.

I remember asking Chris, "Were you's alright?" He'd be like "Nah. Mum would tell us to run from the room because Dad would whack all us out of the way, hit us just to get to Mum. Waste her in front of us, you know, really smack her around in front of us."

The Kahui parents would be drinking at best every day but when times were hard they'd probably only get to drink four or five times a week. They were always having parties at their house. Their cousins to Chris, older cousins, they were around Tracey's age, they were real cruel to Chris and Mona and them. They would make them babysit their kids, when they were having children. Give them a hiding just for a laugh, boot them up the bum just for a laugh.

They always managed to smile. Chris and Mona told me because they hardly ever cried, they were seen, not heard, not allowed to be heard, their cousins and aunties and uncles called them survivors because of it. From what I gathered from how they told the story, that gave them a bit of hope. A bit of faith. And a little bit of endurance to carry on and look for a better life. And look forward to it. That if they could withstand that sort of childhood, once they became adults and were able to do things for themselves, then they would. And they would simply because they were survivors and were called survivors from young. Not a very nice upbringing. I would say similar to mine, although at least my whanau intervened in the end.

When the youngest, Eva and Elvis came along, Banjo and Gwen would hit them too – they were just toddlers. If either screamed too loud, they were smacked for crying. And sometimes they'd had no formula, no anything so they'd just have to drink water and they'd still grizzle and cry because they were hungry. But their only feed was water.

When Chris was telling me all this there were tears streaming down his face. He was crying and genuinely hurt about it. At different times when we discussed it, he'd sometimes be really angry. When he could recall it, when he did recall it, he'd be really angry about the selfishness in his parents. He'd say that.

"My parents, they didn't really care about us, they were pretty selfish. They loved us when they were drunk and happy at first, but once they got too drunk and started getting tired they were just relentless." To the point where their own beds had to be given up for aunties and uncles so that Mum and Dad looked good in the aunties' and uncles' eyes. "Oh, choice, we've got a bed for the night."

"Where did you sleep?" I asked him.

"We had to all bunk up on the couch," Chris told me. "And just sleep sitting up. Me and Mona would hold on to the younger ones and just keep them by us and if any of the fighting went down we'd just keep quiet and pretend we were asleep." And it made him feel real shitty at the time, and he just thought that if he closed his eyes and held on tight then it wouldn't be so bad.

For me, I know what that feels like, to be in that situation. My feelings when I was in a similar situation was that the fear doesn't stop coming to your memory, your hearing is heightened – any little opening door creak and you're fearing that it's going to be a fight coming in the door. Or Dad's pissed off and he's come in with a belt or stick or something to whack the kids. A door. Footsteps. You wonder who it's going to be next.

At night, Chris has been asleep in the bedroom as a child, when through the door has come a couple in heated sexual kissing, just into what they're doing, and they've just fallen on the bed while he's been topped and tailed with his brother on the bed and they didn't care. These adults just kept on kissing and kept on doing the whole business while Chris and William had to just squeeze out from underneath the adults and get out of the room. Sometimes, Chris told me, they weren't even allowed to get out of the room "And we could hear them having sex and we weren't allowed to move and we just had to squeeze our ears shut and close our eyes and turn the other way." That's just gross.

So these were guests at parties, and sometimes even Gwen and Banjo were having sex. Chris told me it happened a lot. Not just once a week, or once a month. Frequently during the week. He'd tell me that it used to make him feel sick. But they would sober up and get it together and clean up the broken mess, broken glass, broken doors. Give the booze a rest for a couple of days and bath the kids and take them out to the park and this would renew his faith and belief in his mum and dad.

Usually after they'd given the kids a treat like this, Chris told me he'd feel stink sometimes for thinking badly of his parents over all their "disgusting, selfish, stupid, drunk, idiot behaviour. But then they take us out to the park and shout us fish and chips and I'd feel stink for thinking that of them earlier."

And I'm going "Oh yeah, yeah." So I could understand as Chris explained what he had to live through as a child, his feelings. They were real, and sad.

He told me all this before we even engaged in a relationship, so we'd never had sex, never partnered up. I think it was just because we came from similar experiences. He would talk lots to me anyway, I don't know why me. He knew me and Atawhai. He didn't say anything to her, stuff all. In general, even his own family members thought him to be a quiet person. Yes he is, he is quietly spoken but if he trusts you enough he talks. He talks quite openly even. Intense. He has a limited vocabulary, but his ability to talk openly and describe it vividly wasn't hindered by that. He didn't have any problems saying how he felt. Distinguishing how he thought from how he felt.

It was an incredibly sad story, and he needed to share it. He talked of love and hate with the same hand. Why do I think that? Well, he would talk about himself and Mona, they would get whacks across the head that would send them flying from one side of the room to the other and they would hit the wall and literally splat and slide down walls. Often. A lot. Especially Banjo. He would do it.

Chris' mum hit him as well, he spoke of Gwen doing it to him one time and it was major and he said that he asked for something, he went to the kitchen, she was doing something or other in the kitchen, cooking. His mum was a little bit furious. Chris told me he couldn't recall what he went to ask her for but she just turned around and smacked him like an underarm bowl, clipping him under the chin, and he went flying and hit the other side of the room, from in the kitchen cooking area to the other side of the dining area. Past the table and chairs and hit the dining area wall, knocking him unconscious. And his nose bled. When he woke up

Mona was crying and hugging him and rocking him, and he just said that "Mum was just swearing her ass off at me" but Mona rocked him back and forth and cleaned him up, wiped his nose. There was heaps of that going on.

When Elvis, the youngest of the five Kahui kids, was born, Chris reckoned he wasn't hit as much, that the frequency of bashings had slowed down. Gwen had started distancing herself from the parties that Banjo was having. Even going out with her sisters, rather than drink at home with Banjo and his family. Started sticking up for the kids when Banjo hit them, or just his general temper when he was hitting, growling, punching, kicking them.

One of the worst things Chris told me about his father is that Banjo has punched him in the face like a man, and then stood him up again and punched him in the guts, and then stood him up and then smacked him across the head, and he was knocked out and lost a tooth – it was a baby tooth and it had come clean out. To be a baby tooth that must have happened somewhere between five and ten, really, but he would have had most of his adult teeth by ten, so probably earlier.

Chris' recollection of the age this happened is not clear, but he remembers being fairly young and it had been happening from as far as he can remember. On the other hand, I remember Chris used to defend his mum and dad for teaching him the importance of a staunch family.

"Wherever Mona goes, you go. And it's your responsibility to look after her if she gets in trouble, if she gets in a fight, if she falls over. Even if you're not near her, you're still responsible for her," Chris remembered Banjo telling him.

Mona told me the same thing much later, she's like "Yep, Chris' job was to look after me, my job was to look after Eva, William's job was to look after Chris, but Chris got to a certain age like three or four and was bullying William. Four or five maybe. So the oldest one would look after the one underneath."

It's a complex thing, because Chris and Mona speak of loving their mum intently, and that in their eyes "she always tried to do something about Dad hitting us". I remember them talking about that. But they spoke fondly of her. So that's why I say that the love and the hate are contained in the same hand, equal to each other, like a duality of the two.

To look back on this now puts some things in perspective. I knew it, but this is the first time I've been asked so deeply about the backgrounds of the Kahuis. The closest police got to asking me that question was "In your opinion, did Chris have a very good upbringing?"

"Nah."

"Did he have loving parents?"

"I know that they do love him, yep."

And that was pretty much it. I didn't elaborate on it and in hindsight maybe I could have. At the time of interviewing my mind was not focused on what I could recall of the Kahuis, it was focused on what happened to Chris and Cru. I didn't see the two events as connected at the time.

The question for me right now is how I should process this in my head. I think it reinforces for me that Chris had survival skills, he has had from a young age a sense of 'knowing', a sense of foreboding. It's a sense of danger or that something is amiss. The sound of raised voices, the hearing of drunken footsteps coming, a change in the wind, like an increase in tension or anger – these are the life skills that we had to learn as children just to survive, and those skills don't go away.

I'm being asked these questions, and they trigger for me things that I'm sure they should have triggered in Chris' mind with our sons. He should have had that natural instinct that he built up, as he grew up with his parents being the way that they were – violent and not very nice to them at times. You come to know certain things that you can feel when they're angry, or you can tell by the things going on that something's going to come, or something's going to happen. Did something happen and Chris failed to detect it in time, or did Chris do this? I wasn't there. I have my beliefs, but we will come to that in time.

So that was Chris' family background, and he told me all this long before we began our relationship in 2004. But the way we hooked up was by accident. We'd been drinking at Banjo's house when one of Chris' cousins, Charlie Hetaraka turned up and invited us to take the party to his house. Chris was actually living at Charlie's house by then, because Banjo would routinely get drunk and throw his kids out of the house when it suited them.

I ended up falling asleep in a bedroom at Charlie's house, but I woke up to find Charlie naked, creeping into bed next to me. He had a monster puku, and the whole idea did nothing for me. I just bailed from the room and went running to a room across the hall, which turned out to be Chris' room. When he heard what Charlie had tried he rolled about laughing, and we joked about it for a while then I lay down in bed beside him and things led to sex.

The next day it was weird. I normally had no worries about going "Thank you for a good time." I'd forget about them and move on. Rude as it was that's how I preferred it. But I felt stink with Chris. I said to him "I know that you're younger than me, and this feels . . . man, am I taking advantage of you? Is this alright?"

He's like "Yeah! Don't go!"

Over the next few days we basically tried to get our heads around whether it was a relationship or not. I kept telling Chris, "You're not my boyfriend and I'm not your girlfriend," but in truth it was more complex. I just felt weird, because I was having emotional feelings again, feelings of wanting to have somebody of my own and not just casually have sex with men. I warned Chris, "I just better be careful because I suck at relationships."

When Chris' big sister Tracey heard about us she practically fell off her perch. She drove around and we had a shouting match.

"What the f*** are you doing here?" she demanded to know.

"None of your business big girl, piss off."

And she was like "You don't tell me to piss off."

"Uh, yeah, I just did. It's none of your business. You pay none of these bills and you don't have the same authority that you have over your brothers and sisters. Not with me."

Tracey got really rarked. "I'm going to smash your f***ing head in."

"Yeah, well, I'm standing right here so you come over here and you do it. I'm not scared of you."

She hit the roof and yelled out to Chris "Chris, get in this bloody car, you're coming with me!"

I learnt then that Tracey was very protective, some might say 'controlling', of Chris. He was looking this way and that, and I was telling him that family or not, her tone and demands were disrespectful of Chris and that he shouldn't just jump when Tracey said so.

"That *thing* there, your sister there, just kicks up a stink, says 'get in the car' and you jump. But if you keep doing that, how are you going to learn how to make decisions for yourself? And all I'm

THE CHILDHOOD OF CHRIS KAHUI

saying to you is if you decide to stay, I'm going to back you. She can't . . . I'm not scared of her. She can't make you do things that you don't want to do."

We must have looked a right bunch to the rest of the street. Eventually, Chris did climb into the car with Tracey and drive off, and I just thought he'd gone weak at the knees, but then he arrived back and demanded I drive with him back to Tracey's house. This was an unexpected and unwanted development and I was making every excuse under the sun to avoid it. But Chris said to me, "I've told her I love you, and that I want you in my life, and that she's going to have to live with it."

My eyes went wide like that cartoon coyote's. Love me? "We've only known each other four weeks man! Love?"

Yeah, he said, and I've told her to accept you and that I'm bringing you back with me. "This is the ultimatum. You said you want to be with me, this is one of the things that you've got to do. Same with her. You've got to accept her just as she's has to accept you. So let's go."

Chris had grown in the space of three hours. So we did, and Tracey even apologised to me when we got there. "As long as you're with my brother you're welcome here and I'll stop doing it."

From that point, things eased up between Tracey, Chris and I. She always kept her distance in regards to me for sure. Whenever she would be having discussions with Chris in regards to family things, I'd never interject. But if she was just flat swearing or whatever, which came up a few times, I would.

I moved out of my Kingsland flat, and moved in with Chris and Charlie.

At the end of 2004, we fell pregnant with Shayne. It wasn't planned, but again it wasn't unexpected. At least, not to me. Chris didn't want Shayne. "I haven't really thought about being a father and I don't really want to be responsible for a child yet. I'm only 18 years old."

"Ok. I hear you," I told him, "but you did not want to wear condoms and I've explained to you my reasons for not wanting to be on the pill while sick, cause it's not safe. Or there's abstinence, and you weren't keen to participate in abstinence either, you just weren't keen on that either. So this is the responsibility that you're faced with. There is a life that's growing within me, and now that you've thought about it, you've decided you don't want it. That's pretty crappy. You knew very well what we were doing and you knew the risks and here we are."

Chris thought about it for a while, then admitted his biggest fear was actually telling Tracey. I was in tears, and suggested he have a good long think about it. Abortion, after my last experience, was not going to be an option. In the end Chris decided to see his sister Mona and talk it through with her.

Mona was really happy for him, very encouraging, told Chris he would make a great father.

"My sister thinks that we should just go for it if we're going to have a baby, and we're already pregnant, abortion's not an option that we should be thinking of. For me she thinks that I'd make a good dad and I want to have a go at it. I'm not so scared now and I'm not so unsure. I look forward to being a dad."

That was the same day. Chris had managed to pull a 180. I was a bit worried that he could swing so easily, but was relieved he'd agreed to step up and be a father. For me, though, Chris needed to go through the kind of steep learning curve I had put Kevin through ten years earlier. Fatherhood meant responsibility, and a change from focus on the one to focus on the family unit.

The Kahui whanau were prone to lying around, and I needed Chris to break that habit.

"Get up and out of bed and invigorate yourself, you're 18 years of age, you should have more get up and go than what you have." That's what I would tell him. It just wasn't done in my day down in Wairoa, 18 year old people, men and girls and boys were out of bed and, if you were jobless, at least get up and take care of the home. You know, there's things to do. You don't sleep all day, half the day away. Look a bit further than just the front of your nose.

That was me, always on his case about that. Chris needed to start thinking about getting a job and thinking as a provider. "This is the time to start practising it, get into the motion of it now," I told him.

Have I walked the talk? I've certainly tried. Everyone has assumed I was constantly on the benefit, never worked a day in my life. Yes, I have taken benefits from time to time, but I have also worked.

I went on the benefit for a while when Sean was two or three and I was a solo mother with the two young children. I really only went back on the benefit when I wasn't working. If I compile them all together about seven years of my 34 years of life have been spent on a benefit, off and on.

With extended families, usually there's kai to be had somewhere, and a roof. I didn't usually want for things. Sometimes, like when I've stayed with my sister Emily, I've done unpaid work for her in place of paying rent and board. That can get a little unbalanced – I once painted her and her husband's house, and it would have cost them about $4,000 to get it done, and she reckoned it was only worth two weeks' board. Times were tight, everyone wanted cash.

I've never been a long-term beneficiary ripping off the system while my partner works, although I was on the sickness benefit during my early pregnancy with Shayne. Chris was on a benefit. In the early stages of our relationship, Chris would not share a dollar with me, not even shout me a $5 Chinese takeaway for lunch. He took the view his money was his money, and because he's had so little all his life, whatever little he got he put aside to pay off his car. Gets $30 in his hand and he'd really like it to himself. I thought, 'well, fair enough. I don't want to complain and my money's mine and yours is yours, you take care of your own bills financially and I'll take care of my own.'

Once I got midway through my pregnancy with Shayne, though, they decided to employ me in paid work, so I chopped the benefit off. When I knew I had a source of income, I always cancelled the benefit, so when people say I was just in a dependency trap, no I wasn't. I used the benefit as a backstop, and never stopped looking for work.

This was the work ethic I wanted Chris to pick up as a prospective father. Fine, you are on a benefit, but lift your eyes higher man.

I gave birth to baby Shayne in May 2005. We were still living at Banjo's house in Maplesden Drive, Clendon. Chris didn't man up like I wanted and we had a fight. "I don't want to be your man, I ain't your man anymore, we're off."

The scrap was over his closeness with Mona, incidentally. I had accused him and Mona of hiding something, because that closeness that they shared was so strong. Their closeness was so strong that they were willing to lie for each other. And between the two of them, they knew something. Hell, he went off the wall when it came to speaking anything untoward about Mona, he would hit the fan. And he did, and it quickly went pear-shaped. The closest he ever came to hitting me was choking me in the driveway while his father was holding me by the shirt and his aunty was trying to slap me and it was the younger sister Eva who interjected there.

It's interesting that Chris' new wife has put her foot down over Mona as well, and told Chris he's not allowed to see Mona as much as he used to. So others are picking up on that. Anyway, it was September 2005 and Chris threw me out, so I took Shayne and left. Ended up having a couple of casual flings while we were apart, but then we got back together again soon after – we were only apart for a couple of weeks.

My life changed again on February 16, 2006. I was working out at Emily's work in South Auckland. I went to the toilet but instead of a wee out came this big solid something, like nothing I'd ever seen before, and it had fallen into the toilet bowl. I then began to bleed heavily. The place was full of men and I didn't want to call out, so I texted Emily. When she came in and saw this thing, she threw up – she was already heavily pregnant with her daughter Ellen. So she was compromised, and I was compromised. Anyway, we cleaned ourselves up and she drove me to Middlemore Hospital.

The doctor did urine and blood tests, went away and he came back a little while longer and he goes "Ok, so we've got good news and maybe some bad news, but still, the best thing is that there's good news."

CHAPTER TWELVE

Pregnant With Twins

I was sitting there looking at the doctor, waiting for the good news. And he goes "Well you're pregnant." That came as a shock, but probably explained why I hadn't lost weight after Shayne.

"Perhaps you've had a miscarriage, and we're going to have to do some further tests."

"You think I might have miscarried, but I'm still pregnant?"

"Yes, you are. But we're just going to check your body out."

They ran me through this new machine that had arrived at Middlemore Hospital's neo-natal unit, worth $120,000 or something. So anyway I went and used it. A short time later the doctor came in and said, "Well we can tell you that you are definitely pregnant and those pregnancies are still highly viable."

"Pregnan*cies*?"

"Yes, congratulations, they're twins."

"So is it likely that the lump that came out was a child?"

He goes "Yes, well the possibility is there, they could have been triplets. I can't be sure."

I only ever shared that with Chris, Mona and Emily. I suspect it was leaked to the public by his family, and I wasn't very happy about that – it was private.

Middlemore Hospital decided to admit me, explaining that my twins were identical, but that they had an extremely rare complication known as MCMA, which was that they shared the same amniotic sac and the same placenta, which fed two cords. But the umbilical cords from their puku entwined as one, and it was causing problems and a risk that the twins would become tangled in each other's cords as they grew and effectively strangle their blood and oxygen supplies.

There were also worries about their organs. Their brain, the liver, the kidney and the lungs. The eyes. In the case of a premature birth, what would they be able to assist with? They came up with a plan where they could definitely give me hormonal injections, three times a day in small doses, which would aid and assist in the development of their internal organs. If they had to do an emergency delivery, they were somewhat prepared.

I had to have scans twice a day. It was going to be a bit much for me to travel, do that, come home, go back for the second one and the third one, which was why they decided to admit me into the wards full time. It was pretty hard physically. And mentally it was hard because I was worried about baby Shayne and parties going on at Banjo's house in Maplesden Drive. At that stage, we hadn't quite moved over to Courtenay Crescent. We'd been planning the shift, but Chris didn't want to be in the house on his own, he wanted to be with everyone else, so he just stayed at Maplesden with his father.

Every second day or so, Chris would bring Shayne to the hospital for visits. I really enjoyed that, because I got to see Shayne's little milestones. I remember when he started climbing, because the old window sills at the hospital, they're sort of like the bay windows but they're smooth with lino on them. I'd sit him on there and he starts going up the curtains at the hospital.

I stayed in hospital for four weeks until they detected a problem in the twins' oxygen levels and decided to perform an emergency caesarean on March 20, 2006.

They were delivered by a team of four doctors. The doctor, Graham Parry, that's his name, he did all my care, he wasn't present at the birth. Because it was an emergency I was taken from Middlemore and straight to National Women's Auckland hospital. And they were delivered in the special ward there.

That whole process was quite sombre. It wasn't high stress. They even had gentle music playing, they had their voices low. It was really well done if I could say that. I had a very, very stressless delivery. Chris was there eventually, he turned up. He came into the operating theatre with me. I watched the procedure so I literally saw them cut and hook my tummy lining skin and lift it over. Chris is like, he won't even look, he's looking at me and going "You're sick, man, what are you doing?"

And I'm like "I'm never going to get this chance, I've always wondered what it looks like."

It was really surreal. Real but not real. While the procedure's going on, it was like I was floating. It didn't feel like my physical body was lying there and that my physical body was on the operating table, cause the doctor, Emma Parry, who delivered them, she got the big clamp things, the things that they use to hold the tool, the instruments with and she's pinching my thighs and she's like "Can you feel that?"

"No, but I watched it, I'm pretty sure it would normally hurt."

She goes "Yep, good, so you're ready."

"Oh, ok."

So from start to finish I watched the whole process. It was an experience. It was weird, I was a little bit squeamish at the time, but only because when she moves my organs out of the way, I'm like "That's my, I just, you just go and put a block there." You know how you hold long grass in a paddock and you pin it there with a tack or something, it was like that. "Woah, easy on my organs!"

The doctor just smiled. "Ok, I know, it looks a bit vulgar, but when you've done it so many times it's like a walk in the park."

This was my first delivery with painkillers – an epidural. For me the squeamish part came when the sac, you could only see a very small part of it and there's organs all over it, but I could clearly see it and I could see the umbilical knots and I could see, like, a cheek and a head. I was just like "They're right there!"

And she just cuts into it in a particular way so the amniotic waters drain away safely, and then I could see their little shapes, the hump of their backs, their little heads, the tiny little things. Just like when you see the scans. The placenta looked a bit weird and it had turned green. The bad news was she didn't take it out but pushed it down into my cervix and told me to deliver it naturally. Something to do with getting the natural birth hormones to kick in.

Then she takes baby Chris out and cuts the cord quickly. The nurse swaddles the baby underneath and goes "There he is!"

Big Chris is just gagging and holding his nose, and I'm like "Whaa! Can I touch him?"

"Yeah, you can touch him!"

It was so amazing. Just quickly and then "We've got to get him in there now and into the …"

"Yep, sweet as!"

So he goes away and they go "Ok, so we're going to get the other one now."

And she goes in, but this time she goes in and she's got these extension things, goes like this and puts these other things on, got new scrubs on and it's like her arms disappears into my body and I'm like "Woah!"

She's got her arm in there up to her elbow, yanking bits of umbilical cord out of me like a magician's handkerchief trick. She's got this silver tray thing, and this nurse is holding it and she's going arm over arm with the umbilical cord which she's got. Pretty soon the first tray is overloaded and she's still going and they call for the big kidney pan.

So the other nurse hands this nurse the kidney pan and she turns it from that little tray into the kidney pan and there's this big chunk, heaps and heaps and heaps of umbilical cord, before she lifts Cru up. When she's at the end of it the surgeon goes "Oh, finally!" And out comes Cru to meet the world. So that's what it was. It was all around him, tucked under him and she had to carefully, pretty much unravel it.

I healed really fast, just three days, and the next day, Ellen was born. Emily's daughter Ellen. I just missed the birth, I had my morphine pack on and was allowed to go. Stuart drove over, picked me up, shot me back out to Papakura and I just missed out on them. She had a home birth, a water birth. Got to hold her and see my sister.

The twins had been born at only 29 weeks gestation – nearly three months premature – about a kilo each. You could hold Chris in the palm of your hand, and from your fingertips to the base of your palm would be the length between his head and his bum.

They were so small their food intake was only one ml, I think, every hour, through the nose. The nurse had to do it because the suction and the compression had to be on and they couldn't allow any air bubbles in there.

It's at this point that Macsyna's narrative begins to intersect with what we now know from the public record. The twins and their mother had been transferred after the National Womens delivery back to Middlemore's Kids First neo-natal unit. In the court record from Chris Kahui's 2008 trial, health worker and child play specialist Kathryn Greenwood told of first meeting the family in April 2006 – at least ten days after the twins were born. Macsyna had already been discharged after just a few days.

Contrary to claims of an abusive upbringing that later ran riot all over a Facebook protest site, Greenwood told the court that when she first saw 11 month old Shayne in April, that he was in very good condition, a happy and healthy baby.[2] Macsyna was by now based at home, looking after Shayne. She elaborated on this in the 2010/2011 Inquest into the twins' deaths, "Shayne always appeared well looked-after and healthy – his hair was always brushed, face washed and he had clothes and shoes which fitted him." Some children, she told the inquest, would arrive at hospital hair not brushed, teeth not cleaned, "drinking coke for breakfast". Greenwood described baby Shayne's relationship with his parents as "warm".[3]

One to criticise, however, was social worker Nadine Ingham – who appeared to be extremely disapproving of Macsyna's admission to her at one point that she would sometimes lightly smack Shayne's hand if he reached for dangerous objects or if he hit other toddlers, but that she would never smack the child in anger. Ingham told the court[4] that an admission of smacking – and this was before the law change – was of concern. Ingham had been scheduled to be a witness for the defence of Chris Kahui.

Ingham first met Macsyna King and Chris Kahui on May 4, 2006, because the twins were approaching the point of being ready for discharge but the hospital was worried Macsyna and Chris had not visited as much as the hospital believed they should have...

It's a 50/50 call, that one. Yes, I could have been there more often while the twins were in the neo-natal unit, but here is the reality I faced. I had a one year old who needed looking after at home. I had to train-up my replacement at work. We were still in Banjo Kahui's cold and damp house, and we really needed to sort out the fresh accommodation at Courtenay Crescent which was warmer, and closer to the hospital. While the twins were in the ward we were living down at Clendon, in Manurewa. "This house," I remember saying to Chris, "it belongs to your dad and whatever he sees fit to do here, who are we to tell him not to? But we've got to get out and get on our own and your mum's offered that house to me and I just want to take it. I want to move."

And Chris was like "well we don't have beds, we don't have couches, we don't have anything for the twins, we don't have anything."

2 Evidence of Kathryn Greenwood, Queen vs Kahui, 2008
3 "Kahui Inquest: Hospital Staff Had No Concerns", NZ Herald, 2 November 2010
4 Evidence of Nadine Ingham, Queen vs Kahui, 2008

So I made it my business to get and collect and go and get all those things. I think it took me like three weeks and I had everything ready, pretty much, for the twins. New car seats. They had to have, they couldn't go straight into the cocoon ones because they were so premature, so I had to have these gel inserts in an upright, and that was just because their bones were still really soft and brittle. So even after the time they were going to spend in the hospital before they came home with me, they still had to be transported in them. I had to have them. So I went about doing that sort of preparation, and I pretty much had to do it on my own.

Chris was just not going to help. We had a number of fights, actually, over that. I remember going out to the Baby Factory in Papakura which had just opened, they had some major sales going on. I got the funding through Work and Income to get two special car seats and just one solid wooden cot. WINZ helped out, but that took a little bit of organisation to arrange at my end with them. But I spent my energy and my time doing that. And looking after Shayne. And I found it a real struggle, physically, on my body. You've probably read what the media say, but I doubt that most of those people in the media have actually had a caesarean section and know what toll it can have on the body. I'd had twins.

Chris Kahui was also asked at the inquest why he and Macsyna had only visited the twins 11 times according to hospital records, rather than 30 times. Kahui told the coroner: "We did not have a vehicle at the time, so it was quite hard to try and get up to the hospital."[5] The couple could not exactly walk to Middlemore all the way from Manurewa, where they were living at Banjo's house while they waited to finalise the lease on the Mangere home they would eventually move into. But where they could cadge a lift, they did. Middlemore's play specialist Kathryn Greenwood had told the court that the twins appeared to have gone four or five days at one point without the parents visiting. King denies it was ever that long…

The nurses were on rotational shifts of six hour time frames. So they're not eight hour shift nurses. They go from there, they spend an hour here and an hour there, they go into this prep room. They do heaps of sorts of things. So for me it wasn't my business to watch out for if

---

5 Evidence of Chris Kahui, Coroner's Inquest, 2010

they were there. Sometimes they didn't even know I was there.

I never went more than two days without seeing them, on the second day I would be there. That's not how they painted it in court, but I know that I visited, and so does Chris. And so does Banjo. Sometimes I'd make Banjo come with me. Actually, Chris' family came with me a lot more than he did. I can recall three times that he came with me. If there was more, well, I just don't remember. Sometimes I'd just take the twins and push them up to a mother's room where you can feed them in privacy, rather than in the ward where they sleep. And I'd do that. Not noted. Not said. Not on record. And nobody cared to ask.

And when I wasn't there, I was trying to get everything together, sort out the house, buy the furniture and everything else. I was so tired all the time. So unlike previous occasions where I was out partying, I guess for once I was actually doing something beneficial. People who don't know me presume to know everything about my case. "You didn't care cause you weren't there enough." Well I was.

The court evidence shows hospital staff may indeed have misinterpreted Macsyna King's apparently irregular visits as "indifference" when in fact it wasn't. Middlemore paediatrician Lindsay Mildenhall told the court how King had "roomed in" with the twins for a few days prior to them leaving hospital and that she had done "very well". He told the court Macsyna's interest in the babies was a surprise given the officially patchy attendance record, and he conceded that the twins had continued to do really well after their discharge to the home, and obviously somebody was looking after them.[6]

When the twins were sent home in early May, the hospital appointed home care nurse Jane Eyres to visit the family in their new Courtenay Crescent home. The last visits were May 31st – two weeks before the fatal injuries were inflicted and supposedly two weeks after some of the historical injuries such as broken ribs had been inflicted, and June 7, five days before breathing failure. In fact, the second of Eyres' visits would have been made almost immediately after the twins had supposedly first been injured, yet the health professional detected nothing in her tests of the twins. Nurse Eyres told Kahui's trial that the family seemed like "a good family", that the babies did not cry when handled, and that there were no bruises or other signs of injury. She told the court the babies

6 Evidence of Lindsay Mildenhall, Queen vs Kahui, 2008

appeared to be making "good progress" under Macsyna King's care, on the four occasions she saw them.[7]

"I handled the babies on each occasion, and I was not aware of any discomfort or anything that concerned me at all," Eyres told the inquest in 2010. "On each occasion I would pick up each twin individually to look at them, to see how responsive they were. When you are holding a baby you can feel the muscle tone of the limbs, you can see a lot by holding the baby."

Eyres told the inquest there were no bruises, no crying when the twins were handled around the chest or when their legs moved, "they were beautiful babies and they were growing appropriately". Under Macsyna King's primary care.[8] If the rib fractures had been inflicted after the children were discharged home, the half dozen broken ribs each child was suffering should have caused pain. Unless they were much older injuries, already healing well.

Another who saw the twins during this time was home care nurse Amanda Retter, who visited the Kahui home on May 11. She told the court Macsyna was paying good and close attention to what she was saying, and she testified at the Kahui trial of Macsyna's "wonderful interaction" with the twins.[9]

Were the twins, Chris and Cru Kahui, being systematically abused and grossly neglected during their time at home, as some Facebook users repeatedly alleged when trying to get this book banned? If they were, the healthcare professionals simply couldn't see any evidence of it.

As social worker Dianne Rainey told the trial[10], she visited twice – once unannounced – and on both occasions the twins were sleeping peacefully, wrapped up "like sausages", and the house was warm and tidy. She gave evidence that Macsyna was "always respectful…always kind".

For all the Facebookers who assumed King was a drunken beneficiary slob 24/7 who kept the twins in disgustingly abusive conditions, what the Coroner's inquest actually heard was:

MR MORRIS: Now, for all her faults that we have heard about, Macsyna was a very tidy housekeeper, was she not?

MR KAHUI: Yeah, she was tidy, yes.

MR MORRIS: And she would often go around tidying up everybody else's spaces too, would she not?

7 Evidence of Jane Eyres, Queen vs Kahui, 2008
8 Evidence of Jane Eyres, Coroner's Inquest, 2010
9 Evidence of Amanda Retter, Queen vs Kahui, 2008
10 Evidence of Dianne Rainey, Queen vs Kahui, 2008, pages 44 to 49 of transcript

MR KAHUI: Yes, if they have left like the kitchen and stuff untidy, she would clean it up, yes.

MR MORRIS: It is fair to say that she would leave the twins room immaculate as well, would she not?

MR KAHUI: Yes.

It wasn't just nurses who failed to detect even one sign of abuse or the historical fractures and head injuries. At one point – the hospital confirms it was mid May and Macsyna thought it was early June – the twins were hospitalised with bronchiolitis. They were under specialised paediatric care for two nights and two days, and Macsyna stayed with the twins in hospital. Not one Middlemore paediatrician or nurse reported finding any hint of the injuries the forensic experts insist were already there.

In truth, there were "five nursing visits, two social worker visits and three other arranged visits, and in total 12 interactions or attempted interactions by phone with the family"[11] in the space of just four weeks. Medical professionals and social workers were crawling all over the twins, and no one saw anything wrong.

On June 7, 2006, just a week before being admitted to hospital with fatal brain damage, family GP Dr Gopinth Nayar gave baby Cru a "thorough" check over. A number of Cru's ribs were fractured, but Nayar detected nothing – no pain response, no sign of abuse.[12]

So why is there such a cognitive dissonance between the expert medical evidence and the public perception? Perhaps because in the early days of this tragedy, the news media were trying to do their job but getting basic facts muddled. Take this example from the *New Zealand Herald*:[13]

Compare this with the house at 101 Maplesden Drive, Clendon, which Chris and Cru came home to in early May. Down a narrow right-of-way, it is small and shoddy. The walls are grey-blue fibreboard, misted with green mould, the guttering sprouts grass and weeds. The carport is sheltered by a plastic tarpaulin, the neighbours are too close. The high back fence is topped with two lines of barbed wire, and someone has put a couple of orange traffic cones at each side of the concrete drive, possibly to warn of children wandering, possibly to stop people scratching their cars. **[AUTHOR: The twins actually lived in a warm Mangere home at Courtenay Crescent, not here]**

Until last Tuesday 12 people and two small babies lived in this cramped

11 Cross-examination of Dianne Rainey, Coroner's Inquest, 2010
12 Evidence of Dr Gopinth Nayar, Queen vs Kahui, 2008
13 "The Kahui Twins – Murder and The Coverup", Caroll du Chateau et al, NZ Herald, 24 June 2006

three-bedroomed house, drinking, smoking dope and cigarettes, partying, fighting – and sleeping in rotating shifts. **[AUTHOR: No, there were not 12 people and two small babies here, the babies lived elsewhere and had their own nursery]**

Chris and Cru shared a cot, their 21-year-old father, Sonny Chris Kahui (known as Chris), a gentle, modest man with a collection of hangers-on, did much of their bathing and caring. **[AUTHOR: Interestingly, Chris and his lawyers spent the next five years trying to argue he had little experience with the twins, and repeatedly told the court Macsyna was the primary caregiver]**

Their mother, Macsyne, known as Macs, is 10 years older than her partner and sometimes jealous of the younger women who hang round him.

Despite the parties she expressed breast milk for the babies – at least intermittently. Her four older children live with another former partner.

And around them, like something out of Once Were Warriors, rages the whanau.

You've seen what the health professionals who visited the twins at home have said. But the idea of 12 drunken and drugged adults and two critically-injured twins cramped into one three-bedroom party house entered the public mindset with this flawed story, and never left. Wrong house, wrong incident. To get a better feel for what was happening in the lead up to the twins' deaths, we return to Macsyna King…

CHAPTER THIRTEEN

It's A Woman's Job

I didn't find Chris quite as gentle as the newspapers describe. Yes, he generally was, but he kept all his anger bottled up inside and when he finally lost it he really lost it. Punched the windscreen and cracked it. During the trial they asked me about it, but I'd forgotten all the other times that he'd spaz out – kick fences in, punch the car mudguards. Smash the door of the shed in, booted it down. Kicked holes in the weatherboard sheds. Smashed the glass doors to the back, cause it was aluminium frames, all that sort of thing. I'd totally forgotten about all the little lash outs that he's had as well.[14] But I've also never seen him hurt the kids.

For her part, King freely admitted at Kahui's trial that she was the more forceful of the two. "I would yell the loudest, I would swear at him and I wouldn't stop until I got what I wanted, to be honest. I would yell and swear at him and kick him in the shins and once I slapped his face."[15]

You've seen that Chris Kahui and Macsyna King actually shared similar backgrounds, but Kahui's has never been exposed until Macsyna's comments in this book. This lack of public knowledge about Chris Kahui's temperament and background allowed Kahui's lawyers to focus the public anger on King, as this account from the inquest shows:

"With respect your Honour," began Kahui lawyer Chris Wilkinson-Smith[16], "these things do not happen in a vacuum, and if one of the caregivers has such a disturbed upbringing, and her immediate history leading up to this event is so distressed and stressful, there may be an

---

14 Macsyna's evidence was corroborated in court by Mona Kahui, who admitted her brother had smashed windscreens and walls when he was angry, "but never people". Evidence of Mona Kahui, Queen vs Kahui, 2008
15 King, Queen vs Kahui, 2008. She enrolled for anger management but failed to attend.
16 Cross-examination of Macsyna King, Coroner's Inquest, 2010

inference that she is more likely to commit an act, and the same would go with Mr Kahui, if he had that sort of background...my suggestion to the Detective Sergeant is that there were many concerning aspects about her background that required closer inspection."

The Coroner was fascinated at this, asking if sauce for the goose was also appropriate for the gander – should we be looking at "Mr Kahui's case" too, he wondered.

"Well, if Mr Kahui had abandoned his first three children and then had been suspected of abandoning his fourth and fifth child, then I think he should also come under that sort of scrutiny," said Wilkinson-Smith. Having already admitted that a "disturbed upbringing" is relevant to explore, Wilkinson-Smith presumably will be welcoming this book's revelations about both caregivers.

The defence lawyer went further a little later at the inquest, rejecting suggestions that a fishing expedition in regard to Macsyna King was "blackening character" in order to make his own client look good. "I think, your Honour, there needs to be a distinction drawn between 'blackening character' and simply revealing aspects of a person's past that is true... blackening character is always out of bounds, exposing a person's true character in a way that may explain their actions is permissible."

Ah yes, said the Coroner, "but you see, the problem there is, you have not got evidence of her actions. It is a 'theory', to use your word...that this witness was responsible for the children's deaths."

There was another burst of anger between us in the final 48 hours before I took the children to hospital on Tuesday 13 June 2006. On the Sunday, June 11, I had Shayne with me and I was over at my sister Ems's. Chris' younger brother and sister, Elvis and Eva, had been staying with us on the Saturday so I dropped them off first when took I Shayne to Emily's. While I'm there, she's like "Sis, Ginta [a friend] and I are going to have a little bit of a get together tomorrow night. Just want to know if you can please sober drive me?"

I went "Yeah. Sweet as."

Shayne and I left Emily's place in Papakura before dark fell. I made my way back to Mangere – stopping in at Banjo's house at Maplesden to get some fresh clothes for Shayne because I had some there and he had spewed a little in the car. Elvis and Eva were there, and Banjo asked if I could stick around while "I just go down the road and have a joint with a mate. Are you going to be here when I get back?"

That was fine, so I just cleaned Shayne up and got him some Pamol. He was just a bit grizzly so I gave him some juice. Got sick with the juice and brought that up so I gave him some water and settled him down. Flannelled him and tidied him up again, rinsed his clothes out and he'd rested in the meantime so I just turned on the TV and just sat there and chilled out with the two younger ones on the big bed that Banjo had in the lounge in front of the telly.

Banjo had come back home by that time. "Thinking of staying the night girl?"

"I'm just having a little break, this boy just had a little bit of a spat."

So we watched TV together and laughed. Eventually, Banjo goes, "You get up here girl, I'll swap you, you get on the bed and I'll get on the couch. Get up there with the boy."

We swap, and Shayne and I go to sleep in the bed. Elvis and Eva crawl into the bed so we're all four of us in the bed. And Banjo's still there beside us on the couch and we all fall asleep. But I wake up to hear this noise. Chris has arrived – this is the Sunday night – and he wakes us up. Well he wakes me up and goes "Get your f***ing ass up, man, get home and come and help me with these boys." And he's like full on swearing at me.

"F***ing don't tell me what to do, bro, I just woke up alright?"

He goes "Get your ass home and get back to those boys."

"No, no. you get *your* ass home. And what are you doing here?"

He goes "What are *you* doing here?"

"Well I stopped, actually, cause of Shayne. He's just settled down, he's not very well."

He goes "Bullshit."

"You're bullshit. Idiot."

We just argue back and forth for a while and he leaves. Slams the door, off he goes. Shayne wakes up. Get back to caring for Shayne and he just starts with these coughing spats again, he's like retching and wrenching and coughing all at the same time. He's going red as. It woke Banjo up and it woke the other two up so I got Shayne dressed and put the bag over my shoulder. They just helped me with the stuff and got him into the car and I shot off to Middlemore hospital.

The doctors reckoned it was just the flu, but said they'd keep us overnight for observation, and give baby Shayne some oxygen and some more Pamol to help settle him down. That was it pretty much.

Shayne was fine by the morning. The doctor ticked him off and checked him off and just said "Best place is home. Rest. See you later." Discharged us. When I got home on Monday morning with Shayne the house is a little bit upside down, but ok. "Hey, what was all of that about?" I asked Chris as he came into the room.

He's like "F***, I needed your help man. With the boys." He's raving about how hard it was to look after them and all of this sort of carry on. So I checked on the twins, and they were fine. Bathed them, fed them, they're just absolutely normal. And they just did all their normal things. Their stool had come solid, good colour. Full wees and nappies. Two number 2's a day and four wets was around about it. They had got to four feeds a day at that point. So Chris & Cru were awake and alert and all of that. I knew I had to get ready to go to Emily's, so I settled the twins back down and started preparing.

"I need help with the boys," complained Chris. For the previous few weeks since the twins came home, I'd been their primary caregiver.

Macsyna may well have been wing commander when it came to baby duties, but she made sure Chris helped out. Basics like feeding, bathing and nappy changing were duties shared. That didn't stop Kahui's lawyers trying to suggest it was mainly the woman's job to notice anything wrong.

"You would expect a mother to pick up on subtle signs of problems with her child," ventured defence lawyer Michele Wilkinson-Smith during cross examination of a doctor at the inquest. Which prompted another female lawyer to spring to her feet and point out "My learned friend put to you that you would expect a mother to see subtle signs of, you know, injury or unwellness in a child. Now, if a father was involved in having taken a lot of care of the child for a year, and then was involved in feeding and changing and, on his own, looking after the twins, you would expect the father to also notice subtle signs, would you not? "

It took the good doctor a bit of umming and ahhing, but eventually he conceded, "Yes, I expect that."

When Kahui's lawyer had later persuaded Mona Kahui to name Macsyna King as being in charge of all things baby, the Coroner felt compelled to help set the record straight:

CORONER: But the feeding was shared between the two of them on occasions wasn't it?

MONA: Yes.

CORONER: And other things that need to be done with babies?

MONA: Yes.

CORONER: Changing their clothing, their nappies and bathing and so on?

MONA: Yes.

CORONER: Both of them helped each other there?

MONA: Yes.

Of course, the ultimate kicker is that only Chris Kahui knew how long the babies had gone hungry, because he had lied to everyone else and said he'd fed the babies. Chris was an experienced baby feeder. He chose not to tell the doctor his children had not fed in 24 hours. If these medical problems were truly not his fault, why did he keep that key information secret?

"If two three month old babies had not fed for 24 hours, certainly you would expect to be told that?" police counsel Simon Mount asked the doctor.[17]

"Yes, I think it would be pretty obvious."

"Christopher Kahui did not say anything to you about anything unusual in baby Cru's feeding pattern?" probed the lawyer.

"No."

Chris and Mona were regularly up at Middlemore visiting their ill mother Gwen who'd been in critical care but had just come out of danger. While she'd been critical, I'd taken on the load, and I reminded Chris of that. "Yeah. I've needed help with the boys over the last few weeks. And now that your mother is not in intensive care, I just want to go out with my sister."

So he knew I was going out. Stu knew, I told Stu. Ems knew, of course. And I think Mona and Stu also said to Chris, "Bro we're here, we'll help you. I'll help you. Ok so it'll be alright." It's not like Chris didn't have childcare experience – Shayne was now 13 months old – it was just that he preferred seeing his mother, to be frank, rather than child-minding.

All the witnesses agree, Macsyna King left the house after lunch to go to Emily's. Chris Kahui's older cousin April Saunders testified that she and her husband arrived sometime after 1pm and Macsyna wasn't there. She heard one of the babies crying, and picked up the twin making the noise,

17 Cross examination of Dr Gopinth Nayar, Coroner's Inquest, 2010

underneath a sign at one end of the cot saying "Cru".

April told the court, and this is crucial to the case, that she fed baby Cru the remains of his milk bottle that had been beside him – about an inch of milk left – and that the child opened his eyes during the feed and responded normally, there were no breathing difficulties and his eyes were normal.[18]

Why is this crucial? Because if Cru – who would later suffer the worst injuries – had been harmed prior to Macsyna leaving the house, the experts are confident he would not have been feeding properly or – more significantly – looking alert, as it usually only takes 10 minutes or so for symptoms of the brain injury to kick in. Saunders told the court she fed Cru for around 10 to 15 minutes, then put him back to sleep.

"About the time that April fed baby Cru," police counsel Simon Mount asked Mona Kahui, "you saw your brother Chris go into the twins room with a full bottle of milk?"

"Yes."

"And then, some time later he came back out of the room with the same bottle empty?"

"Yes."

"At the trial," asked Mount, "Macsyna was asked how the twins were, when she left the house on that Monday, and she said this at page 85, line 1, 'They looked normal, as normal as I remembered, fed normally, they were alert when they were awake, their eyes had just started following sound, their movements were not absolutely controlled but not floppy and limp so I left them and they were good, they were fine, there was nothing wrong with them, I wasn't worried and they were in the best condition that I remembered leaving them in.' Do you accept that Macsyna's description of the twins as being fine and good, at about that time on the Monday is an accurate description from your own observation?"

"Yes," agreed Mona Kahui.

April Saunders was not only Mona and Chris' cousin, she was a mother and grandmother with extensive childcare experience. Hers is the last independent testimony that the twins were normal. It was around 2pm on Monday, 12 June 2006…

I'd driven from Courtenay Cres in Emily's grey Subaru, which I'd borrowed, went to her home and we picked up the work truck, a

18 Evidence of April Saunders, Queen vs Kahui, 2008

Safari or Pajero or something, a big ugly beast with a chrome-dome looking top and the number plate HORSES.

She's got to do some painting and renovation quotes for this home in Manurewa, with one other lady who worked in the office and who did cleaning of any homes that were vacant. It was a rental property business with Shane Wenzell. While Ems was meeting this woman, Des, I stayed in the truck with her daughter Ellen. About half an hour to an hour later she comes out and goes "OK, I've done my whole job. Now I'll just txt this to Honey (*husband Pou*) and we'll go out to Ginta's."

"Oh, ok then."

"I'll drive us out there," said Emily, "but once we get there I'm going to have some wines with Ginta and you can drive us back. Does that still suit with you?"

And I'm like "Yep."

"Ok well first I've got to go and drop Ellen off to Honey". Incidentally, she calls her husband Honey.

We dropped Ellen off. I think we eventually dropped her off at the office on the way to Ginta's, because when we got to their home in Papakura, Honey's not there so she rings Honey from home at Rolleston[19] cause he's not there and Emily says, "I'll drop her off in Takanini."

In her testimony at Chris Kahui's trial, Emily said that Macsyna initially went to sleep for a while at Emily's house, probably understandable given a) the late night wake-up the previous evening when Chris had burst into Banjo's house demanding help with the twins, and b) the 4am visit to Middlemore hospital with a sick baby Shayne earlier that day. Emily told

---

19 Cellphone records show a call from Emily to husband Pou at 17.31 that evening. She appears to have been home in Rolleston – the Papakura street they lived in – while he was nearby, but clearly not close enough to physically speak to rather than phone. Pou testified at the inquest that he was driving around dropping some of his staff at their homes in various parts of South Auckland during this time. An hour passes, presumably dinner is made, and then Pou calls Emily at 18.47 from Takanini, where he worked, presumably to tell her he's there. Eleven minutes later, at 18.58, Emily calls Pou – presumably to tell him they're leaving now. She and Macsyna are on the move. See cross examinations of Emily Hepi and Pou Hepi, Coroner's Inquest, 2010. So as not to corrupt memories of the incident, I deliberately did not put the call times to Macsyna or indeed reveal that I had them. I wanted to see how they fitted her story. The sequence fits so well it actually clarifies some particularly lengthy exchanges during the inquest, when counsel were trying to get Pou Hepi, whose memory by all accounts is poor, to remember exactly what had happened that night and how baby Ellen had ended up in Pou's care. Macsyna remembered dropping the baby off at the office, which others had forgotten, and that salient fact not only proves Macsyna was with Emily, but it fits the call records. It also explains why Pou remembers seeing Macsyna with Emily, even though he could not have made it home.

the court they went out and did the painting quote only after Macsyna woke up several hours later.

So, having called Pou at 6.58pm to say "we're on our way with Ellen", they drive to the office to meet Pou in Takanini, drop off the baby, then sometime soon after that they rejoin Auckland's southern motorway at Manurewa and begin tracking north to transfer to the Northwestern motorway at Spaghetti Junction in the city. It's a Monday evening, but the worst of the rush hour is long past. From there it's off at the Waterview exit...and a sudden change of plans caused by a phone call at 7.38pm...

We go past Carrington and it goes down like a horse shoe, and around. The first garage that we came to, I can't remember if it's a Caltex or a BP, but we stop there because cause Ems needed gas and smokes. Suddenly her phone rings – I'd forgotten to bring mine, which was unusual. We're still slowing down to enter the service station forecourt, and I can see it's her husband calling. She goes "I'll speak to him as soon as I stop."

Which she does. "What's the matter?"

"You need to bring that bloody truck back. The boss has just given me a good bollocking over it."

"Why, I'm a fully licensed driver, I wasn't speeding, any tickets I get I'll be responsible."

And he's like "nah, It's just he just doesn't want it to go out unless it's on business, and you've gone out for something personal and you're going to be back late. We can't do that."

They have a little bit of a "thing" on the phone, and Emily was really annoyed. We got the gas anyway because the truck was on E. She bought smokes and other bits and pieces, and then we pulled out of the service station and took the back way through Avondale, and I guess Mt Albert and eventually Mays Road, until you join the Southwestern motorway out to the airport and Manukau.

Emily's spitting tacks and going "f***ing stinking so and so's," and she's booting it in this bloody truck, she's giving it death. We get back to Emily's place in Papakura, swap cars, jump into the Subaru, and off we go again to Ginta's.

While the women were driving back to return the car, Emily's husband had phoned again to check on their progress. That cellphone call went through at 7.54pm, and was routed through Vodafone's Mangere cellsite.

This was late-breaking news at the Kahui trial in 2008, and became one of the key pieces of evidence that drove the jury to acquit Chris Kahui. Defence lawyers argued strongly that the cellphone records meant Macsyna King must have returned to Courtenay Crescent, and bashed the children before being driven away again by Emily.

"Courtney Crescent is in Mangere, is it not?"

"Yes."

"You did not go to Mangere that evening, is that your evidence?"

Macsyna King replied: "I did not go anywhere else. I did not go to Mangere."

The issue of motive, and precisely why Macsyna would drive from halfway across town to sneak into a house normally full of people, and beat her babies senseless, was not credibly explored by Chris Kahui's defence lawyers. They didn't need to explain anything, they just had to plant the seeds of doubt about Macsyna's credibility as a witness, and a mother.

"You returned home and you lost it," defence lawyer Lorraine Smith argued. "What happened to make Emily suddenly go back? I put it to you that you did something terrible to the twins."

Addressing the jury, Lorraine Smith hammered the point home: "The defence says there is something very wrong about this. The defence says Emily King and Macsyna lied."

Despite the rhetoric, there were some sizeable evidential holes in the defence argument. Not the least of those was that if a cellphone call had indeed been made while the phone was at Courtenay Crescent, it would not actually have gone through the Mangere cellsite but a different one, Papatoetoe West. Far more likely then that the cellphone call was indeed placed while Emily and Macsyna were driving past Mangere on the Southwestern motorway, which is covered by the Mangere cellsite.[20]

Smith was right about one thing though – Macsyna King had testified strongly in court that there had been no return trip to the Mangere home, and then been forced to explain the cellphone call placing her in Mangere. King argues that she did not technically return to Mangere, and she is right, but such subtleties are lost on juries: if the cellsite is named Mangere, and your house is in Mangere, you must have been in Mangere.

The other problem with Lorraine Smith's carefully constructed conspiracy theory, is that it relied a lot on chance. For a brief period, around 7pm, there was only one adult in residence at Courtenay Crescent – Mac-

---

20 Evidence of Thorsten Teichmann, Vodafone, Queen vs Kahui, 2008

syna's brother Stuart. A short time later it was back up to the full quota of four adults. Macsyna had no way of accurately pinpointing, from half a city away, the best time to arrive at Courtenay Crescent without being noticed. It's a small house. Stuart King is adamant that his sister never came home that night. And there's still that issue of motive – why would a mother drive halfway across town to bash her babies, when she was having a girls' night off with her sister?

Why would the sister knowingly cover up a double murder of her own nephews, and then allow the killer to look after her own baby Ellen, born just a few days after the twins? As Crown Prosecutor Simon Moore put it to the jury, "When Emily gets up [the next morning] she finds Macsyna feeding her baby. The known baby-killer is feeding [Emily's] baby. Not only is Emily not concerned that this baby killer is feeding her baby, but she [then] asks if her sister will look after her baby while she is at work."

If the jury believe the defence claim, warned Moore, they need "a reality check".

The credence given to the cellphone records by the jury however was clearly reflected in a New Zealand Herald analysis of what led the jury to acquit Kahui in a record one minute verdict: "Denials by Ms King that she did not return to the south Auckland home for a brief time while Kahui was out dropping off his sister to visit their mother at hospital, were clearly not supported by cellphone records which showed Emily King had returned to the Mangere area that evening."

In other words, the jury believed that King's denial she had been home was overturned because of a call through the Mangere cellsite. Never mind Vodafone's evidence that the Papatoetoe West site was the one that actually covered the Kahui home.

When the cellphone and alleged secret trip resurfaced at the inquest in 2010, even Coroner Garry Evans was openly sceptical: "You've got to get her into the house, you've got to give her time to injure the babies – it's a long stretch, isn't it?"[21]

The coroner's disbelief didn't prevent Chris Kahui's lawyer, Chris Wilkinson-Smith from continuing to flog a dead horse: "You went to the house and did violence to the twins. You were annoyed the house was untidy, annoyed [Kahui] was visiting his mother. It would have only taken a few minutes. . ."[22]

Given that Kahui had regularly visited his mother while other family

21 Coroner's Inquest, 2010
22 Cross-examination of Macsyna King, Coroner's Inquest, 2010

members like her brother were left babysitting the twins, that discovery is unlikely to have set Macsyna off, even if she had turned up. More to the point, though, the 2010 version of the conspiracy theory suggests Macsyna didn't sneak across town to deliberately kill the twins, but entered the house normally – yet without attracting the attention of anyone there – and only then did she supposedly lose it when she saw Chris wasn't home. But instead of going into the rooms to see who was there and asking where Chris was, the public are supposed to believe that Macsyna blamed the twins for this turn of events and slammed them against a wall or the cot without making any noise that would attract the attention of her brother across the hall, then snuck out again.

Believe that, you'll believe anything. It violates the K.I.S.S principle at so many levels, and it's astounding that the trial jury in 2008 got sucked in by the smoke and mirrors surrounding it. We'll return to this in a moment.

So what did happen at Courtenay Crescent the night the twins stopped breathing?

Chris Kahui gave an exclusive interview to the Sunday Star-Times newspaper in 2006, which may have helped trigger his arrest just a few weeks later. Kahui told the paper that "every four hours" he had fed the babies that night, the last feed being around 1am.[23]

Kahui gave three statements to police, however, where he said the twins had last fed in the evening between five and 6pm on the Monday night, and that their behaviour had been "just like normal".[24] In the first two of his videotaped statements to police, Kahui claimed Cru had drunk a full 150ml bottle of milk after being given CPR. By the time of his third statement to police, taken after the Sunday Star-Times interview, he no longer mentioned the 1am feed.

In his first police statement, taken only a day after the incident, Kahui says he also fed the babies again at six in the morning after the incident. Again, this claim was dropped from his third statement to police.

Then, after his arrest and on the eve of his murder trial, Chris Kahui changed his story again. He coughed to the changes in his stories while his defence team quietly de-emphasised the later feeds and concentrated on the last normal feed everyone could agree on, when cousin April Saunders fed Cru between midday and 1pm on Monday afternoon. This was crucial for the defence case, because if the jury believed it then they could argue that Macsyna must have harmed the children before she left

23 "I Did Not Kill Them", Sunday Star-Times, 1 October 2006
24 Closing submissions by prosecutor Simon Moore, Queen vs Kahui, 2008

the house that day – that the children were already brain damaged and that's why they couldn't feed.

The defence lawyers had to come up with a plausible backstory on why Kahui kept changing his statements. Defence lawyer Lorraine Smith told the jury in 2008 he was a simple boy who had made errors (others would say 'lied' and indeed the prosecutors labelled him an outright "liar") in his police statements because he was "desperate" to look like a "good father". Chris Kahui himself told the Inquest last year the same thing, "I wanted to look like a good father".[25] You don't make mistakes for a reason, you make mistakes unintentionally. If Kahui was telling the police something with the intention of making himself look good, it was deliberate and he was lying in my view. Without casting judgement on Kahui at this point, it is a general truism that offenders frequently lie to the police when being questioned so as to make themselves look better.

Crown Prosecutor Simon Moore told the jury that if this was true, if Kahui was really "a good father", why was it always Macsyna King who had taken the children to get medical attention when they needed it, not Kahui?

At the 2010 inquest hearings, Coroner Garry Evans extracted yet a different excuse for the changed story in regard to feeding the twins: "Why is there a completely different story in your statement to what you told the police?"

"Because I wasn't sure if I had fed them."[26]

So which is it, did Chris Kahui initially give false evidence because he wanted to look good, or because he remembered better four years after the event than when he first spoke to police 24 hours after the event?

In one early statement, Kahui had said the breathing incident happened around 11pm. Subsequently, that was changed to 9pm. Pinning down what actually took place and when inside 22 Courtenay Place was like trying to herd cats – different versions were flying in all directions.

In my view, Kahui's legal advisors would have realised that they had no hope of successfully getting the client off if he stuck to his story about regular feeding through the night. That's because they knew the prosecution's forensic experts were going to testify that the onset of rolling eyes and breathing difficulties would have been within minutes of any attack. If Kahui had fed the children at five or six pm normally, then the injuries could only have been inflicted after that, and one of the four adults in the home – Chris Kahui, Banjo Kahui, Mona Kahui or her partner Stuart King – must have been the killer.

25 Evidence of Chris Kahui, Coroner's Inquest, 2010
26 ibid

Only by ditching the later feeds and changing his story could Kahui's defence team push the blame elsewhere and create "reasonable doubt" for the jury to acquit. Even Kahui's change of story placing the breathing problem at 9pm, rather than 11pm, would have helped, particularly in light of the cellphone debate. But if Kahui was lying and being shielded by close family members, or collectively the four adults in the house were covering for one of their number, then the cellphone debate becomes irrelevant, regardless of how much heat it generated.

At the trial, Mona Kahui testified to seeing April Saunders feed Cru at 1pm, and how she had also seen her brother Chris walk up the hallway with a full bottle of milk and come out later with an empty bottle, suggestive of baby Chris having a feed as well. Chris later confirmed to the inquest that he had indeed fed baby Chris when Mona saw him. That evening, Mona says Chris drove her to Middlemore to see their mother, around 7pm. Cellphone records placed Emily and Macsyna in Papakura at 6.58pm, some 25 km away and evidently en route to Takanini to drop off baby Ellen. Mona says Chris left the hospital immediately after dropping her off, she says, presumably to return home. If that's the case, then Chris should well and truly have been back at the house at the time when defence lawyers claim Macsyna supposedly burst in after a mad dash across town, found him not there, and beat the babies senseless for reasons unknown. In the defence scenario, Emily and Macsyna have to be doing an average speed of 100km an hour through suburban Papakura and Mangere streets, in order to get there before Chris got home. Given that they didn't know Chris wasn't there, they wouldn't have been speeding like that. A diversion to suburban Mangere would also have made it impossible for Emily to have reached Avondale in time to receive a phone call there at 7.38pm.

At 8.15pm, Mona says she and her father Banjo left the hospital in his car and drove back to Courtenay Crescent, where they caught up with Chris. According to Mona they all went outside for a smoke, and when she'd finished she went inside to see the twins and found Chris holding baby Chris. She told the court Chris asked her to pick up Cru, but that when she did so his face was pale, lips were blue and his eyes were rolling into the back of his head. He was not breathing.

Mona testified she called out to Chris about Cru's eyes and his failure to breathe, but that Chris thought she was "over-exaggerating...he didn't think it was that serious."

There are clear conflicts, now that we've had a trial in 2008 and the inquest in 2010/2011, in the evidence from those in the house that night.

For example, Banjo Kahui told the 2008 trial that he saw Chris Kahui go into the twins' nursery, and then Mona followed in right behind him "almost immediately". Banjo's evidence conflicts with Mona's 2008 testimony immediately above, but it gets worse.

In June 2011, Mona admitted to Coroner Garry Evans that "it was probably about ten minutes from the time Chris went inside until I went in."[27] Chris Kahui had said exactly the same thing, "about ten minutes" in his initial police statements.

Ten minutes alone with the children before Cru was found by Mona not breathing and with his eyes rolling back. Perhaps realising it wasn't a good look, Chris Kahui again changed his story, saying he was only in the room alone for three minutes before Mona came in.[28] Either way, Banjo Kahui's testimony that Mona and Chris entered the room together is clearly wrong.

But think about it for a moment. He told police he had gone in to feed them. What was he doing for ten minutes (or even three) before Mona came in? Counsel assisting the Coroner, Chris Morris, wanted to know some answers when he got the chance to cross examine Kahui at the inquest:[29]

"I think I was picking up stuff on the ground," Kahui responded.

"It wouldn't take three minutes to pick up stuff, would it?"

"No."

"So what else were you doing?"

"I can't remember what I was doing in there."

Given that defence counsel Lorraine Smith had a field day convincing the media that Macsyna should have noticed evidence of historical injuries, it is bitterly ironic that her own client failed to notice the much bigger elephant in the room. Did Chris Kahui see that any of the babies were apparently lifeless and scream for help? No. Mona was the first to see anything wrong, the instant she walked in.

Chris' initial response when Mona told him about Cru was to suggest giving the baby a pat.

"I told Chris that Cru had stopped breathing, but he thought that I was over-exaggerating," Mona told the inquest, which is similar to what she told the trial in 2008.

When Mona finally convinced Chris Kahui to do something about the

---

27 Evidence of Mona Kahui, Coroner's Inquest, 2011
28 Evidence of Chris Kahui, Coroner's Inquest, 9 October 2010
29 Cross examination of Chris Kahui, Coroner's Inquest, 11 October 2010

lifeless Cru, she told the trial her brother put baby Chris back into his cot, took Cru from her and laid the baby down and initially just stroked his arm. Only after that, Mona says, did it look as if he was about to perform CPR. At that point Mona ran screaming from the room to alert her partner Stuart, and Banjo Kahui came in.[30]

Banjo denied on oath seeing eyes rolling back or blue lips.[31] However, Stuart King – who'd come into the room after Banjo, told police, "Cru's lips were purple and he kept getting darker and darker", and that the Cru's eyes rolled back in his head. Additionally, says Stuart, every time the baby tried to breathe his tiny hands shook and twitched as he took in a breath. "It sounded like sucking in drink through a straw," Stuart King told police. When King asked Chris Kahui if he wanted an ambulance, Kahui said no. "Nah, nah, he's breathing again. He should be fine."[32]

Banjo Kahui told the 2008 trial he'd gone to assist Chris with the CPR, and "he looked alright…otherwise I wouldn't have passed him on".

Mona Kahui says when she re-entered the room shortly after Stuart, Chris had picked up Cru to cradle him and was saying "Oh my son, don't do that to me again."

But Stuart King's testimony to the 2008 trial is even more interesting.[33] He says he took Cru off Chris Kahui because he could see Cru still wasn't breathing. Kahui and Banjo had been in the room, supposedly performing CPR (although no one else appears to have actually seen this), but Stuart saw what the other two men had not – whatever the pair had done it hadn't worked. "His lips were dark purple. They were getting darker and darker. His body was so flimsy. You could tell it was not normal." How long was Chris going to cuddle a baby still turning blue, whilst saying "don't do that to me again" even though the crisis wasn't over?

Yet the Kahuis were all playing it down. Here's what Mona told the Coroner:[34]

"What is the reason Cru was not taken to the hospital?"

"Because my brother thought that he had come to and that everything was going to be okay."

"So do I take it that, you were happy with that situation?"

"Yes."

"Banjo was happy with that situation, your father?"

---

30 Evidence of Mona Kahui, Queen vs Kahui, 2008
31 Evidence of William 'Banjo' Kahui, Queen vs Kahui, 2008
32 Evidence of Det Sgt Chris Barry, Coroner's Inquest, 4 October 2010
33 Evidence of Stuart King, Queen vs Kahui, 2008
34 Cross-examination of Mona Kahui, Coroner's Inquest, 2011

"Yes as far as I knew, yes."

"So the situation was normal as far as you were concerned?"

"Yes."

The odd one out in these witnesses is Stuart King – Mona's partner and the only non-Kahui. Banjo says he was satisfied Cru was breathing and handed the baby back to Chris, and Mona walks in to see Chris saying "don't do that to me again", implying the crisis was momentary, fleeting and solved. It is only Stuart King who tells it differently.

Stuart, however, described Cru's body as "limp…just hanging there", and reckons breathing may have initially ceased for "between five and ten minutes"[35] while he was there, and when it resumed while he was holding the baby it was far from normal, with 40 second heavily-laboured breathing "in short bursts, like he was sucking air through a straw"[36] then stretches of silence.. "He [Cru] was cold. His hands were all floppy, his whole body was limp."[37]

Stuart told the court he personally did not perform CPR, nor did he see Chris Kahui or Banjo perform CPR. Instead, the two men looked "freaked out, scared." Mona has already testified she had left the room before Chris began CPR.

So we are left with only two people who definitely claim to have seen CPR performed: Chris Kahui and his father – and both of them have now been forced to admit to police and/or Macsyna that they lied about the events of that night. Was CPR actually performed, and if not, why did they pretend that it was?

Contrast Stuart King's graphic description of the breathing failure with this statement to the court from Banjo Kahui: "If his eyes were rolling or something I would have immediately taken him to hospital. He didn't look like he was gasping or anything."[38]

Not even one tiny gasp? According to Stuart King, Banjo was in the room watching Cru virtually die in front of them, hands twitching with every straw-sucking breath. According to Banjo, it didn't happen. Yet Stuart King says "Banj[o] wanted to ring an ambulance."[39]

There's another piece of evidence that's been overlooked in this CPR debate as well. Chris Kahui was not confident handling the tiny twins, so

---

35 Stuart later conceded on cross examination that five or ten minutes without breathing it was what it felt like, but two or three minutes would be more accurate. Coroner's Inquest, 2010

36 Evidence of Stuart King, Kahui Depositions, 2007

37 ibid

38 Cross Examination of William 'Banjo' Kahui, Coroner's Inquest, 2010

39 Evidence of Stuart King, Kahui Depositions, 2007

how likely is it that a man frightened of changing their nappies in case he damaged them would be confident enough to perform CPR on a prem baby? How confident would any of us be? That's why Stuart didn't perform CPR but tried to rub Cru back into life.

Chris Kahui at one point told police "he looked like he was just fading away", which he later confirmed meant "dying".[40]

So if you didn't really know how to perform CPR, and your baby has stopped breathing in front of you, what would be the normal, natural, immediate reaction of any parent who wanted their child to recover?

Even Mona couldn't keep the story straight under questioning from the Coroner, gradually retreating from her claim that no one called an ambulance because everything was hunky-dory, to an admission that there had been some talk about it.

"But you've already told me that it was suggested by others in the room that baby should go to hospital, haven't you?," asked the Coroner.

"Yeah."

"Yes. And that suggestion was not accepted by your brother was it?"

"No," admitted Mona.

The question has always been, why did no one in the house call an ambulance? Perhaps the answer lies in the transcript of a bugged phone call between Chris Kahui and his father Banjo, released for the first time ever at the inquest, where Chris said: "See, f***, if we never went into the hospital that time we went to the doctors, f***en they probably never would have found out!"

"Who?" asked Banjo.

"The police, when they ain't even, you know, if we never had checked up on anything and then we still probably, you know, if the boys, you know," Chris was recorded saying.[41]

It displays a naivety about the ability of forensic science to work back-wards from an incident. If Kahui truly believed that avoiding medical assistance would prevent detection by police, that would explain a lot about his reluctance to go to hospital. It also raises questions about how much Banjo Kahui really knew, and whether in fact anyone has yet heard the real story of what went on in that house, that night.

---

40 Cross examination of Chris Kahui, Coroner's Inquest, 2010
41 Cross Examination of Chris Kahui, Coroner's Inquest, 2010

CHAPTER FOURTEEN

I Want Straight Answers

As Kahui's lawyer jumped to object to the use of evidence that had never been used at the 2008 trial, and therefore never considered by the jury before they acquitted Kahui, he was overruled by the Coroner.

For Garry Evans, the reluctance to get medical attention was the final straw. "Any normal parent would take the babies to the hospital. Why did you not act like a normal parent would have?"

Evans said Kahui had been given "a great deal of latitude with his answers...It's time for him to give straight answers to straight questions."

Suppose you owned a puppy, said the coroner, that stopped breathing and turned blue, "Would you take it to the vet?"

"Yes," agreed Kahui.

"So why did you not take the babies to a doctor like everyone said you should? What is your answer? Take as long as you like."

Chris Kahui looked blank and said nothing for a few moments. "I don't have an answer to that."

For all of his apparently stellar ability to give police false information without blinking, there is one piece of evidence Kahui can't get around. Nurse Jane Eyres told the inquest she had personally visited the Kahui twins at home just five days before the breathing failure, and specifically discussed with Chris Kahui what to do if a baby stopped breathing. She testified explaining that in such an emergency, or even merely "showing signs of respiratory distress", the parents were to "ring 111" and call an ambulance immediately.[42]

Chris had been told by a nurse just five days earlier exactly what to do in exactly this emergency. He decided not to do it. Nurse Eyres said

---

42 Evidence of Jane Eyres, Coroner's Inquest, 2010

Chris' failure to call 111 was a surprise, "because they had carried out the advice we had given them until then...using saline drops...to try and keep the nose clear, they had gone to the GP...so no, they were following our instructions which we had recommended." For a family that had previously done what was asked, one member was now refusing. Why?

The record shows that despite Stuart King urging an ambulance, Chris Kahui said no, that he could drive the twins to hospital if he needed to, and that he'd rather everyone went to look for Macsyna. His sister Mona was heading to the hospital five minutes away, but Chris did not want the twins going with her.

"I thought he meant it would be faster for him to go to the hospital than wait for an ambulance. I thought he would know what to do," Mona now says.[43] But Chris had no intention of going to the hospital.

"Find Macsyna," he told them. "Tell her that Cru stopped breathing but he's breathing again and he's alright."[44]

I didn't know any of this was happening that night. We got back to Emily's house at Papakura sometime around midnight or 1am. As the designated driver I had nothing to drink, but I was tired, and I hadn't had much sleep the night before, so I crashed. When Emily got into bed Pou apparently told her that Banjo and I think Mona had come around looking for me, and left the message that "something's wrong with Cru. He stopped breathing or something, but he started breathing again and he's alright."

Emily told the police that she tried to wake me up and tell me, but I don't remember that. Must have happened but I was out to it.

When I wake up in the morning eventually, Ems goes "Sis, drop me off at work." She told me about the breathing incident but that everything was OK. I just assumed if it had been anything serious they would've gone straight to hospital. But she runs around, does things anyway, we jump in the car, and I drop her off in Carbine Road, Mt Wellington, then I go home to Mangere. Stu wakes up to me because he had to open the door and I say "What's happened bro?" And he goes "Oh, that boy stopped breathing."

"Which boy?"

"Cru."

"And?"

---

43 Evidence of Mona King, Coroner's Inquest, 2011
44 Evidence of Mona King, Queen vs Kahui, 2008

"Nah he's alright. He came right, so we just kept an eye on him and he's sweet."

"What do you mean he stopped breathing?"

"He just held his breath."

Which is a lot different from 'he went blue, couldn't breathe, they had to do CPR.' Stuart didn't tell me that.[45] I walked into the nursery and the room was still warm. They just were breathing and sleeping, their chests were rising and falling. I put my head down to hear the breathing and I couldn't hear anything irregular. I couldn't even hear a snuffle actually. As I'm pulling the nursery door closed Chris turns up. "What the hell's going on?" I asked.

He's like "Man, I just went to go and get some baby formula milk powder, we ran out of milk powder."

"I mean with the babies!"

And he goes "Cru just held his breath for a bit. Second time. He just held his breath for a bit and I panicked."

"Then what?"

"Just Dad was like 'this son's alright, we should go and tell Max what happened.'"

"Why did he think that Chris, what happened?"

And he goes "I don't know. Cause he was worried."

"Worried about what?" I kept pressing.

"Oh just cause he's never seen Cru hold his breath before." We'd seen it one time. One time only in the neo natal unit at Middlemore, when he was probably two weeks new. Different. He's at this stage now. March they were born, well this is in June. Different.

So I said "What do you mean he held his breath?"

"He just held his breath for a second and I freaked out and Dad was there and Mona was there and they all just tried to tell me what to do."

He was pretty vague about it. At this stage I still had no idea that they had to administer CPR, or that Cru's holding the breath was more than just holding a breath, he went blue. Could not breathe for a wee while.

---

45 If Stuart King had not actually seen anyone performing CPR, and that's indeed what he has told the court, he is unlikely to have mentioned this aspect to Macsyna, and he may have been unaware that anyone was claiming to have done it until later discussions with Banjo, Chris and Mona. For the record, I don't believe CPR was administered. I believe Chris and Banjo Kahui lied about this which is why their stories weren't straight and why Banjo initially hid it from police. And if there was no sustained effort to resuscitate Cru, I'll leave readers to join the dots.

My Shayne comes crawling out of the lounge. And he's just got his nappy on and it's so see through, the plastic, you can see where the filling on the inside of the nappy has fallen away – it's sodden. Chris had not changed him, and his nose was as snotty as. I just unleashed on Chris as I was prone to do, "You freaking idiot! Shayne's sick! Keep him warm, keep him clean and keep him changed! What the, you don't got a hell of a lot to do. You don't have to clean, you don't have to chase after other children, Shayne is the only one who can walk. Him and the twins, they're your priority and nothing else. What the hell's going on?"

I started an argument, and Chris is just like "Ah just shut up man! Everything's sweet, I just forgot to change him. I was going to change him when I got back."

"What? Look at the state of his nappy! And look at his nose!"

Shayne's none the wiser, he's just toddling along. "Mum!"

Mona gets up and she's unusually quiet. Mona is a chatterbox, likes to talk about everything. Loves to be the first to tell about everything. Likes to be the first to the gate with the goss. And anything that's happened, whether it be a dumb joke, if people came over, whatever, if Mona was around, she likes to be the first to say so. But this morning, nothing. She's just "Good morning."

My brother Stu seems a little bit blasé. Not really here, not really there. He's not usually like that. He's either hungry, bored, or keen for a drink. It's a thing of habit, that boy.

None of them had told me about CPR at this stage or how long Cru had not been breathing for. I'd checked on the twins already, and they seemed to be sleeping and breathing fine. So while I knew I wanted to get them checked out, I didn't have the heightened sense of urgency that I would have if the four in the house had told me the truth. So things were a bit weird and unusual, Mona's not talking like she normally does. And as I subsequently found out Chris had lied to me by not fully disclosing what had taken place. Holding your breath is one thing, but stopping breathing, turning blue and needing CPR is absolutely different. I know I would have gone "F*** man, help me get them in the car." And I would have just taken them to the hospital. But that's not what he said.

So I just planned my day, with Chris and Stu. I scooped Shayne up and brought him into the nursery. Ran some water for a hot flannel and wiped him down to clean him up. I asked Stu to flip the gas stove on and the gas top on to heat up the kitchen so we could at least do bottles and things like that. I remembered asking Chris about the babies' feeds. And he goes "They don't want their feeds yet, they're just not hungry."

He was maintaining this line that he'd fed them regularly like I'd told him to do, which is also what he told police, so I had no obvious reason to disbelieve him. The only thing I noticed with the babies was a new bruise on Chris' cheek.

In his first videotaped police statement, Chris Kahui claims to have also noticed a bruise on Chris junior's cheek, about three hours after their six am feed. I now believe Kahui was lying, because the babies did not feed at 6am and he retracted those earlier statements when he got to trial. However, on the police video Chris claims baby Shayne may have entered the nursery and "done something…whacked him or something." Shayne was only 13 months old.

Kahui gave the same answer to Macsyna when she asked about the bruising, that Shayne had gotten into the nursery and roughed up the twins a bit. Macsyna did not make a connection between the bruise on the cheek and the head injuries at this point, because she was unaware of the head injuries, and unaware how serious the breathing episode had been. Nor was she told that her babies had missed all their feeds for the previous 21 hours.

MR KAHUI: No I do not remember telling her.

CORONER: You do not remember telling her?

MR KAHUI: Yes.

CORONER: Was that not most important information both for her and Dr Nayar?

MR KAHUI: Yes.

CORONER: Did you tell any other members of your family on the Tuesday morning that the babies had not taken any milk since midday, the day before?

MR KAHUI: I am not too sure if I did…

So anyway, I told Chris we needed to get the children checked out by the doctor. They've asked me time and time again why we didn't go straight away, and I'm sorry, I just didn't understand that the babies were in such a bad way. They seemed to be just asleep and breathing normally, not distressed or anything, and Chris hadn't told me they hadn't fed normally. And so we grabbed some McDonalds on the way to the doctor. It's a decision I quickly regretted.

The couple spent maybe half an hour at McDonalds. Stuart was with them and told police the twins looked normal when he saw them open their eyes. Neurologists later told the court it was possible for the babies to briefly drift in and out of 'lucidity' and appear normal for a moment or two.[46] A similar thing happened when they were first seen at Middlemore.

Stuart left for home, while Kahui drove Macsyna and the babies to the family doctor, Gopinth Nayar. There would have been a wait in the waiting room, and then the eventual call through to the surgery around 1pm. Because Chris wasn't the world's greatest communicator, Macsyna did most of the talking, based on what she'd been told by Chris and Stuart earlier. Cru had had a breathing episode around midnight, she told the doctor. Nayar told the court his first focus was actually baby Chris because of the bruise on his cheek. He says one of the parents explained how baby Shayne had apparently caused that injury. When he lifted Chris' eyelids, he told the court, there was an "abnormal pupillary response" and that he knew immediately that the baby had suffered a significant head injury.

However, Dr Nayar also told the court he believes Chris Kahui had volunteered information about having to give CPR to Cru overnight. Macsyna King is adamant Chris never revealed CPR at this stage because "I would have remembered that! I hit the roof later when I found out about this at the hospital"[47]. Could Nayar be confused? It is possible, because it often happens in court cases, that a witness' memory can become corrupted during police or court questioning. The University of Sydney last year released a study on what it called "false memory syndrome":

"Memories can't be trusted and become contaminated when people discuss their memories of an event with others," says a University news release. Lead researcher Dr Helen Paterson found that sharing memories can contaminate people's recollections and create false memories.

"A false memory is the recollection of an event, or details of an event, that did not actually occur," said Paterson. "My research focuses on how people can contaminate each other's memories for an event by discussing it with one another." Paterson said a key finding of the research was

---

46 Cross examinations of Dr Jane Zuccollo, perinatal pathologist, and Dr Patrick Kelly, child abuse specialist, Queen vs Kahui, 2008.
47 To be fair to everyone, it is also possible that after five years of questioning Macsyna King's own memory on this point has been damaged – that she has come to believe she wasn't told about CPR.

that misleading information presented through discussion with another person who observed the event can also lead to memory distortion. "That is, witnesses who discuss an event with a co-witness are very likely to incorporate misinformation presented by the co-witness into their own memory for the event. Once their memory has been contaminated in this way, the witness is often unable to distinguish between the accurate and inaccurate memories."[48]

This false memory syndrome is bound to have affected numerous incidents in the immediate investigation of the Kahui case, purely because so many people were involved at multiple stages. The adults in the house at the time would have compared stories and in doing so contaminated each other's recall. The nurses and doctors who worked on trying to revive the twins would likewise have discussed their experiences with each other. Macsyna's testimony about aspects of the events leading up to and afterwards is also likely to be tainted in places for the same reasons. These are not conscious errors on the part of these witnesses – just a natural side effect to keep in mind.

We know that Dr Nayar, for example had a second conversation with Chris Kahui and Macsyna King two days after the twins had been taken to hospital, because he confirmed this to the court. He said both parents were anxious to further discuss what had happened. The conversation was only brief, and Dr Nayar says he declined to go into any detail with the parents because it had become a police matter. However, it's quite possible, even probable, that memory of a discussion about CPR has flowed from this second conversation, rather than the first.

What is interesting is that the doctor recalls Chris telling him baby Cru held his breath only briefly, and he noted in his referral letter to the hospital, "Witnessed episode last night lasting under one minute". If that's what Chris told Dr Nayar, then it is massively different from the five or ten minute episode that Stuart King testified about in court. Why would the father of the twins lie to a doctor about the breathing incident?

Middlemore Hospital was not advised by Dr Nayar that one of the twins had already required cardio-pulmonary resuscitation. Nor is there any reference to Macsyna discussing CPR with the nurses or medics when she was asked what happened, as will become apparent.

There's also the intriguing police interview with Banjo Kahui from June 20th 2006, two days after the twins died, which hints at a cover-up involv-

---

48 "Sydney study finds false memories are common", University of Sydney news release, 9 August 2010

ing those in the house when Cru stopped breathing. For a start, Banjo has now admitted to the inquest that he lied to police when he told them he and Mona went looking for Macsyna but they didn't know whose house they were driving to. In fact, he knew it was Emily's house. More significantly, Banjo Kahui admits he didn't reveal to police that Cru had stopped breathing and required CPR.[49]

"You knew if you told police what happened with Cru stopping breathing, it was damaging to your son," police lawyer Simon Mount asked him at the inquest.

"Yes," admitted Banjo, who could not explain why he had lied to police.

Given that intention to keep the full details hidden from investigators, and given Chris Kahui's cryptic bugged phone call to Banjo where he said, "If we never went to the doctors, they probably never would have found out", it's not unreasonable to suspect the CPR incident was not being widely talked about. Both Chris Kahui and his father knew full-well that an ambulance should have been called immediately, and they chose not to. The question is why.

I'd gone into the doctors worrying about Cru's breath-holding, and come out after hearing Dr Nayar ask whether we had dropped the babies on their heads, and that we needed to get them to hospital. When we got to the car I'm going, "What happened man?", and Chris kept going that it must have been Shayne climbing onto the couch. I still didn't know exactly what was wrong, because Dr Nayar didn't go into much detail, and I still didn't know Chris had performed CPR on Cru.

Dr Nayar's evidence at Chris Kahui's trial backs up King's version of events. Nayar says when the parents gave a definite "no" to his query about whether the babies had been dropped, that he did not continue that line of questioning, and wanted to avoid a "confrontation" with the parents. He avoided discussing injuries, and told the inquest he merely told the parents the babies were "sick or unwell".

The doctor was not told the twins had not fed for 24 hours, and Chris Kahui as we've seen has admitted to the inquest that he can't recall telling Macsyna that either.[50]

In Dr Nayar's judgement the exact cause of the injuries was not worth

49 Cross examination of William 'Banjo' Kahui, Coroner's Inquest, 2010
50 Cross examination of Chris Kahui, Coroner's Inquest, 2010

discussing or being delayed by, it was better simply that the parents take the children to hospital, and given the hospital was five minutes away he assumed they would go straight there...

It was the "Nah!" The tone. The tone and the way he said it to me. "Nah! I'm not coming to the hospital." Stern. Firm. Not loud, but firm. It was just creepy. Scary. Unlike the Chris I knew. I mean, I was the dominant one in our relationship. This wasn't like him. So I push him and go "Well why? I need your help, I can't carry both their car seats and both of them in out of the car at the same time and I can't take one out, put one down. Our twins, newborn, gentle, careful, hello?"

"So? I don't care! Take me home, I just need time to myself."

I was just stunned. 'What the?' is what I was thinking. 'Who the hell's this jerk talking? I don't know this person.' I started to suspect that maybe Chris knew more about it than he was saying. These are some of my thoughts going through my head and I'm starting to panic a bit. I knew that it had not been cool with us because I'd been going "The house is a freaking mess and this is going on and Shayne's crawling around cold as."

Chris agreed to stop at Countdown[51] so I could get some fresh nappies and other things for the babies from the pharmacy, if they were being admitted, but he wanted to go home and I needed to grab their medications and Plunket books. When he pulled up at 22 Courtenay Cres, I told Chris to wait in the car with Chris and Cru while I got their things. "Just wait here in the car with the kids then, I'll be back in a second."

In hindsight, I don't know why I thought their Plunket books and medicines were important. It was so trivial in the scheme of things. All I know is that at the time I had no true understanding of just how critical a condition they really were in. If I had fully been aware of what had gone on, I would have acted, and I wouldn't have bothered with going to the supermarket and going to get their Plunket books, but I did. Those books had the notes from their last admission into the hospital where they had croupy coughing. That water on the lungs thing. I just thought it might save time.

---

51 Security video footage shows Macsyna paying for nappies and baby wipes at Countdown at around 1.40pm. More security footage shows her at a nearby pharmacy just after that. The till receipt confirms she purchased teats, pacifiers, and a baby overnight bag.

So I go into the house, I grab the baby bag and run out to put it in the car, and bloody Chris has gone! Nowhere to be seen, while the two twins are in the car outside all on their own and he hadn't even told anyone. I just lost the plot and started running back inside in a panic.

"That f***ing c***, he's done something to my babies. The f***ing asshole." And I was crying, angry, and freaked out. Really freaked out, because he's just gone. He'd never done that before, never run away and left the twins alone. I tried to ring him on his cellphone but he wasn't answering, so I grabbed their medicine out of the fridge and asked Stu, "Please could you watch Shayne? I've got to take the twins to the hospital, I don't know what's going on but the doctor says I've got to get them there now. Chris has just pissed off and I'm freaked out."

Stu looked at me and nodded. "Just go, sweet as. Just go."

Before I left, I rang Chris' sister Tracey. And I said "Tracey I need your help."

She goes "What's the matter?"

"I need you to ring Chris and get his ass back here."

"Well what do you want me to make him do? What am I going to do?"

I lost it at her. I was like "You can, you know you're always bossing him around, you can get on the phone and tell him to get his ass back here and help me to get the boys to the hospital." And I start crying on the phone.

"What the f***'s happening?" she wanted to know.

"I don't know Tracey! We just left the doctor's, he said 'get to the hospital.'"

And she goes "Well why the hell don't you go to the hospital?"

"Cause Chris didn't want to come and I wanted to grab the other stuff."

Tracey just huffed. "Well you should have just not bothered, who cares what he wanted?"

Yeah, right, I said. "Pretty hard to make the driver – what am I going to do, turn the wheel for him? He drove from the doctor's."

And she's like "Ah f***."

And I went "Please man! If you could ever help me, this is how you can help me. Now ring your brother and make sure you get it done! I'm not f***ing going to go through all of this on my own.

He helped me, now you help me. These are our kids, and you're part of it, so f***ing do something."

So I hung up on her and she did. She did try and get a hold of Chris. I heard that she actually drove over and went to go and find him. She arrived at the house, talked to Stuart, he said "Yeah, nah, Chris just pissed off. Max said that she had to go to the hospital because her and Chris went to the doctor's, but then Chris took off and left the babies."

Macsyna King's version of events is again supported in testimony given to Kahui's 2008 trial. Mona Kahui says King was trying to make a phone call and "crying…yelling", while Stuart King says his sister had been furious with Chris, and that Chris had walked off[52]. King told police that his sister was crying, and that Chris' refusal to take the babies to hospital left her looking like "somebody had ripped her heart out and stood on it".[53] So having collected what she thought the babies might need for hospital, Macsyna drove off. What followed when she arrived at hospital became the subject of much media speculation and formed part of the bad press that has plagued King ever since the deaths: a witness claimed she looked utterly unconcerned when they saw her. What most people don't know is that King had been working for months with self-proclaimed New Age "business and life coach" Shane Wenzell in South Auckland, and appears to have picked up a few beliefs about transferring bad vibes. I specifically didn't raise this with Macsyna in our interviews as I wanted to first hear her own description of the trip to hospital, rather than flag any issues ahead of time. We know that Macsyna had been furious with Chris for deserting her, and weeping, because other witnesses have testified to this. But by the time she got to the hospital something had changed…

So I get to the hospital and I think 'no, calm down. Just calm down. If I'm going to put that out there, then maybe I'll make them sick.' I don't know, I thought it might help if I did. So I tried to put a brave face on and believe my little boys are going to be alright. 'If there's anything wrong,' I thought, 'I'm in the right place. It'll be sweet.' So I get out, get the kids there, little bit nervous and there's one family

---

52 Police, the court and later the inquest all had great difficulties getting accurate times out of the Kahui and King families, because wearing watches was not a common practice. "I just observe at this point that the difficulty with many of these witnesses is that they have shown that they really only have a very vague sense of timing," police lawyer Simon Mount told the inquest at one point during Kahui's cross-examination.
53 Statement of Stuart King to police, 2006

in front of me in admissions so I just put one of the babies up on the stretcher and Cru in my arms and I'm trying to look at him and he looks like he's sleeping. They both look like they're sleeping. Things were ok at that point. Sort of ok. Then the lady with admissions, it's my turn at the windows, I just said, "My babies."

The 'lady at admissions' was Fleur Paulsen, a charge nurse at Middlemore's Emergency Department. She told Kahui's trial she was the first person to see the twins, as she was based at the triage desk. She told the court Macsyna was polite and calm, and did not appear to be overly concerned about her twins and says she found this "unusual"[54]. Evidently, though, the hospital doesn't appear to have been overly concerned either – despite having been phoned in advance by Dr Nayar[55] to say the twins were coming in with neurological damage – because the triage desk assigned the twins only a "Category 3" on the priority list – condemning the twins to a wait of up to half an hour before they were seen by a nurse. The hospital could have given the twins a Category 1 status, which would have told paediatricians to deal with the babies immediately.

In light of the criticism over half an hour spent at McDonalds – which happened before Macsyna was told to get them to hospital straight away – the willingness by the hospital to make the twins wait up to half an hour once they got there was bitterly ironic. Paulsen told the court she inspected the twins, they were breathing normally, and their eyes were half open as if drowsy, but otherwise unexceptional. One of the twins had a small bruise, about 15mm long, on his cheek. A doctor, remember, had already advised Middlemore that he had inspected the twins and they had neurological damage. As a potential lesson from this tragedy, it may be that Middlemore's own bureaucracy could improve its prioritisation – does an ED nurse have greater medical expertise than a doctor in general practice, and should a doctor's prior opinion take precedence over standard ED procedures?

And she goes "just get an orderly to help you, just go straight around to the paediatrician thing." So the orderly comes along, he's got Chris and I've got Cru, and as I'm holding the carseat, because it's an upright carseat, I've got it like that and he's facing me, he just opens his eyes for a second and he's got his eyes, they're upturned

54 Evidence of Fleur Paulsen, Middlemore ED, Queen vs Kahui, 2008
55 Evidence of Dr Catriona Slater, Middlemore ED, Queen vs Kahui, 2008

and they're rolling. And then they're back and down and then they're rolling and then they're back and down. I saw his eyes and I just froze. I guess I didn't really react immediately. I don't know what I did except for carry on walking. Then the nurse comes in and I went "Here's the doctor's recommendation. But I've just seen my son's eyes and they're rolling."

The nurse she's talking about appears to be Claire Dillon, a nurse at the KidzFirst unit at Middlemore. In court she described Macsyna "swinging" the babies in their capsules as she was coming towards her. This sounds harsh and could be a fair summation, but parents reading this will know how unwieldy carseats – particularly the big ones – can be to carry. Dillon also describes King as "elated" when she first saw her walking towards her and seemingly unaffected by the conditions of her children, which at this stage had been given a "Category 3", half-hour wait priority by the front desk.

Given that the children had been seen at triage by a nurse who didn't seem overly concerned, perhaps that "she'll be right" attitude from the front desk had given King some reassurance that maybe her babies weren't so sick after all.

Unlike the triage nurse who saw only one bruise, one and a half centimetres long on the cheek of Chris, Claire Dillon told the court she could see bruises extending from the temple down to the mouth on both babies. No other witness reported seeing similar bruising on both babies. There is something else anachronistic about Claire Dillon's testimony, and to me it may be an example of false memory syndrome at work again. She talked in court of telling Macsyna that baby Chris had a broken thigh bone, yet the twins had not yet been x-rayed or seen by a hospital doctor. Indeed, Dillon says she was the person who first unwrapped the babies from their carseats so she could weigh them. There's no indication in Dillon's testimony that Macsyna alerted her to rolling eyes, but that's what King says she did.[56]

When I told the nurse she just goes "Ok," and keeps reading the referral letter from the doctor's and then she just slams it down.

---

56 Evidentially, of course, it's one person's memory against another's. But I wonder in the drawing up of their evidence for court, two years later, how much testimony from hospital staff had been subconsciously contaminated by re-examining their experiences through the lens of hindsight and talking to each other about the case. You can listen to Macsyna's recollection of this dramatic encounter at www.investigatemagazine.com/macsmiddlemore.mp3

And I go "I've just seen his eyes rolling." The nurse didn't look at me, she just quickly got the light and opened his eyes and she just hit the red button and all the nurses from the station they come running in, he comes flying out of the car seat, she's got her scissors and just cuts him open and runs with him, down to the corridor weighing thing and onto the stretcher and is just yelling all these things and before I know it, I would say about two minutes they've got X amount of things stuck to them. Things here, oxygen there, and the anaesthetist is trying to get a line in their hands and it's just panic. It's just hard out panic.

They're yelling at me, "Get out!"

"I'm trying to see what's –"

She's going "Get out!"

I lost the plot, I started crying. I ran to the room where their nappy bags were and grabbed my phone and rang my sister and said "Sis, I'm at the hospital, and I'm panicking. I just took the boys to the doctors and now I've arrived at the hospital and they're in the operating room and I'm not allowed in there and I'm scared, I don't know what to do."

And she's going "Well where's Chris?"

"I don't know."

She goes "Have you tried to ring him?"

"Yeah, I rang, no answer, but I rang you and I need to talk. I need to say things, I need to know, and I feel alone. Can you come?"

She's just "Yep. I'm at work but I'll talk to Ginta and take a car." Because I had borrowed her car for Stuart. So essentially Ems was at work with no vehicle, which was at my house at Courtenay Cres, with Stuart.

It was a mess.

As I waited for Emily to get there I tried to ring Chris again, but he just wasn't answering his phone. I sent a txt instead. "It's really urgent and serious, our boys are in some sort of danger but I'm not allowed to know, can you please answer the phone? I'm ringing you now."

So I ring, ring, ring, no answer. Still no answer. Getting more and more angry and more and more scared. 'You f***ing c***! You must have known that this was happening, that must be why you wouldn't come with me and why you said "Nah, I'm not coming to the hospital." F*** you!' That's all I can remember thinking.

It was 2.55pm when the babies were sent to the resuscitation room – around 40 minutes after they first arrived at hospital. In that room, paediatricians struggled to stabilise babies Chris and Cru Kahui. Paediatric registrar Melanie Ang was one of the first to tackle the resuscitation. She told the court the babies began to fit, twitching and jerking, and she diagnosed a broken leg on Chris because it was at an unusual angle. This raises an important question – Dr Nayar hadn't noticed the broken thigh when he took the baby out of his carseat to examine him, so could it have been caused when Chris was grabbed out of the car seat and rushed to resuscitation by the hospital medical team? For Melanie Ang to find the leg in that position, when a senior doctor who examined Chris an hour earlier had not[57], allows the possibility that this injury, and this one only, was caused in the emergency room.

Baby Chris died at the age of what paediatricians call "term plus one" – medical terminology that places premature babies on a time scale relevant to normal delivery. In real terms, although he'd been born three months earlier, he was effectively a newborn at one week of age – small and fragile.

It is speculative, and there's no hard evidence one way or the other, but consider the evidence of an Australian forensic paediatrician hired by the Kahui defence team. Dr Terry Donald is the head of the Child Protection Unit at Adelaide's Women & Children Hospital, and he told the court here that there are two mechanisms that break thigh bones: direct impact or bending. The autopsy found no sign of external force on the leg – no bruising above the fracture point – leading Donald to suggest the reason Chris' leg broke is because it got bent.[58] Did that happen while he was being freed from his special car seat? Just how easy is it to break the thigh of a newborn?

Dr Jane Zuccollo is a specialist perinatal pathologist, meaning she primarily conducts autopsies on babies who die during pregnancy, up to children as old as five. She testified at court that something as simple even as pulling the leg of a newborn a little too hard could break the bone, and that it was not a difficult bone to break.[59] Zuccollo added that the broken femur was extremely fresh, with absolutely no evidence of scar formation around the wound site.

Paediatric radiologist Sally Vogel told the court the bone break was so

57 Evidence of Dr Gopinth Nayar, Coroner's Inquest, 2010
58 Evidence of Terence Donald, forensic paediatrician, Queen vs Kahui, 2008
59 Evidence of Dr Jane Zuccollo, perinatal pathologist, Queen vs Kahui, 2008

fresh there was absolutely no sign of new bone growth or healing.[60] Timings on the injury ranged from immediate, to back as far as ten days, but forensic experts made the point that if the break had occurred before the brain damage, baby Chris would have been in excruciating pain and would have screamed every time his leg was touched. There was no evidence from anyone suggesting the babies were unsettled. Instead, everyone had described them as placid and easy-going children. That makes it likely the break either occurred at the same time as the fatal injury, or afterward, when the baby could no longer respond to pain. If Chris had been able to cry out in pain while nurses were yanking him from the carseat straps, the warning cry might have averted a break. But with Chris brain dead and silent, the nurses had no reason to suspect they had hurt or injured him. No bruises were found over the broken thigh site, no fingerprints, which again lends weight to the theory that something soft and pliable, like a carseat strap spreading pressure over a wide area, was the trigger for the break.

Vogel's evidence was based on skeletal scans taken on Thursday 15th June, three days after the fatal injuries were inflicted, and she told the court the femur fracture was so recent it could "easily" be only one or two days old at that point. So the weight of the evidence suggests baby Chris had not been enduring a broken leg for days or weeks – the injury is most likely to have happened either during the fatal assault or at the hospital.

While medics were trying to stabilise the two babies at Middlemore, others were trying to find out what had happened. Kathryn Greenwood, who had played with baby Shayne during hospital visits when the twins had just been born, discussed the bruising and says Macsyna told her Shayne may have climbed onto the couch near the cots and "got them". Nurse Claire Dillon, the one who'd pushed the panic button, appears to have asked Macsyna at some point later that afternoon about the "bruising"[61], and also been told the story about Shayne. Although it was now being passed off as Macsyna's story, it had begun with Chris, along with his fictional accounts of continuing to feed the babies regularly, and the incident happening at midnight (when really it was before 9pm). Dillon told the court she'd also by this stage raised the issue of the head injuries and brain damage, and that Macsyna's reaction to news that Chris' thigh was broken was one of obvious sadness, and that King then asked, "that's terrible isn't it?".

60 Evidence of Sally Vogel, paediatric radiologist, Queen vs Kahui, 2008
61 Evidence of Claire Dillon, Queen vs Kahui, 2008

Middlemore's KidzFirst unit's clinical director, Wendy Walker, says she also asked Macsyna what "might" have happened, and King again repeated what Chris had told her about Shayne. When Walker got the results of the CT scans confirming the twins were suffering brain haemorrhages, she confronted Macsyna about child abuse, and called the police...

CHAPTER FIFTEEN

We're Blaming You

By the time I'd rung Chris' phone for about the tenth time,[62] these two female officers in three-quarter length black overcoats approached me. "We're police officers, we're here to talk to you about the abuse of your sons."

I just looked at them and the nurses in disbelief. "You heartless people! Abuse? I've just got here with my sons from a follow up from the doctor's, and you're saying to me straight away words, abuse?"

"What was going on before you got here? Where were you?"

And I'm going "Can you see that I don't give two shits that you're police women and that you're saying to me it's abuse!"

Those were my initial words to them, I told them to go and get stuffed and I told the nurses, "I'm pretty sure I've heard that I can have an advocate here with me to speak with me and to let me know what my rights are, I want one anyway because I'm not allowed in there and I want one too because I don't think that dealing with you is the right thing to do right now. I want to worry about them, not worry about answering your questions!"

Everyone had told me to get out, I wasn't allowed to see my babies, and suddenly I had the police accusing me of abusing the twins. They kept on pushing me for answers, and all I wanted was to be with the children, and I got real aggro with the police officers.

"Look, you're forcing me, and right now I don't need it. So you need to get out of my way or I'll push you out of the way!" And I walked out of this room that they had secured for us. It was an

---

62 As well as attempts to call Chris Kahui's cellphone, police found a call at 15.38 to brother Stuart, which is believed to be Macsyna's first successful voice contact with Chris, who was beside Stuart. There were calls at 16.06 and 16.07 which didn't get through, then successful calls again at 17.02 and 1706.

observation room with all the medical things but I walked out of there and stood right by the theatre door waiting to hear something, waiting for news of the twins.

The two officers hung around, waiting for me while I waited for news. I ended up crying on the shoulder of a woman I'd met before when the twins were born. She'd recognised me and went, "Hi Max, how's Shayne?"

And I said "He's at home with his uncle Stu."

"Oh, what are you doing here then?"

"I brought my twins in and they're in trouble. They're hurt and I don't know what's going on and there's two police officers over there and they're trying to make me talk to them but I want to know what's wrong with the twins."

Wendy just hugged me and goes, "You don't have to do this right now. You can do what you're doing, which is worry about them first. You are entitled to do that. I'll go and tell them that they have no right to do this to you."

I just sobbed on Wendy's shoulder. "They're saying to me, 'we've got questions regarding the abuse of your two sons'." And I told Wendy "I've just got here with them and they're. . . ."

It was horrible. Really, really horrible. I immediately felt attacked, I felt cornered and angry at Chris for just abandoning us. Did I see the warnings in him? Or did I see the signs that something was amiss? No, I didn't. Even now I'm struggling to see where I missed something. But I do have suspicions that there was something going on between Mona, Chris, Banjo and even my brother Stuart. Which of these four had a knowledge of what went on when I wasn't there. And that's where it lies. And that has never left me. I still think it to this day. I thought it then, I think it now.

Between the three Kahuis in particular, between Mona, Chris and Banjo, I believe they have made a pact to keep each other safe. I don't know why, I just believe that I'm right about it. I have no evidence to support it bar that they've told me and the court too many different stories that contradict each other and make each other look like liars.

Macsyna King, however, is not without her share of criticism, most of it boiling up from her apparent attitude inside both Middlemore and Starship hospitals, where later cross-examination of witnesses by Kahui's defence lawyers created the impression this was a mother who just didn't care. It was a mythology that grew and effectively became self-fulfilling – practically everyone had a Macsyna King story to tell. Those who know Macsyna well, however, will tell you that back in those days she was quick to get her back up when she felt picked on. King herself is the first to admit it…

As childish and as petty as it sounds, and my reaction was stupid – I'll admit that – from the moment I got into the hospital I was openly treated as the prime suspect. The doctors had come out and asked me "Have you dropped them?"

"No."

"Well it's only just happened. What happened last night?"

I said "I don't know, I wasn't at home."

"What do you mean you weren't at home?"

This is leading up to them telling me that they're going to transfer my sons over to Starship hospital. I was not treated with respect. Wasn't spoken to very nicely. I behaved and reacted badly to that. I did. When they said "We're taking your children to Starship, you can come in the ambulance if you want," to me it felt like they were sneering, that they didn't really want me there and were saying it because it was in the rulebook.

I reacted badly to that. Why? Because I was a mother who'd suddenly been told my sons had been abused and were badly ill, because my partner had done a runner without explanation and was nowhere to be found, and because I was being investigated all of a sudden by police and treated like I was guilty – and I didn't even know what had happened. I was emotional as and hurt and didn't know so many things.

In the course of investigating Macsyna King's account, I came across an Auckland medical centre that had sent its nursing staff on a child abuse training seminar run by Starship Hospital. "The starting point for Starship, whenever a child comes in with injuries," the attendees had been told, "is that all parents need to be treated as liars and potential abusers. Our starting point is that nothing parents tell you should be believed."

All parents are liars? Little wonder this award-winning attitude was shining through at the frontlines. I was told this by highly respected doctors, and am satisfied the account is true. It is a fundamental of our legal system that people are presumed innocent until proven guilty. The barely concealed hostility towards parents in child abuse cases from the get-go, when information is scant and co-operation is desperately needed, probably does more to harm inquiries than help them.

That Middlemore had such an approach is probably proven by the testimony they gave against Macsyna King in the trial and inquest. She was an easy target at the end of the day, her every move and every word scrutinised – whereas Chris Kahui never came to Middlemore at all. As the absentee parent (and, it turned out, the accused killer), Kahui escaped the character blowtorch King was subjected to. There were many pairs of accusing eyes inside the hospital, and all they thought they needed to know was that this mother had failed in her fundamental duty to protect her children. The possibility that this mother was an unwitting victim was a mere technicality. A bird in the hand was worth any number in the bush.

And what was the bird in the bush doing while all this was going on? As crown prosecutor Simon Moore told the jury, while Macsyna was bearing the wrath of the hospital system over child abuse – literally left 'holding the baby', Chris Kahui was calmly sitting at home playing on the Playstation, "while his babies are slipping away to death".[63]

You ask me how the health system could handle this better? The job of nursing, from my outlook, is to administer and give care. Compassion is part of that and a non judgemental view towards the parent. Even if that parent has been abusive, what is the role of that nurse? What is the role of that doctor? Within those guidelines, stick with them. When it comes to interacting with the parents, I found judgement to be one of my first thoughts of what was happening. Judgement before they even knew what had happened, and certainly before I knew what happened, but they expected me to know. It carried on through what I saw. From their facial expressions or the tone in their voices. A tone and a facial expression and the choice of words and the delivery all in one and you send that to that receiver, and if it's sent in not a very nice way, that's how they're going to receive it. For me, that was something that was key, it took my focus off helping to do what little I could for my sons. It wasn't helpful, and for want of a better word I would call it distracting. Like, the energy could have been used elsewhere, instead of there.

---

63 Closing submissions of Simon Moore, Crown prosecutor, Queen vs Kahui, 2008

There is one other serious aspect to medical evidence: butt-covering. I've seen Middlemore Hospital try to falsify medical records to cover its backside – something I never would have previously believed had I not experienced it personally.

Just before Christmas, 2009, my three year old daughter's finger was chopped off in a see-saw accident at daycare, and crushed to a paste before being lost in the dirt underneath the see-saw for 20 minutes while staff dealt first with the injury and the blood loss. When they finally found the remains of the finger in the dirt, they placed it on ice and waited for the ambulance.

Due to a communications error by St John's, an ambulance was sent from the wrong depot and took half an hour to arrive. When my daughter finally arrived at Middlemore to be assessed by the plastic surgery team, it was 100 minutes after the initial accident. Middlemore Emergency Department staff – the same unit that assessed the Kahui twins, forgot to take the finger off the ice. Not only was it squashed flat and covered in dirt, it was becoming frostbitten. Over the next six hours we were seen three times by social workers dancing around the possibility of child abuse – we kept telling them it was an accident at a registered day care centre – but we were not seen by a surgeon until very late in the day.

It wasn't until I kicked up merry hell with the head of the ED that she told me ED had decided early on that there was no hope for reattaching the finger, so they had assigned the case a low priority. ED had told us nothing as parents. At this stage I said 'stuff protocol', and reminded them that I worked for Investigate magazine and that Middlemore had better produce a surgeon rapidly to discuss reattachment options.

They finally agreed to attempt reattachment surgery at 7pm – nearly eight hours after the initial accident. The hospital told us there was no hope, we told them we had faith in miracles. The operation, to Middlemore's shock, was a success.

But here's the rub: when our daughter was discharged, the hospital tried to get us to sign papers stating that the child had been seen rapidly and her finger "immediately reattached". The discharge papers were clearly inaccurate, and we refused to sign them until the massive time delay was entered into the official record.

We had to endure social workers for Africa before we saw an actual surgeon, and surgical decisions were being made behind closed doors, without reference to the family.

Now don't get me wrong. The staff we dealt with were pleasant and polite and, once we insisted, Middlemore did some great surgical work, but its bureaucracy was happy to create a false paper trail that in the event of a formal investigation could have been problematic.

If there was a recommendation to come out of this, I would argue that hospitals need to remember that the parents who bring an injured child in might not actually be the abusive party, so treating them as automatically guilty might be counter-productive. It was in King's case.

"Nah, I don't want to go in the ambulance with you, with my sons. I'll come in my own car." I snapped back at them. Emily was with me, and I would ride with her to Starship.

When Emily turned up I'd been asked to move away from the normal waiting room close to the paediatric unit, and instead go out to the public waiting area out by the security entrance. The twins were still inside and hadn't been transferred to the ambulance yet. Ems comes through the door and I just broke down in her arms. I said, "All that I heard was trauma, head injury, they need a cat scan. The boys' breathing is fluctuating and they still won't tell me anything." And that's about as much as I could tell Ems without blubbering.

She goes "Where's Chris, why is he not here with us?"

"I don't know. I really don't know."

"Just tell him to come."

"He doesn't want to come."

So we just talk about that and she goes "has something happened, have you had a major fight?"

And I went "Yeah, but only when we left the doctors and he told us to come to the hospital. Chris refused and ran off."

I hadn't had any luck reaching Chris on his own phone, so I rang my brother Stu who was looking after Shayne.

"The twins are in critical care at Middlemore hospital, I'm not allowed anything, the police are here to talk to me. they're saying things like abuse and I really need to get hold of Chris. I need him. I need him here for support and I need him to come and answer some questions, they're still here so maybe he can talk to them or whatever, but I need him anyway, bro, is he there?"

He goes "Yep."

"Can you put him on the phone?"

He goes "Hang on." Goes away, comes back, he goes "He doesn't want to talk."

"Bro, make him get on the phone. Tell him how important it is."

Chris gets on the phone. I say to him, "Chris, where are you man? I've been ringing you and ringing you."

He goes "Yeah man, I know! What do you want?"

"What do you mean what do I want? I txted it to you, I told you! But anyway I need you here, the twins are in critical care. They're in major danger and I don't know what to tell them and what's gone on."

And he goes "It was Shayne!"

"It was Shayne what?"

"Shayne, I left the door slightly open to the nursery and Shayne got in there and jumped all over them."

I'm going "You told me about a bruise, you never said anything about Shayne jumping on them to me!"

And he goes "Oh, I just forgot man!"

He starts getting all angry. Yeah, I'm not helping, but. He's like "Ah, f*** man, I just, I don't have a car."

I said "You've got Ems' car, you've got my sister's car."

He goes "Well I haven't asked her if I could use it."

"I'm telling you that you can use it! She's sitting here right with me! Get here and come to us!"

And he goes "Nah, I'm not."

"What do you mean 'Nah I'm not'?"

And I'm arguing on the phone with him. I remember just being gobsmacked. I was silent for a bit and cried and pleaded with him. "Please can you just get here? I need you here. I need you now. Are you going to come?"

And he goes "I'll come later."

"If they died before you got here, I'm going to have trouble forgiving you, so just get your ass here man!"

And he's like "ah nah, f-you."

That was my second attempt at trying to get him there.

Mona Kahui later told the inquest her brother was holding the phone away from his ear, and responded with, "Whatever" when Macsyna told him the babies were critically injured. He then returned to playing Playstation in the lounge with Stuart [64] although his game was interrupted an hour later when police knocked on the door and began their first 40 minute

---

[64] Evidence of Mona Kahui, Coroner's Inquest, 2011

interview with Chris. Kahui later testified to the inquest that while Macsyna had been merely "angry" with him when he first refused to come to the hospital, she was "hysterical" and really upset when she later phoned him to say the twins were critically injured.[65] Even though the hospital was within walking distance, he told the inquest he didn't feel he should have to go there.

CORONER: Was she worried about the twins' health?

MR KAHUI: Yes, she was.

CORONER: And she wanted you to come to the hospital to be with her?

MR KAHUI: Yes.

CORONER: Because you were the father.

MR KAHUI: Yes.

CORONER: Well, why did you not go?

MR KAHUI: I did not really want to be walking up to the hospital.

CORONER: You did not really want to be walking up to the hospital?

MR KAHUI: Yes. I would have rather her come to pick me up...

"Something's up, I don't know what, but something's up. They're just a bunch of shit-kickers," said Emily, referring to Chris and his family. "See I told you that you can't trust them. As soon as you take your eye off them, if you're not cuddling them and telling them they're doing good, they're going back to their stupid ways again."

I let her talk, I was still trying to process this claim that our son had jumped all over the babies. They didn't have major bruises on their faces that I could think of. There was one on Cru's cheek that was like a perfect little round spot. Chris said that Shayne had done that. I accepted that because Shayne would reach out with his unsteady hand to touch the babies, but that was minor.

As is turned out, the forensic experts were not convinced the bruising amounted to anything significant. Pathologist Jane Zuccollo told the court the bruises on the babies's cheeks were not in areas underlaid by bone structure, meaning they may not have been impact bruises.[66] Pathologist James Ferris told the court the bruises were "most unlikely" to be related to the head injuries at all, and were a common side-effect of people pinching babies' cheeks, or "chubbing".[67]

65 Phone records show Macsyna's first successful call to Chris was 15.38 in the afternoon. There were two more calls after 5pm
66 Evidence of Dr Jane Zuccollo, perinatal pathologist, Queen vs Kahui, 2008
67 Evidence of James Ferris, pathologist, Queen vs Kahui, 2008

The words that kept going around my head were the ones the police officers used, that word 'abuse', and the reaction of the nurses, "Get out, just get out!" All of that is just brimming up in my memory, in my head. And I cannot, for the life of me, decipher any of it.

Police officer Jane Ingram told the court that Macsyna wasn't just upset, she was nearly inconsolable. "She didn't want to speak to us to begin with, but she was really upset. As I say, she wasn't just crying, she was sobbing, and anything she did say was almost incomprehensible anyway."[68]

Detective Ingram added that Macsyna's overprotective sister Emily was a hindrance to police inquiries, with Emily telling detectives Macsyna wouldn't speak unless she had a patient advocate or cultural adviser available. Emily told the inquest she was concerned about Macsyna's emotional state. "I was more worried about her not really knowing what had happened, not being able to deal with things in a proper way and if she could not talk to me, my concern was how is she going to talk to these people, these police officers?"[69]

Ingram remarked that when they managed to get Emily out of the way, Macsyna was fully cooperative with police and was "happy" to answer some initial questions. In the court records there is reference at one point to Emily being allowed to come back in after promising to "behave"...[70]

"Have you eaten?" Emily asked me.

Brunch at McDonalds seemed so long ago. It was getting dark. I muttered something.

"OK, you've got to keep your strength up so you've got to get dinner. So we'll go and get some McDonald's and then we'll follow them to Starship. So you just calm down and you just talk to me about things you can remember. Whatever you think you can remember. Think about what's happened."

Weirdly, we're walking out of the hospital and I just lost it at her. "Nothing happened man! I don't know what happened! Except that we left the doctors and came to the hospital! I told you!"

The security guys, the nurses, people at the entrance of A&E,

68 Cross-examination of Detective Jane Ingram, Queen vs Kahui, 2008
69 Cross-examination of Emily Hepi, Coroner's Inquest, 2010
70 For all of her attitude, Emily Hepi gave an initial undated statement to police, and another eight page signed statement dated 19 June 2006, the day after the twins died. On 29 June she gave a further 11 page statement to police, and an 18 page handwritten statement on 3 July. There were two smaller statements given to police just before Chris Kahui's 2008 trial.

they're just gawking at this mess of a woman with the mouth on her, so I turned on them as well.

"Don't stare at me! I'm having a hard enough time dealing with those idiots!" I was just reacting to everybody and everything, even to people who weren't doing anything to me. I lashed out, attacked, and if you were on the end of it can I say now that I'm sorry.

We followed the ambulance but pulled into the drive-through of McDonalds in Otahuhu for a couple of minutes, then continued on the main road out to the motorway. We arrived at Starship in time to see the twins unloaded from the ambulance, so we weren't far behind, but it was another ten minutes or so before we found a carpark and got inside ourselves.

I walk in and I go to go touch the boys and hold them and the nurse goes "You're not allowed to handle them."

"What do you mean I can't touch them? They're my sons! Get out. Don't f***ing tell me anything. Just get out."

Two seconds, I don't know how long later, maybe a minute, two minutes, a lady who integrates with the hospital and CYFS, named Kaufoou, comes in and she goes "I have documentation here that says that we have now taken custody of Chris and Cru Kahui, we've taken them out of your custody."

This day from hell was getting worse. "What do you mean they've been taken out of my custody? I have only, four hours ago, less than that, they were in my care and custody, I went to a follow up at the doctors, I've come to the hospital now and now I've lost custody. Why?"

"Well your children have the symptoms and are suffering symptoms and classic signs of severe child abuse."

And I'm like "You f***ing a**hole bitch, f*** you. How dare you assume that? I just landed here, and that's straight away what you've got to say to me. I've abused my sons. You haven't investigated, you've talked to the doctors, they've had less than four hours."

She goes "Well they're skilled people, they know what to do, we've seen this before and these are all the same symptoms and this is a classic case of child abuse."

I was going "I don't believe this shit, how can you even say that to me? You don't know me! You don't know what's gone on!"

"Would you like to talk to me about it?" she asked.

And I go "No I don't! I'm wondering how this went from, I'm

mum four hours ago to I can't hold them without supervision."

I became really hostile and it affected my dealings with the hospital all the way through. Starship was acting like I was guilty, and that's how they treated me. When I got on my high horse, they wouldn't so much talk to me as talk at me, like they were reading from a script.

"OK, so I'm not allowed to what?"

"You're not allowed to handle them unsupervised, there will be a nurse in there at all times acting in our capacity, and they will have responsibility for care of the twins 24/7, they will be doing the supervising."

"Oh, so now a nurse can double up as a supervisor for CYFS?"

"Yep."

"And I don't have any rights?"

"Nope."

So straight away, she was certain that it was child abuse and by assumption that it was me. Yes, something has obviously gone wrong. No, I don't know what caused it, but that doesn't mean that I'm a child abuser.

And she's going "Ok, well, this is the state of your sons. Look at them."

"I f***ing can see that." I'm swearing at this poor lady who coordinates with CYFS. Taking out all my anger on her. She never swore at me, she talked to me properly and with respect and was pretty cool, when I look back. It was me that wasn't cool. I didn't like what she was saying and I didn't agree with what she was saying. And I took that out on her.

So I'd just been told I wasn't allowed to touch my sons, and that custody had been taken away from me, and I was still talking to the CYFS coordinator, when suddenly the person on the nursing desk of the critical unit comes over and goes, "We have a room and a bed for you if you want to stay the night with your sons."

The words were perfectly polite but the tone was cold, and it was the straw that broke the camel's back for me. "Nah, you go get stuffed, stick your room, I don't want anything to do with you."

Every nurse and doctor all day had looked at me as if I knew something about what happened, and it got too much. I complained to the coordinator and told her what I felt, and she goes, "Well we really need some answers…we're not really facilitated to help you, we're here to help these children cause they're the ones in need."

Fair enough, but who really wants to stay around knowing that you're not really welcome and with the way that they speak to you, you hear that there's no welcome in their voice, you know it. Who the hell wants to stick around and stay in that?

"Well that's what we've got to offer," the woman told me. "So you bite the bullet or you can go back to your place, it is your choice." I did have to bite the bullet and I did stay, regardless of that lash-out at those poor staff. None of them deserved that from me.

Despite knowing that Macsyna had stayed at Starship's Ronald McDonald House that night, the testimony of the CYFS coordinator Kaufoou Palu Filita – "I heard the mother say 'I don't give a shit. I'm going. I need my sleep'," has reverberated through the public arena, fuelling claims that the mother abandoned her children in their darkest hour of need. The simple truth, that she reacted badly to having custody of her children stripped from her but got over it, never made the headlines.[71]

Across town, meanwhile, Emily's husband Pou had turned up at the Courtenay Crescent house to add his weight to demands that Chris front up to the hospital. Stuart King told the court Pou warned that the boys were seriously injured, 'there's going to be a big investigation'. King says that got Chris Kahui's attention, and that Chris just "freaked out".[72]

Chris turned up at Starship a little bit later, maybe 10pm or 11pm. He'd stayed in the hallway, and when I came out of the room I saw him standing there. I just ran to him and cried and hugged him. He didn't say anything, just "F***…" He walked over and looked at Chris and walked over and looked at Cru, and walked back out. We were shown where the whanau room was so we could talk, because Tracey turned up with him. She had picked him up and physically brought him to Starship.

He wasn't angry and he wasn't happy. He wasn't sad and he wasn't pissed off. He was just . . . blank. That's the best I can recall it. There was some video or a photo of Chris taken at the urupa (cemetery) and the pastor is reading the final rites and the dirt's being put on and I was in tears at that moment – everybody was. Except Chris.[73] His face is up and he's just looking around and angry. He makes

---

71 Evidence of Kaufoou Palu Filita, Kahui Depositions, 2007
72 Evidence of Stuart King, Queen vs Kahui, 2008
73 Kahui held his composure at the inquest as well.

direct eye contact with the cameras. At the time this was happening, I don't recall it. The funeral was a blur, but in the photos there's one where he's just blank, and I look terrible. My hair's a bloody mess. I think I'm in jeans and this ripped jumper. I don't think I even made an effort to dress the day that they were being buried. I wasn't ready to say goodbye.

So I looked like a mess and he looked blank, as he did when he turned up at Starship that night. He never cried with me. When we got to the whanau room I just bawled my eyes out.

"I just don't understand it Chris. They were fine. They had just started being able to do this. Grab and hold a finger, following my head with their eyes and turn their heads in their cots, smile. They were starting to, I think their nerve endings were coming through because they were starting to get ticklish and react to under the cheek things and under the arm things. So they had just got those going. And then they were lying there practically lifeless. And I'm talking to him going, "So they were fine Chris."

"Yep."

"So what happened?"

"I don't know."

"Well, something's happened, so . . . ?"

And I think initially I just tried to step it through and talk to him, not yell at him and not scream at him, just talk to him. "What happened, were you home with them all the time?"

"Yep."

"You never left their sides?"

"No."

Later, he remembered that he'd gone off to the hospital with Mona or something and Stu was home with them.

"Dad was there, Stu was there, Tina (Stu and Mona's four month old daughter, name changed) was there. Shayne, the twins, and me and Mona had just, I forgot, I'd just been to drop Mona off and pick her up from the hospital cause she's visiting Mum."

"Ok, so, and no parties? Mona and Stuart and your dad weren't drinking?"

"Nah."

"Ok. Nobody else there?"

"Nah."

"Well then it must be with youse, so what happened?"

And he goes "F***, I don't know man, I think they just might be hurt from when Shayne got in there!"

I looked at him closely. "Well, they're saying 'brain injury', Chris. Severe internal damage. The doctor out there just said it's similar to when you've got that whiplash effect going on in a car crash or a car accident or in that sort of situation." If a child was in that sort of situation, they can get the whiplash effect going in their body. And sometimes that can have effect on the brain's attachment to the skull, so I had a vague idea.

And he's like "Yeah."

And I'm like "Ok, so even if Shayne did jump up on the couch, not going to happen man! Not going to happen! Are you saying that Shayne did it?"

And he's like "Nah. I'm just saying that that's like the only thing…"

That's how he was talking to me. Evasive and resentful as soon as I questioned him on it. I remember turning to him, "You better not be saying that our son did this because that's bullshit. He's not one of those kids. He's a happy child, a bonny child and he's . . . . not possible. And Chris has got a broken leg man!"

"Oh f***, I don't know anything about that! You changed their bums and all of that."

And I'm like "Yeah Chris. Yeah. And I didn't notice that he had a broken leg why? Cause he's got snap domes on."

He's like "Well yeah, you never picked it up." It just became a debate.

It wasn't until the next day that I remember finding out about the historic injuries. They might have told me earlier, but if they did I hadn't taken it in. We were given this briefing in the whanau room by doctors and specialists, the social workers and the coordinator who'd told me I'd lost custody. They were all there the next day in the whanau room, and they started talking about "historic injuries". I was like, "what?!"

They explained that there was a bruise on Cru's head that was about two weeks old and just healing and the bruising was well on the mend. The bruise was under his hair. There was another bruise on Cru's cheek, and that one I knew about because Chris had explained to me that he was feeding them and let Shayne crawl in the nursery while he was feeding the twins. And Shayne just poked his cheek.

But there was a fracture, a skull fracture, hairline skull fracture on Chris' right side. So exact opposite of Cru. Chris was here and Cru was there. And the hairline fractures and they're the result of something blunt, not sharp, something blunt or large that has struck their head. And that's how delicate their bodies are. But historic injuries nonetheless.

There was an enormous amount of debate at trial amongst the medical specialists about the scope and nature of these apparent historical injuries. Radiologist Sally Vogel performed an ultrasound on June 14, the day after the twins were admitted to hospital.

In regard to Chris' apparent hairline fracture, she believed it was a crack but added that it could also have been a natural skull feature known as a parietal fissure. There was also a second apparent fracture site at the rear of Chris' skull – at least on the ultrasound.[74] And this, along with the CT scan taken at Middlemore, formed the basis of the data Starship was running with before the children died.

The problem at a forensic level is that when the actual post-mortem was performed, none of the skull fractures was found to exist. The one at the rear of Chris' head appears to have been a natural deformity in the skull. Nor did the autopsy find any evidence of a "high right parietal fracture".

Adding corroboration to this, radiologist Sally Vogel conceded under cross-examination that she could find no evidence of any soft-tissue swelling over the supposed fracture sites – no bumps on the head. There was indeed a bruise on the back of Cru's head, so he'd suffered some damage anywhere up to a week or two prior to admission. The bruise did not match any suspected fracture site. So skull fractures? They couldn't find them.

In other words, and this is important, although media reports talked extensively of these historic skull fractures based on various scans, the actual autopsy found none.[75] There is plenty of debate amongst expert witnesses based on scans and ultrasounds, and that debate continues to this day. However, it is a matter of record, if not widely publicised, that the twins did not show any hard forensic evidence of fractured skulls, once pathologists were able to examine the bones close-up. No one in the whanau room knew any of this on the Wednesday...

74 Evidence of Sally Vogel, radiologist, Queen vs Kahui, 2008
75 Evidence of Jane Vuletic, forensic pathologist, Queen vs Kahui, 2008

CHAPTER SIXTEEN

The Extent Of Their Injuries

The doctors spoke to us about the twins' current injuries, like the damage to Cru's brain and its extent. It was explained that if you imagine a tennis ball in a jar and there's room in the jar and you shake the tennis ball around, it can jiggle around. There's a little bit of give and a little bit of room and it bounces around. That is the similarity, that's the analogy that was drawn for me to understand what's happened to Cru's brain. So there's his brain, the cerebral cortex, and it has tendon like things that attach the brain to the insert or inside of the skull. The cerebellum. And in essence, it keeps the brain from bouncing around in the skull and causing damage. Now all of those tendons, all of those things that attach Cru's skull to his brain, had all been severed. He explained that is why they related it to whiplash because that's something that they know can happen to a child that will cause that sort of damage internally, for those things to detach.

Although this was the paint-by-numbers version of brain injury given to the family and the news media, behind the scenes – as with the bruising and the vanishing skull fractures – it was a little more complex and creating some interesting debate.

Cru died from traumatic brain injury. No question, that's what the autopsy found. Forensic neuropathologist Janice Synek, a specialist in brain dissection, told the court that there was no evidence of severe general swelling of Cru's brain. While it was certainly possible that there had been some, the swelling had gone by the time of death. There were signs of tiny subdural blood clots, which may result from a knock to the head or violent shaking, as tiny blood vessels are torn. However, Synek could not find any evidence of a large subdural brain haemorrhage. Again, she wasn't ruling out that there had been one, but she simply could not find any fingerprints left behind inside the skull.

Synek did find "some small clefts", or contusional tears, under the surfaces of the frontal brain lobes, which again indicate some kind of primary trauma to the brain.

"There were no haemorrhages in the callosal bridge spanning the large cerebral hemispheres or in the brain stem or cervical spinal cord of the neck." In English? Haemorrhages in those areas, particularly the brain stem and neck, would be strong indicators that baby Cru had been violently shaken. While their absence did not completely rule out shaking, it was reasonably strong evidence he had not been shaken. Under cross examination Synek agreed Cru was most likely to have either struck something, or been struck, rather than shaken – his brain injuries were consistent with impact. It is always possible that the offender was supporting the baby's head when shaking, meaning the brain would still be harmed by the rotational forces, but the neck would not suffer the damage of a head flopping back and forth.

Whatever happened, the real cause of brain death does not appear to have been the impact, but the apnoea or breath-holding that followed it. Synek found "reddening, swelling and patchy tissue death" consistent with cerebral ischaemia – similar to the effect of a stroke. She believed this had been caused by hypoxia – where the brain was essentially starved of oxygen during the breath-holding. If the brain is deprived of blood for ten seconds unconsciousness results. After 20 seconds, the brain's electrical circuits begin powering down. With witnesses saying Cru didn't breathe for between five and ten minutes (and even allowing an exaggerated sense of time in a crisis), it seems likely that the breathing incident on Monday night, and the Kahui family's collective failure to call an ambulance while it was happening, sealed the baby's fate.

Synek confirmed at autopsy that Cru's brain damage from ischaemia and hypoxia were far greater than baby's Chris'.

Cru had the most severe brain damage of the two. There is no way that medical science at this point in time, this was in 2006, they cannot do a procedure that allows them to open up the skull, and they're so delicate and they're so little, there's no such thing as reattaching those things to the skull. And even if they could, the damage that has been done. And it was around about, and they couldn't exactly pinpoint it, but they said around about a 10 to 12 hour window period where that damage has been done.

There was a time period of about half an hour to an hour [after the injury] to get the twins to the hospital, and they would have been able to sustain breathing for the rest of their life, but they would need 24 hour round the clock care and never ever be able to live a fully functional life of their own. They would have needed assistance all the way through.

I just burst into tears. I think they carried on and told me about Chris' injuries. I think they did. I'm sure they would have, but I don't recall it.

In court, neuropathologist Janice Synek remarked that even though baby Chris' brain damage was less extensive than Cru's, baby Chris suffered more blunt force trauma and contusional tearing. It had been said that Chris had suffered from a head injury and brain haemorrhage at an earlier occasion, which would indicate historic trauma. However Synek stated under cross-examination that although there was evidence of some bleeding in the frontal orbital region some weeks previously, the source was "an insignificant lesion" and it wouldn't be safe to draw conclusions from it.[76]

Complicating matters, premature babies are more likely to suffer intraventricular haemorrhages naturally.[77] Another study suggests "20%-30% of asymptomatic neonates [no other symptoms of child abuse] have small subdural and sub-arachnoid haemorrhages which rapidly resolve spontaneously."[78]

"Neonatal haemorrhage is common and may be a source of confusion," warns the child abuse research paper. "Such haemorrhage usually disappears by eight days, but can persist as long as three months."[79]

Away from the autopsy itself, perinatal pathologist Jane Zuccollo had spent some time examining the initial CT scans of Chris' skull. The scans from the day of admission, she said, showed evidence of an old subdural haemorrhage but that there was evidence it had been "surgically drained"[80]. The twins had spent a lot of time in hospital. Zuccollo believed the old injury to be older than three weeks, meaning it must have happened either just as the babies came home for the first time, or possibly while

76 Cross examination of Janice Synek, neuropathologist, Queen vs Kahui, 2008
77 Evidence of Jane Zuccollo, perinatal pathologist, Queen vs Kahui, 2008
78 "Shaken baby syndrome", I Blumenthal, Postgrad Med J 2002; 78:732-735
79 Ibid
80 Evidence of Jane Zuccollo, perinatal pathologist, Queen vs Kahui, 2008

they were still in hospital. The babies had been readmitted to Middlemore Hospital for two days and nights with a bronchial problem in mid May – exactly four weeks prior, could the haemorrhage have happened then?

Although experts believed baby Chris would have shown earlier symptoms from a historic subdural haemorrhage, that international research paper states, "Infants also frequently have a subarachnoid haemorrhage, which like subdural haemorrhage is small and of little clinical significance."[81] In other words, the symptoms of these small haemorrhages may be impossible to detect for clinicians, let alone caregivers. "Often, the patient may be asymptomatic [no obvious symptoms]," warns one medical textbook in regard to infants with these kind of haemorrhages.[82]

"What kind of mother doesn't see the signs?" Kahui's lawyer Lorraine Smith had asked the jury, implying that King must have known and that her failure to report it proved she must be the killer.

The status, then, of "historic" head injuries remains extremely murky. While child abuse specialists waxed lyrical in court about the nature of these injuries and their implications – based on scans and ultrasound images – the problem remains that the autopsy itself was nowhere near as definite and if your case hinged on proving historical injuries it's hard to see how you could push this particular aspect beyond reasonable doubt. Pathologists had been unable to find the "historic skull fractures" (or in fact any skull fractures, new included) that Starship and Middlemore's paediatric teams insisted were there.

Of the "historic" injuries, the only clear, unambiguous evidence related to the bruise – believed to be fresh – on the back of Cru's head and the twins' broken ribs. There is absolutely no medical doubt the twins suffered multiple rib fractures, which are often classic signs of child abuse. However, even here some complications arise. Scientific studies have shown that the bones of premature infants "are severely undermineralised compared to infants born at full term".[83] This means the bones of prem babies are often substantially weaker than a normal infant's. Another medical study found nearly eight percent of infants presenting with rib fractures were not victims of abuse but in fact sufferers of "bone fragility".[84]

81 "Shaken baby syndrome", I Blumenthal, Postgrad Med J 2002; 78:732-735
82 "Intracranial Hemorrhage In Children, Radiology Cases in Pediatric Emergency Medicine," Volume 5, Case 7
Lynette L. Young, MD, Kapiolani Medical Center For Women And Children, University of Hawaii John A. Burns School of Medicine
83 "Rib abnormalities arising before and after birth", Hannam et al, European Journal of Pedatrics, DOI: 10.1007/s004310050067
84 "Cause and clinical characteristics of rib fractures in infants," Bulloch et al, Pediatrics Journal,

Pathologist Jane Vuletic, who conducted the autopsies on Chris and Cru, found Cru had six cracked ribs which were healing, and which had some scar tissue around them, indicating they were some weeks –between two and at least four – old. Chris likewise had cracked ribs dating from the same time. Perinatal pathologist Dr Jane Zuccollo has a similar time estimate, based on the amount of scar tissue. Zuccollo adds that it's possible the cracked ribs would not have caused much discomfort in the infants, possibly none at all. Which may be why none of the nurses on home visits or doctors picked up any hint of the injuries. Paediatric radiologist Sally Vogel estimated the ribs had possibly been damaged for less than seven days.[85]

The ribs appear to have been cracked by someone compressing the baby into them, as if cuddling too hard, which could make a direct connection to abuse more problematic, given the number of eager aunties, uncles and cousins who had access to the twins in the weeks they were at home. In other words, yes it is an inflicted injury, but it may have been inflicted accidentally rather than intentionally. Having said that, cracked ribs are one of the classic signs of infant child abuse, and a cuddle type injury could also result from deliberate squeezing. The cracked ribs could also have been caused by someone picking the babies up with their hands around the chest, and squeezing, or from CPR – which may become relevant later in this book.

Although Chris Kahui routinely had access to the twins as their father, he was looking after them overnight alone, 9 days before the fatal injuries were inflicted (14 days before the children died).

A review published in one medical journal notes:

"Children are usually shaken in response to prolonged inconsolable crying. In a fit of rage the child may also be thrown down. The perpetrator is generally of limited patience and experience in handling a child. Some have admitted using shaking as a technique for stopping the child crying. Such individuals are most frequently male, fathers, boyfriends and babysitters."[86]

We know Chris Kahui found it difficult to cope with the twins, even though they were just effectively tiny newborn babies confined to a cot, because by his own admission on Sunday, the night before the breathing incident, he had driven all the way to his father's house in Manurewa

2000; 105 e48
85 Cross examination of Sally Vogel, paediatric radiologist , Queen vs Kahui, 2008
86 "Shaken baby syndrome," I Blumenthal, Postgrad Med J 2002; 78:732-735

to wake Macsyna up and demand she come back and help him with the twins. What could two newborns possibly have done to provoke such a reaction from their father that he drives halfway across the city? Kahui's sister Eva recalls her brother saying "the boys are hurt, you have to come home".[87] What did Chris know, why did he say the boys are hurt? Why couldn't he cope?

What hasn't received any attention in the media coverage of the trials and inquest, from what I can see, is the fact that contrary to witness testimony, the babies may also have been crying before they were found injured the following night. And if they were crying, then at that stage they were still conscious.

Why do I say this? It's an argument from inference, not from direct testimony. Chris Kahui and his father Banjo were heard arguing loudly, before Chris went into the babies' nursery on the Monday evening. Kahui's sister Mona has testified that Banjo was angry, wanting to know why Macsyna wasn't around to look after the twins. The argument became quite heated, by all accounts. This much has been entered into the court records, but what triggered it?

There was some cross-examination on whether the twins had cried. In his statement to the inquest Chris Kahui stated that baby Chris had not fed or cried at any time after Macsyna left on the Monday afternoon to go to Emily's, and Macsyna King's lawyer Marie Dyhrberg wanted to clarify, "certainly up to the time you took Chris to the doctor? Is that right?"[88]

"Yes," answered Kahui.

"But that is not what you said in your police statements, is it?" challenged the lawyer.

"No, it is not," admitted Kahui.

"No. So what you are saying is that what you said in your police statement is not right, what you say in your Inquest deposition is correct?"

At this point Coroner Garry Evans jumped in. "But you told, Mr Kahui, you told Mr Mount that everything you had told the police was true, did you not?"

"Yes."

"You told him that," continued Evans. "And the supplementary statement that you put before me says that 'this statement is true and correct to the best of my knowledge and belief'."

"Yes."

---

87 Cross examination of Eva Kahui, Queen vs Kahui, 2008
88 Cross examination of Chris Kahui, Coroner's Inquest, 2010

"Now," exclaimed Evans pointedly, "the difficulty I have is I do not know what to believe, whether what you told the police was correct or what you tell me in this statement is correct. Do you see the difficulty I have?"

" Yes."

"Because there is two versions, is there not?"

"Yes, there is."

We don't know if baby Chris was crying but, as any parent knows, a sleeping baby is a quiet baby is a happy parent. If the twins had already been unconscious, or even just asleep, Banjo Kahui would not – I believe – have had cause to get angry at Macsyna for not being there to look after them. Yet he was angry, and he was angry before the children were found brain-damaged.

If the twins were quiet, they would have been out of sight, out of mind as far as their grandfather was concerned. There would have been no obvious reason for Banjo to complain. Yet the jury was asked to believe that Banjo Kahui just became randomly angry about the sleeping twins specifically and the absence of their mother. The same Banjo who'd had Macsyna and Shayne staying with him the night before, when she was also away from the twins, and hadn't kicked up any fuss then, even when Chris came around demanding she return to help him with the twins (she ended up taking Shayne to hospital instead).

What pushed Banjo's buttons on that crucial Monday night in June 2006?

Far more likely, I believe, that the argument resulted from the children perhaps crying for their feed or not settling well, and Banjo getting frustrated with Chris' inability to shut them up. If that's the case, then the documented argument and "why isn't Macsyna here to look after them?" makes perfect sense.[89]

We know, through witness testimony, that Chris entered the nursery hard on the heels of this argument and was in there alone for up to ten minutes[90].

Nearly everyone agreed, however, that the injuries that finally killed Chris and Cru must have been inflicted after the twins last fed and behaved normally. Zuccollo told the court case, and later the inquest, that in her experience the symptoms shown by Cru in particular must have shown up only minutes after the primary brain trauma was inflicted, and witnesses are already on the record that Kahui was alone with the twins for up to ten minutes before the breathing incident.

89 Evidence of Mona Kahui, Coroner's Inquest, 2011
90 Initial statement of Chris Kahui to the police, and also Evidence of Mona Kahui, Coroner's Inquest, 2011

Did Chris get overconfident and attempt to pick up both babies at once to play or feed, then simply drop them, accidentally? Did his father see it and is that why he lied to protect Chris? Is that why he and Chris argued? Or did Chris – wound up by his argument with his father, simply snap when he got inside the nursery, just like when he smashed the windscreen on his car in anger?[91]

Did Banjo lie to protect Chris – as he has now admitted at the inquest – because he knew his argument may have contributed to whatever went on?

The lack of any major bruising or impact points on their skulls indicates the twins may have connected with a soft surface, like a mattress. The contusional tears in the brain are symptomatic of the brain suddenly being forced to decelerate inside the skull, such as when the head meets the mattress too fast and the brain keeps moving, becoming injured in the process. Remember, these premature twins at three months were effectively only newborns in real terms. They were tiny. Only Chris knows what happened in those ten minutes, and he's admitted giving police untrue information about the events of that day, as has his father. Were police really dealing with the 'tight 12', or should we re-define it as the 'tight 2'?

I just remembered looking at Chris and thought for a split second 'F***, I want to kill *you*. I want to do that to *you*. I want *you* to feel that. How can you just sit there and go, 'No, no, no'."

He looked at me and he knew that I was angry. My sister, she knew that I was angry. Tracey knew that I was angry. At that point my aunties and my uncles, three or four aunties and uncles that lived in Auckland, they came in the room. They just hugged me and said "Look, just gather yourself. Pull yourself together, because this isn't the end. It's not cool for the boys but it's not the end. You've got to see this through for now. Best thing you can do is pull yourself together and come back over here. Don't wander off over there. You look like you're going to kill that boy and that's not the best thing."

A clear difference between Chris Kahui's and Macsyna King's demeanours was emerging. At Starship hospital, staff reported Kahui as staying calm and collected, while the mother of the twins was said to be an emotional wreck, hovering between extreme friendliness and irritability and everything in between.[92] None of the Starship or Middlemore staff

91 Evidence of Mona Kahui, Queen vs Kahui, 2008
92 Evidence of Carl Horsley, Queen vs Kahui, 2008

who later criticised Macsyna knew that she had been the one who always sought medical attention for the children. None of them knew that while they were judging her mothering skills in a crisis, the babies' father had brazenly stayed at home on the Playstation, having done a runner from the car, remarking "whatever" when told the babies were in critical condition.

Kahui's defence counsel went to great pains under cross-examination to get detectives to admit that Kahui had "fully cooperated" with police and answered all their questions, whilst painting King as erratic and evasive. Chris Kahui was indeed "fully cooperative", if your definition of the phrase is elastic enough to include giving police false information, which is what he now admits he did. And he did it so calmly, so coolly, that for months police believed him. He even changed his story again when the inquest began last year.

Under pressure, even with detectives in his face and a video camera rolling, Kahui silver-tongued his way through three police statements taken between June and October 2006.

The man who could tell these stories so smoothly was given credit by hospital and social workers for his seeming dignity and honesty, and his lawyer even turned it into a PR coup at the trial, saying he'd given false evidence because he was a "simple" boy who just wanted to look "like a good father". Whereas King, on the other hand, was indeed trying to hold herself together, and sometimes failing, and got classed as a flake for her troubles. For example, the police who attended at Middlemore the night before reported that Macsyna was "sobbing"[93], but the Starship staff who came out to pick up the twins in the ambulance told the court Macsyna was "indifferent".[94] Was this because of Starship's starting point – that "all parents are liars" – and were they subconsciously looking for any signs that matched their preconceptions? Or was it simply because of King's abrasive personality?

At the time I couldn't help but feel what I feel and when I think about these things now I still feel a real strong rising anger and I want to do something about it, I want to action my anger, I want to put action into my hands and make something happen. But I can't. After I heard the medical briefing, I realised that there was very little I could do in regards to my sons' care. I could pray all I want. I could talk till the cows come home. I could question every-

93 Evidence of Jane Ingram, detective, Queen vs Kahui, 2008
94 Evidence of Vicki Harris, paediatric nurse, Queen vs Kahui, 2008

body and they could find out, but there was no way to turn around what had happened. What had been explained to me at that point, I knew that every minute from here on out, I'm really just biding my time. I'm saying goodbye. I'm just saying goodbye to my sons. For what that may be worth.

Social worker Marlana Maru told the court Macsyna became "distraught" when doctors indicated her babies were not likely to survive...[95]

I just had this strong urge to just bail Chris, Banjo, Mona and my brother up in the room and threaten them and if I had a way that I could have physically forced them to do it, maybe even now I think I might take my chance with that and do it. But I can't give in to that anger.

It's really hard to explain. When you know, beyond any shadow of a doubt, that this doctor sitting in front of you is not lying, is presenting you with facts, and he's doing it with compassion, in such a low and gentle tone. I could not be angry at him. I couldn't. I just felt like a little kid being stuck in a cage and told, "Here, just listen." Like watching somebody you love being hurt right in front of your eyes and being absolutely unable to change it or do anything about it or lessen the effects of it. Nothing. I just felt so powerless and useless.

As I sat there my mind began flooding with old memories of failed motherhood. Leaving Sean and Narelle with their father, when I couldn't see it through. Things had got tough and I'd quit. And here I am in this situation again, two of my children in one go are in need but it's too late this time. This time it's too late. I couldn't ring their father and go 'can you come and get them?' The despair hit me like a train. I just kept picturing this black, hollow, with a light, that had little tiny bars. 'Not for you, you don't get to touch the light.' And I remember thinking and feeling like I was just sinking in sand and my world was starting to turn back around to the nightmare of the life that I had lived as a younger mum again. I just was overwhelmed with all these emotions. All the old habits and all the old mistakes I'd made in the past seemed to have, at that point, severely booted me in the ass, and I couldn't even move.

95 Evidence of Marlana Maru, Queen vs Kahui, 2008

I couldn't stand up. I didn't even make an effort to wipe my nose. I was a mess.

My sister kept trying to wipe my nose, I didn't give a toss. I was absolutely detached in a sense, from caring about myself at that point. I suppose physically, but in there mentally, a million and one thoughts. And of all the thoughts, the strongest one was 'You, Chris.' And regardless of if he did nothing, I still thought, 'You.' He was still answering me "I don't know."

"Well it's your f***ing job to know. And regardless of whether you did nothing or you don't know what happened, I charge you with making it your business to know."

I still didn't know that he'd performed CPR on baby Cru, but I was about to find out. It was Mona who first told me what happened that night at the house, when I cornered her a bit later.

"Sis, I went into the nursery and Chris had just put Chris down and walked out and asked me to go back in and check on them a little bit later so I did." And so she goes in and sees that Cru is blue. And she yells out to Chris, and Chris comes back in and he's freaking out and doesn't know what to do. And then she says that dad comes in and does CPR on Cru.

There's no mention from Mona at this point, the first time she tells me, of Banjo and Chris having an argument before Chris had gone into the nursery for ten minutes.

So I confronted Chris about this, and he told me he had fed Cru, Mona fed Chris, both him and Mona put the babies back down in the cot, he went off to the kitchen to put the bottles back in the kitchen sterilizing unit, and Mona went to check on Tina. He said Mona had then gone back into the nursery room and yelled out to him. Then he told me he'd done CPR.

They were telling me two different stories, and I said that to Chris. "But Mona just said to me that your father did CPR, now you're telling me that you did it."

And he goes "Nah, I did it."

Then Mona goes, "But after a while, Cru started breathing again."

And I go "Ok then. And then what happened?"

"Well we all, Stu came in by that point and we all started talking about what did we think was the best thing to do, and we thought the best thing to do was to come and find you."

"Hospital is less than five minutes that way but you'll drive 25 minutes or whatever from Mangere to Papakura south to find me? But help is necessary and needed, he went blue, he held his breath and you think to find me was the best thing? What's wrong with that picture?"

"We just didn't know what to do?" They got angry when I asked it that way, they were angry at me for asking them that, asking it that way.

But my common sense goes, "Stuff whoever lives that way or anything else, the best help are doctors who work, and that's their skill, that's their trade, that's their job. Take the babies there." I couldn't believe that they chose not to call an ambulance or drive the babies to Middlemore, where Mona was going anyway. When Tina was sick, when the twins were sick prior to being critically ill, we had just been discharged the week before, we spent two nights in the hospital with them and all they had was a slight cough. But it turned out that lucky we did, there was a little bit of oxygen on the lungs and they really needed to have the respirator clear out their breathing. Increase a little bit of water then go to the milk feeds, even if it was only 10ml of water just to see if it made a difference, it did. So we learnt, any little thing. A sniffle, a cough, they're irritated for more than five minutes, just go to the hospital! I always told them that, they always knew it, I would just not muck around.

Shayne was the same. The day before the twins were critically injured, he just had an overnight fever for longer than I was comfortable. I couldn't cure it with Pamol and keeping him in just his nappy and a cool singlet. The temperature just wasn't coming down unless I kept the Pamol up and gave him water and sat up with him. When he relaxed and his temperature came down a bit, kept him cool with a wet cloth, but more than twelve hours was a bit long yards for me, and we also had to care for the twins. So I just took Shayne off to the hospital.

So they'd seen me do this with Shayne. Even before the twins came along they'd seen me do it with Shayne. I was pregnant with the twins and living in the hospital full time. Shayne needed to go to the doctor, he just had this continuous green thick, coughy phlegm coming from his nose, but a thick, croupy sounding cough. For two days straight I'd ask Chris, "Have you taken him to the doctor yet?, because he'd bring him for visits. "Nah."

"Why not?"

"Oh, just had other things to do."

"The boy is sick Chris, what were you doing that was more important?"

"I was just at home playing the games, man!"

To say I was a bit irritated would be an understatement. Even pregnant with the twins, when it was really hard to walk, I would still come out of the hospital and take Shayne to the doctor, get his prescription, get him home, give his first dose, then take myself back to the hospital. So they knew that I was going to all these lengths before the twins got there, with Shayne. When the twins are born, I had the same view, take no chances. Nothing ever changed in regards to the care of the kids. Take no risk. Yet in this one instance with the breathing, where it was really vital, they decided that looking for me was the best option. I don't know why. They won't answer me why.

Later on in the hospital, after my sister had picked up Banjo, I got a different story again about the CPR. He goes "Girl, I just walked in, Chris is freaking out about Cru cause he stopped breathing and he's blue and Mona's trying to do something with the other one and Chris' trying to do something with the other one so I did the CPR."

And I go "Mona said you did it."

"Yeah I did."

And I went "But Chris said that he did it."

He looks at me for a second and goes, "Oh girl, I lied. I said I did cause I don't want anything to look funny for Chris."

And I'm going "Why? Nothing is funny. What the f*** man? What's happening? Why are you's lying to me?"

Then he goes, "I'm not lying girl! I just freaked out. I just thought it was better to say that I did it cause if anything should happen because of that CPR then I'll get the blame."

And I go "Yeah, and you just make all of you's look like liars and I just don't trust you right now. Which one of you three is telling the truth?"

"Chris is telling the truth."

"Yeah, Chris is telling the truth, so why are you and Mona trying to lie for him? I don't get it." So between those three I immediately knew that between the three of them something had gone down, but to extract it or to get it, I didn't know how. I didn't know what. That was just the talk of the CPR thing.

The stories were changing so much I wanted to see if the hospital could tell when the injuries happened.

That later became a bone of contention at trial. Defence counsel for Kahui argued King was acting suspiciously by asking hospital staff if they could tell her when the injuries were inflicted, or release copies of the twins' medical files to her. Macsyna argues she was suspicious, all right, and it was no act: she wanted to know when and how this had happened. Crown prosecutor Simon Moore got sufficiently annoyed at the stream of hospital witnesses claiming it was odd for a parent to want to know when their children had been injured, that he asked one of them, "don't you think it would be logical for Macsyna to need to know?"

"Could be," the witness finally conceded.

The changing stories surrounding the Cru breathing incident continued to bamboozle police and the inquest. Banjo Kahui told the court trial that he was standing at the front door of the Courtenay Cres house and could see into the nursery when Chris Kahui went in, just before the injuries were discovered.

"And am I correct that you could actually see through into a nursery from where you were standing?"

Banjo: "Yes."

"Did you see your son Chris pick up baby Chris?"

"Yes."

"You did not see him do anything violent to baby Chris, did you?"

"No."

"You did not hear the twins screaming or crying at all?"

"No."

"You did not hear any bangs?"

"No."

"Chris did not seem in a boiling rage?"

"No."

"Your daughter, Mona, went into the nursery almost straight after Chris, didn't she?"

Answer: "Yes".

All well and good, but it then emerged from the house plan that it would have been impossible for Banjo to have seen the nursery from beside the front door where he claimed to have been. His evidence was clearly questionable.

At the inquest, nevertheless, Chris Kahui's lawyer asked him if Banjo was right.

"I just in particular ask a suggestion that your sister went into the nursery almost straight after you. Do you want to comment on whether you think your father might be right, or do you remember differently?"

MR KAHUI: "I remember Mona walking in after me, yes."

MR WILKINSON-SMITH: "Okay, and the suggestion it was straight after you, what do you think about that?"

MR KAHUI: "Yes, that is quite right, yes."

So we're clear…both Banjo and Chris Kahui have stories saying Mona came in straight behind him. But here's what Mona said at the court trial:

Question: "You have told us that you saw Chris taking Shayne to the lounge, did they both go into the lounge?"

Answer: "Yes."

"Did the lounge door remain open or closed after they went through?"

"When Chris went in because you can see through the glass door, I seen him walk in and pick up Shayne, walk into the lounge door and kick the lounge door closed."

"And you say that the other three of you, your dad, Stuart and you finished off your smokes [outside]?"

"Yes."

"And then you went inside?"

"Yes."

"Did you notice whether the twins' door was opened or closed once you got back inside."

Answer: "I cannot remember."

"Where did you go once you were back inside?" "I went into my room to get my gears ready for the hospital."

"Where did Stuart go after you got back inside?"

"Into the room."

"Into which room?"

Answer: "Into our room."

"So you went together back to your room?"

"Yes."

"What about your dad, do you know where he went?"

"I am not sure."

Question: "When you left your room to leave the house where was Stuart?"

"He was in the room, in our room."

Question: "What was he doing in there?"

"Playing Playstation."

Question: "And do you know where your father was?"

"No."

"When you left to leave the house?"

Answer: "No, I am not sure."

"Before you left the house did you decide to go and do something?"

"Yes. I went down into the boys' room to say goodbye to the boys."

Question: "So you went from, as we look at the plan, from bedroom 1, out the door, turn left down the hallway and went into the bedroom 2 which is the twins' bedroom, is that right?"

"Yes."

"Do you recall if the bedroom door was open or closed?"

"It was pulled to."

Question: "Pulled to but not shut?"

Answer: "No."

"Do you know where your father was at that stage?"

"No."

"Did you actually go into the twins' bedroom?"

Answer: "Yes."

"Who was in the bedroom?"

"Chris and the twins."

"Whereabouts was Chris in the bedroom when you saw him? He was standing by the cot holding baby Chris?"

Answer: "Yes."

So many different versions, it's hard to keep track of them all. Even police lawyer Simon Mount sighed after reading this and commented, "Needless to say, it is yet another version which is different."

And yet the jury deliberated for only one minute before finding Kahui not guilty, the changed stories meant nothing to the intellectual giants serving for that trial...

At no time did Chris tell me that his cousin April had been there that day, for example. The twins had died and been buried when Chris finally told me about April being there. April gave the last full feed to the boys that Monday afternoon, and they drank it.

She told me herself, I went to talk to her, banged on the door, confronted her "Did you hurt my twins? Did you hurt my sons?" Really just put it to her.

She goes "No Max. Come in."

I said to her, "I just need to know what you did when you went there."

And she goes "Banjo and Shane" – her partner, her husband Shane – "were talking."

"Yep."

"And I asked Chris if I could come in and feed the twins."

"Yep, ok. Was he there with you when you were feeding the twins?"

She goes "Nope. Nah, he just got things ready for me and he was out in the lounge playing with Shayne."

Chris told me that he never left April's side and he sat in the room and fed the twins with April. So there was something up with that there cause April said that she had fed Cru. Chris had already fed Chris, baby Chris, had put him back down, and only Cru needed feeding, and April fed him, and Chris wasn't there. So does that make a big difference that he wasn't there? Yeah it does to me. He said that he was there with her, all the way to me, that first time he spoke to me about her being there.

He told me she turned up just after lunch on the Monday, soon after I'd left.

Which fits with what the court heard as well. The substance of April's evidence is critical, because virtually all the medical experts agreed it was the last independent testimony that the babies were awake, alert and feeding happily, when Macsyna had already left the house, therefore they must have been injured after this final feed, which is why police concentrated on those still in the house.

"This child had a very severe primary brain injury," Professor Carole Jenny told the inquest. "He had tears in the actual cortex of his brain and I can't imagine that a child with that severe an injury would have been able to do a complex motor event like taking a normal feed."

This is also where the issue of dehydration kicks in. By the time the babies got to Middlemore Hospital on the afternoon of June 13, 2006, they were described to the news media as "malnourished". Most young TV reporters or news journalists have not yet had children, so the intricacies of childcare whizz over their heads to a certain extent. Infants like the Kahui twins rely solely on milk to survive. Their bodies are tiny and the feeding cycle at that age is probably every four to six hours. Miss one of those feeds entirely and a baby can become dehydrated, having urinated away most of the fluid from the last feed. Miss two or three feeds in a row and those children are now in serious trouble. I've seen babies who can't keep a feed down through illness having to be hydrated through an intravenous drip within just hours of the illness appearing.

Chris Kahui has given authorities utterly different stories. In his first two statements, on June 13 and again on June 21, he told them he'd fed the babies normally twice after the breathing incident, and that they had fed well. He gave the same impression to the twins' mother, Macsyna King, leading her to believe the boys had been fed at 6am and were not due another feed until around midday. In his third statement, delivered to police in October 2006, Kahui said the last time the children had fed was between 5pm and 6pm on the afternoon of the injuries, that was his position going into trial – he dropped the claim that the babies had fed after the breathing incident. Then he altered his statement yet again, for the inquest, claiming that in fact his previous statements were all wrong and that in truth, the twins had not fed since 1pm the previous day.

Now, it's important to remember that Chris maintained his feeding "errors" for months, and there was no evidence from his immediate family that contradicted that and led police to the truth, so they must have accepted Chris's word that he'd fed the babies and they were OK.

If they hadn't fed for 24 hours, as is now claimed, they would be more than a little malnourished, they'd be at death's door, or in medical speak, "extremely hypoglycaemic and dehydrated and potentially running into problems".[96] If the last time they fed was actually 6pm the night before they were admitted to hospital, they'd still be showing signs of advanced dehydration. And if they fed at 6pm, the fatal injuries were inflicted after that.

"Why in the third interview [taken in October 2006] did you say that they were not fed at that time?" Coroner Garry Evans asked Kahui.

"Probably because I had more time to think about it."

CORONER: "You had more time to think about it?"

MR KAHUI: "Yes".

CORONER: "But the interviews that you gave in June came immediately after the breathing incidents, did they not?"

MR KAHUI: "Yes."

CORONER: "The two interviews."

MR KAHUI: "Yes."

CORONER: "Was what you told the Police in June, at those two interviews, your memory of events, that is what you remembered?"

MR KAHUI: "It would have been what I remembered – well, my memory would have been better then than it is now, yes."

---

96 Evidence of Jane Eyres, Coroner's Inquest, 2010

CORONER: "Your memory would have been better then than it is now?"
MR KAHUI: "Yes."

It still is not certain when the babies last fed normally. Not only were they brain-damaged, they were starving to death, and only Chris Kahui knew the truth about the feeding cycle.

Despite internet speculation, we know the babies were not malnourished prior to this because the home care nurses who visited, sometimes unannounced, were delighted at their good health and good progress.

If Kahui had told Macsyna King when she arrived home about 10am that the twins had not fed since 1pm the previous afternoon, and that he'd had to perform CPR on Cru at 9pm, is it likely that the woman who'd rushed a boy with a runny nose and a cough to hospital at 4am two nights earlier would not have leapt into action and bypassed McDonalds?

But Kahui didn't tell Macsyna that, and he didn't tell the police. He didn't call an ambulance, and he didn't feed the babies. He might well have changed them and changed their outfits at 6am, but their failure to feed would have been a harbinger that his own nightmare had not ended with the breathing incident the previous night, it had only just begun...

CHAPTER SEVENTEEN

Their Final Moments

Police were wanting to move quickly on finding out what had happened, and understandably so. The twins had been admitted overnight to Starship, and the next day we'd all been invited down to Harlech House, where the Manukau Police CIB are based. Colin Higson was the detective sergeant and he invited us in for a cup of tea and this 'hui' thing. Present was Tracey, a kaumatua Ani Hawke who I think was there (she was related to the Kahuis), me, Emily, Stuart, Mona, Banjo and Chris. Definitely us. About eight of us. And Det. Sgt. Higson's going "Right, we need to know who's done this."

That was the first question he asked. Now I have an equal opportunities mouth and I'm prepared to insult anyone when they ask me what I think is a stupid question, so I gave this poor cop the Macsyna special: "You're a f***ing idiot! You stupid dick! Who's done what? Enlighten us, you know a few things, just like the doctors know a few things, so how about you tell us what's going on?"

"Well your sons have been critically hurt Max. We have the best people on the job right now and they are saying to us the twins have less than three days to live. So you pretty much have three days to think up your story and come up with a good one, or you can tell me the truth."

I'm like "What a dumb approach, you idiot. You want to get something out of people and that's how you think you're going to get it? Give me a break."

After giving Colin a blast, I needed to go to the toilet and asked for directions, then off I trotted, leaving the others behind in the room. But I got a little lost and ended up outside a nearby office, and I could hear the voices inside.

"So, how're we going to get the car bugged? What are we going to do about that?"

"Well," said the second voice after a moment, "after this convention with this family, if we find that they are uncooperative, that's what we can use to put forward to the judge. To get a warrant for surveillance in regard to the assault on the twins."

And I'm like 'f*** me!' And I'm gobsmacked, cause I've lost my way. Colin Higson pokes his nose out the other door, realises I'm lost and points me in the right direction. "The toilet's just down there."

When I got back to the room I whispered, "Ems, I just heard them say that they're going to bug the car and the phones."

She goes "Yeah, probably. Good. We'll give them the run around and we'll have a little game too, but they can listen to what we've got to say, I don't really got anything to hide. Neither have you. You should just come out and tell them everything."

I go, "I bloody did!"[97]. Not that I realised in that early stage that Chris had told some significant lies.

And she goes "Just saying!"

I gave police a fuller statement further down the track, after the twins had died. It took me days because I was bawling so much. My lawyer Marie Dyhrberg told me to take my time, take as long as I needed.

When I researched the Arthur Allan Thomas story, one of the things I discovered was how conspiracy theories had grown around Jeannette Crewe's father Len Demler, supposedly because he had failed to help out on the search for his daughter and her husband. It wasn't until I accessed the police files that I discovered all those occasions when locals and the media were sticking the boot into Demler for not being there, were times when he'd been called away by police to help them with their inquiries. The man could not physically be in two places at once, but everyone assumed that where they were was the place where Demler should have been, and they caned him for it.

A similar phenomenon has occurred in the Kahui case. Defence lawyers made much of hostile hospital staff who noted that Macsyna was not at the twins' bedside 24/7 as they lingered on life support. It's easy for hospital workers to make moral judgements, but both King and Kahui

---

97 Police testified at the trial that King had been happy to answer their questions after the initial stand-off at Middlemore Hospital, once she'd been separated from her sister Emily's influence.

were called away on police business. Chris' older sister Tracey turned up at the house, exclaimed, "What a pigsty" to her brother and gave him a hard time.

In the 24 hours since the twins had been admitted and Macsyna and Chris had ended up at Starship, baby Shayne had not received the care he normally did. When CYFS arrived they took away Shayne, who'd earlier been frolicking in a police video as Chris made his first statement, and Mona and Stuart's daughter Tina, stating the children had been poorly cared for.

By the time Macsyna got back to the house and ordered the family to clean up, it was too late.

In truth, CYFS and police wanted to check the other children for any other evidence of physical abuse and needed a mechanism to do so. Given the mystery over who had done what to the twins, a little bit or erring on the side of caution was probably a good thing, but let's not over-egg the pudding by exaggerating the significance of the CYFS seizure. Middlemore Hospital staff later admitted in court they'd then checked over Shayne and Tina and found no evidence of abuse.[98]

The CYFS child-seizure story was out the gate and running, however, and the two children were removed from those family circumstances as publicity grew.

Again, in the wider media coverage this was seen as more proof of chronic child abuse, but the evidence from witnesses is that prior to the twins being injured, all the babies had been well-cared for and – surprisingly – to a standard higher than many families in the Middlemore hospital catchment zone. As health worker Kathryn Greenwood told the inquest:

"Shayne always appeared well looked-after and healthy – his hair was always brushed, face washed and he had clothes and shoes which fitted him." Some children, she told the inquest, would arrive at hospital hair not brushed, teeth not cleaned, "drinking coke for breakfast". Greenwood described baby Shayne's relationship with his parents as "warm".[99]

It was Greenwood who helped assess Shayne again for CYFS. In the space of one visit at the hospital she managed to determine that the child had not progressed since the previous visit. She could be right, but I would lay good odds that any 13 month old child taken from his parents by strangers, after a night of substandard care by relatives while his parents were at the hospital, and recovering from the flu, wasn't exactly going to

98 Evidence of Claire Dillon, staff nurse, Queen vs Kahui, 2008
99 "Kahui Inquest: Hospital Staff Had No Concerns", NZ Herald, 2 November 2010

shine like a star. Babies can have bad hair days too, and one snapshot assessment is not exactly peer-reviewed science.

I think I slept two nights at the hospital, I can't remember how many nights there I'd slept. Maybe two, I went home one night and then I came back and checked back in upstairs.

On the night they were admitted, the next day I went to the police Hui with everybody at Harlech House. After that I shot over to Courtenay Cres to get some clothes and some personal items, to gather some photos and things.

My time away from the hospital was spent doing random tasks, like cleaning the home, mowing the lawns. It might seem strange but what I would normally do when things were bugging me, was cleaning. Keeping myself busy. Too much idle time on my hands when I felt that way was just no good. Not in any situation was it good for me, especially when I was highly emotional.

When I was at the hospital, I'd sing with the twins, play with them, hold on to them, rock them as we sat in the lazyboys in the room – I filmed their days once they were in hospital. I filmed their days there every day. Changing their nappies was really difficult to do. The first time I changed them when they were critically ill, I went through this weird thing, where I changed Cru's bum. The feeds were just intravenous things and up through the nose and then do that. And they had hats on. I can remember the first sort of tests they ran involved coming in and shaving a patch of the twins' heads.

I asked if I could keep the hair that they shaved off their heads and they said no. They swept it up and binned it, so I just waited for them to leave the room for a moment, got the hair back out of the bin and kept it.

The Police have got the hair now. That, and all the video footage of the five days that they were there. The Police also took all my photos and videos of Shayne's first birthday on 10th of May. We'd taken the children to McDonald's for a big first birthday for Shayne, we got heaps of those sorts of things. Family photos with everybody holding onto them. Them when they're awake and them when they've got toys. The police have got all of those sorts of things, and I pray they don't lose them. They are all the mementoes I have left.

Once they'd run their tests, they came back with results of the brain activity and explained that there was just not enough oxygen getting to the brain. I already knew the basic fundamentals of the need for oxygen. It was really, really daunting. Another huge blow, another kilo of loneliness added on top of the burden of knowing all these things that are going on and have gone on. Then there's this grey period, this unknown period, the stuff that Chris said he doesn't know. Doesn't know how they got hurt, how that happened.

So there were moments like that and then there were moments when Chris and Cru would need resuscitating. I watched the nurse and asked what's going on and she just hit the panic button and asked us to get out and we'd have to get out, and it was really hard.

"Nah, I'm not going to get out actually, I don't give a rats if I don't have custody. I'm not touching them, you're present. I'm not going to get out if these are their last moments. Sorry. Not leaving." I had to argue with them to let me stay whenever they did any procedure like that, they kept asking me to leave. It was really hard. I was getting angry again, reacting hard out and badly to people. If they said anything remotely judgemental towards me I would be ten times as hard towards them.

On the fourth day, this nurse removed the oxygen mask, the ventilating thing, removes it off him. "What are you doing?" I asked, worried.

"I'm not allowed to resuscitate him anymore. I've been told I'm not allowed to do it. Those are my orders, those are my instructions."

"What the hell do you mean you can't resuscitate him? This is what takes care of their breathing, what keeps them alive, and this is why they come here. And you're saying now that you're not allowed to do it? That's why we bring them here!"

And she goes "I can't. I'm not allowed to do it anymore. I have to remove it Max."

I flew off the handle again, went storming down the corridor. "Ring the doctors, I need to know who made this decision!" I remember one of the hospital staff referred to me in court as "irritable". Irritable didn't even begin to cover it. About 20 minutes later the CYFS coordinator turns up and says, "We've decided to let nature take its natural course because they cannot have a decent quality of life."

I just couldn't let go, and kept arguing the point. "Who the f*** are you to describe a quality of life fit for any person? Who are you to delegate and say that to?"

"Well, I know it sounds like euthanasia, but that's what we've decided to do. We can and we've got the power to, that's our decision." That was pretty much it.

I looked at her in sadness. "You're just not going to try. You're just going to quit."

She goes "It is the most compassionate thing that we can do for them. They are going to just exist. We cannot by any means see any activity of the brain whatsoever, Max. Which means that they are not able to distinguish anything from anything."

"Yeah," I said, "but they still have that percentage where they know, they sense. Just like when you know you're in a good place, you feel happy there. It's like that. And when you're in a place that gives you the willies you feel that thing. There's still that there for them."

"We are not reconsidering. That's final."

I was, I don't know, I guess grasping at straws. Maybe exploring the possibility of continuing their life. As I explained earlier, I had already experienced abortion as well. That pigeon – the feelings I'd gone through back then – was coming home to roost again, and that home truth was hitting me hard.

This time around, however, I didn't have control of that decision at all. Legally had no effect on the decision at all. It was gutting. It was really, really gutting. It was the first time that I realised what being powerless in a really, really severe situation was like. Again and again and again, and blow after blow from Middlemore hospital, had dragged me powerless to that point there.

I couldn't help but look at my sons and think 'I've only just got to know you and I'm just starting to enjoy the reactions from you, and now I've got to prepare to say goodbye because these people are by no means going to resuscitate you.'

What could I do? Nothing, just be there at the end. All the family were called, my uncles were called and they baptised the boys for me. I don't even know why I asked for that, I just thought any little thing I could give them, whether it was right or wrong I was going to give it anyway. That's what I thought should happen so my uncles did that. They asked if we'd baptised the twins yet and I said "Nah, they haven't been."

Cru kept having these seizures and his breathing stops. The longest one lasted for about two minutes or something and then he just breathed and he was back to breathing on his own. Every time it happened it was just really, I can't describe it. I got, from that experience though I can say I have drawn a respect for life, the breath of life, I know how important it is. I now have a much stronger appreciation for that through watching my sons labour to breathe, work really hard to fight for every single breath.

I just watched his chest rise and fall for a long time and then I just had to get out, cause it was starting to do my head in. I was starting to think negative again and starting to go 'F***, if it happens again and Chris says one more negative thing to me I'm going to just do something stupid, and I know it.'

So at the back of these rooms at the critical care unit, there's like this corridor like room, like the corridor that you enter in. It's tucked out of the way, down the back. You can see windows, car parks and the city out there. After half an hour of trying to sleep someone burst in the door. "It's Cru, wake up, wake up. Come back in."

He's doing it again, he's starting to labour his breathing, he's starting to get all groggy. The nurse starts taking the IV's off and the monitors off and I'm going "What the hell are you doing now?"

She goes "It's time."

"It's not time!" I'm going.

And she goes "It's time, he's going to go."

That nurse got a broadside from me. "F*** you, f***ing, get the f*** out of the room. Get another nurse in here, get your ugly ass out of here, I don't want your shitty negative intentions in this room. Whatever last breaths they take they'll be by their decision, by God, not by you and by your negative shit. You think you're going to do that?"

Poor nurse, I just unleashed on her. She did it anyway. She's crying as she's doing it, "I'm sorry, I've just got to do it. These are my instructions." She does it anyway and she goes "Please don't be angry at me, it's just what I've got to do. But believe me it's the kindest thing to do."

"Kind? They don't even have any pain care."

And she's like, "well, they can't even distinguish pain, Max, that's how severe it is. You don't really understand."

But I do. And I'm just crying. I picked Cru up and walked up the hallway, and the security and the nurses and the doctors go "No, you can't take him anywhere, you're not allowed."

"Get the f*** out of my way. If he's going to have his last breaths they're going to be fresh air, not this shitty ass room, fake air. It sounds stupid but it means something to me. Let his last breaths be fresh, fresh air."

They said no, they were going to stop me and I begged them "Please, please, please let his last breaths be fresh air, It's stupid Auckland air but let it be fresh air!"

> At the trial, intensive care consultant Fiona Miles described this incident to the court as "tense", and says she told King her actions in holding her son for his dying breaths were "not appropriate". For a while it was a Mexican stand-off between the mother, and the system…[100]

They let me go and I just told them, "Stand right there, follow me, I'm not going to go anywhere and do something stupid. Please."

So they did, they let me. Cru took his last breaths in my arms, in the darkness just before an Auckland dawn. And I curled him over and he grabbed me for a little bit, then he let me go. He let me go and I knew that he'd passed at that point.

I just stood there and held him, remembered, and "Thank you for the short little time that I got to know you and all the little joys that you gave me while you were here. I've learnt heaps from being here with you and I'm really sorry that I wasn't there for you to stop what was….I just, I love you."

It was real gutwrenching, real emotional. But I felt this over-whelming feeling of love come over me. I believe it was from him. I believe in his last moments he said "I love you too", because I felt this strong elation, it was really, really strong in my chest. It was overwhelming. And I felt relief and for that little time I never thought of anger. I never thought of Chris and what he did. I never thought how sad it was, I never thought of my pain and I never thought of myself, I just had this overwhelming feeling of love. I couldn't stop hugging him.[101]

I just walked back into the ward and asked if they could just let me bathe him and dress him. The coroner was coming in to pronounce him dead and confirm it. So I just held Cru for a while and put a blanket over him and wouldn't let him go until the coroner came.

---

100 Evidence of Dr Fiona Miles, Queen vs Kahui, 2008
101 To hear Macsyna talk of these final moments, download www.investigatemagazine.com/macsynalastmoments.mp3

I laid him down and said "I'm going out there, when you've done what you've done can you call me back. I want to bathe my son."

Even in death, the CYFS coordinator was trying to claim my child. "No," she answered.

"He's dead now," I argued. "Now you have no jurisdiction over a dead child. He's mine now."

So she, the coroner came in and pronounced him dead, and they came and let me know. I went back in and bathed him and sang to him. Just what I normally would do when they were alive. The nurse had to stay in there for 'supervision'. I didn't care. She listened to me singing and watched me bath him and dress him. I was only allowed him for a little while and then they were taking him down to the morgue.

I held him for I don't know how long. There was no appreciation of time for me at that point.

When baby Chris passed, it was much the same. They had such different little personalities. Chris was the little, he was the mouth-piece. Cru was lazy and fat. If he was hungry, he would just grab his brother's chest and Chris would cry. Cru would be awake and just looking around the room and then he'd clutch Chris and make Chris cry and then let it go. If nobody turned up it was like the kid knew, and he would do it again. Then Chris would cry and Cru would take his hand off and Chris would be alright. That's how they worked, that's how they knew each other.

So when the nurse disconnected Chris from life support, I was ready for it this time.

"This is it Max. This is it," the nurse was telling me. Their attitude seemed to have changed as well. "Are you going to go outside with him?"

"Yep."

And they were obliging. They helped me, just had everything cleared. The doors were open and the security were there. They had cordoned off this area where the termite media couldn't get to. And they had this little wall partition thing where I just stood there with him for a while. And when he took his final breath, he smiled. He just seemed to peacefully slip away. He didn't labour or breathe, his chest didn't rise as high and didn't rise as high. He never gasped before his last breath. It seemed to just simmer down. So it was just rise and fall, but every time it rose it would be a little less than the last one. He was just real peaceful. I like to think that anyway. Despite the injuries that's what I think about.

Everyone was there for their final passing, Chris, Banjo, everyone. But all those faces in that room faded to nothing and in those final stages I can only remember me and the twins. I know the family was there, but I can't recall their faces or what they were doing. It's just not how my memory wants to remember it.

Kahui's lawyer Lorraine Smith was in the room at the end, and told the New Zealand Herald, "All I can think about is what I saw at Starship on the Saturday…the grief, the absolute, unrestrained grief. He [Chris] was holding the baby that had just been taken off life support and he had his arm around the mother and they were just weeping in each other's arms."[102]

When I think about the physical injuries and when I think about them and their lives, it's almost, for me, unfair to think of them in that way. I don't like attaching the negativity and all the hurtful things towards the small memories that I have of them. They just weren't around for that long. I can't really say why I do that. I like it that way when I think of my sons. I like it to be happy. I like it to be simple. It's not full of heaps of memories, unlike Shayne and unlike my other children.

In those corners of my mind where my most treasured memories live, my little boys play there, good and healthy. Good for me to think of, healthy for me to think of. At the moment that's what's best for me. Being able to talk about them is still hard, but it's not as hard. When I did try to do this while the whole investigation was going down, I would be, I think it took me five days to give my first statement. I just could not stop welling up with tears. I know that the police were frustrated. Marie Dyhrberg didn't really care, she was quite supportive. She never pushed me or urged me or anything. She just said "The truth needs to be how you remember it, say it in your own time. I don't care how many days it takes you. The police might, but I don't."

The police, however, were indeed getting frustrated. Macsyna King was formally interviewed by police shortly after the twins died, and her lawyer Marie Dyhrberg later told journalists that Macsyna was "absolutely

102 "Marae farewell to battered twins in lone white coffin", NZ Herald, 23 June 2006

committed to doing what she can do so that whoever has done this is brought to justice."

Police by now had interviews with Chris Kahui and Macsyna King in the bag, but it seems the Kahui side of the family were not being so cooperative. Ani Hawke, a Bastion Point protest veteran and relative of the Kahui side, had ended up as a "family spokesman" and kaumatua, and it was Hawke who had coined the phrase "the tight 12".

Chris Kahui and Macsyna King were not members of the "tight 12", having already chosen to speak to police on the day of the tragedy and make formal statements within a week. Mona Kahui and Stuart King also spoke up front[103]. But inquiry boss Detective Senior Sergeant John Tims was decidedly unimpressed at the rest of the whanau, telling journalists there had been a meeting only a short time after the twins were hospitalised where a pact of silence was agreed to.

"The family made a decision that they would be uncooperative with police and they would not come forward and assist us with this investigation until they were given the go-ahead by a spokesperson and by their lawyers.

"These actions by stonewalling this inquiry says to me the family and extended family are supporting the individuals that have inflicted these serious injuries," said Tims. Somewhere along the way, a newspaper headline writer combined "silence" with "stonewall", and the mythology grew, although police later told the inquest that eventually everyone gave "multiple statements". By the time of the inquest in 2011, Coroner Garry Evans had had enough of hearing about "the wall of silence" in the media and on Facebook: "It perpetrates what is a canard, that is that there was a complete silence by the family whereas in fact there were statements made by family members. As to the integrity of those statements that of course is another matter," remarked Evans perceptively.[104]

John Tims' remarks were published the day the twins were laid to rest at the Mangere Lawn Cemetery…

When the twins died, like I said, it was another reminder of everything I had ever done wrong in my life. If I wanted justice for the

---

103 Stuart King gave a 6 page statement to police the night the twins went to hospital, June 13, 2006. He gave a 12 page handwritten statement to police on June 20th, exactly a week later. Then he gave a 22 page typed statement to police on June 27th. He also gave a video statement on 2 August, which ran to 100 pages once it was typed up, and followed that up with a further 16 page statement on 28 August. If King was a member of the 'tight 12' he was certainly its most loquacious member.
104 Coroner's comments, Coroner's Inquest, 2011

twins, I had to be open and honest about what I had done wrong in the past. I was forced to confront myself. Was I like that? Did I do that? I focused on all the horrible and stupid things that I did.

The best thing I could do was reveal it and be – not vulgar – but absolutely honest about it and not hold anything back. And if I was willing to be myself to that point and allow myself to be abused and battled and accused and whatever, in my mind, that was enough for me – I was making what little effort I could to help. Because there was no way the rest of them were being up front and honest about things at any stage of the game. They continued to change their statements. As far as I know I'm the one that made a statement to police, stuck with it, never ever had to make any additional changes or retract it or anything. That means heaps to me. That matters heaps for me.

Pretty much the day that I buried Chris and Cru is the day that Chris and I were over. If I'm being absolutely honest with myself, that burial marked a finality for me, although I did make a pact with myself to keep him close because I needed to know a few things. I needed to know what had happened, and Chris was the clue.

So I had to maintain some kind of relationship with him, if I was going to get anything out of Chris, let alone Mona, Stu or Banjo. Devious as it may sound, that's what I decided to do. In my mind I knew that that was the only way, if I was going to make an attempt to find out some things from them and ask them anything, that was how I was going to do it.

I did not have sex with Chris once the boys were buried, ever. I just couldn't do it, my heart wasn't in it. Just the thought of sex repulsed me. I did not want to be touched by him again. Putting up walls helped, I just was rude and aggressive.

"Max, would you like a hot drink?"

"Don't ask me if I want anything, ok? Not now. Not right now, just piss off."

I was rude and cruel and mean, keeping him at a distance. "Just stay out of my face man. Piss off. I need to go and get stoned." Once I was stoned I was a lot more approachable. But quiet and reserved, and I did it on purpose. It was my way of coping with the loss of the twins and the removal of Shayne by CYFS, and it enabled me to wind back the aggression enough so that the whanau would open up.

When I was in my straight and sober mode, I was a thunderstorm in waiting. Not long after the twins died we had all gathered at Emily's place in Papakura, and who should turn up but my older half-sisters, Denise and Fiona.

They came under the guise of a supposedly humble heart, crying and hugging us and going "Man, just want to hug you first and tell you that we love you and we're really sorry for your loss. Why didn't you tell me that you were going through this and all of that?"

It seemed genuine, and we welcomed them in, along with my oldest half-brother Robert who we'd seen a lot of after the twins were born.

Chris, Banjo and Mona are there. Fiona and Denise come in and they sit down in the lounge and they start asking questions. "Ok, we just want to know are you fullas ok?" So first question, sweet. And then they get straight into it. Fiona goes "Ok, well, I want to know what's happened. Macsyna, tell us man, just tell us. Who cares who it is?"

It was a stupid question, obviously we all cared who did it and we were already asking those questions, but in far more careful ways. The change in the room was like ice, everyone's like "shit!".

"Please, I just want to help you and just ask you a few questions. I'm your sister and I want to know. Are you happy to tell me?"

All eyes were on me, so I went, "Ok then, let's sit down over here."

Fiona and Denise sit down with me, and Robert's sitting in the lounge with Banjo, Mona, Chris and Ems. And Ems is making them cups of tea while I'm sitting at the table with Fiona and Denise. And they're going "What happened?"

"Look, I don't know, ok? I was away from the house and I was with Ems all the time and I never left her side. Chris was looking after our boys at home. The next day I took them to the doctors after doing my own thing. Then we went to the hospital and it wasn't until we got to the hospital that I realised it was something major and something severely wrong with them. I only knew that because they were just in a panic station, the doctors and the nurses."

Fiona snorted at me. "What do you mean you don't know what happened? What kind of mum doesn't know what happened?"

I was trying to keep my patience and keep my temper down, so I used a low, slow voice. "What I just said is what I meant. I went out with my sister Ems. Ok? My sister, our sister Ems. And I wasn't home and I left them home with their dad. From there to the hospital I've been trying to find out what happened."

"Yeah, well you're just not bloody trying hard enough. What do you mean you don't bloody know? How f***ing useless are you?" yelled Fiona. Off she goes swearing. I just stood up and pushed my chair backward.

"Yeah, well, first of all you can calm down, eh. You can either calm down and talk better, or I'll start swearing at you. This isn't how to sort it out and I'll remind you that I have just buried them. I'm still trying to cry about it, but you and every other bastard wants me to tell them and tell them right away, exactly what happened. And when I do, as I just did with you, I keep on getting the 'yeah well, there's bits and pieces missing.' I clearly know that, but to gather it all right now – and you're talking to me like that – it's not going to happen!"

And she's just like "Ah well, I'm trying to help you and you're not trying to do anything. You're just sitting here defending him! Do you know something and are you protecting him? Are you scared of him or something? I'll hit him now, I'll punch him now. And Banjo, I'd hit you Banjo!" she yaps, eyeballing him.

Fiona is in full flight, just verbally attacking everybody. The other sister's going "Fiona, Fiona, Fiona. Settle down, settle down."

She's like "Yeah well, I'm bloody pissed off. I want to know now!"

"Well f*** you, bitch!" I snarled at her. "I want to know right now too. How dare you think that you have more right to know before I do? First of all. So you line up and take a ticket, and if you don't like it you f*** off."

Fiona stood up to go and Denise and Robert tried to settle her down. "Hey, hey, hey, you can't come here and attack them." Robert tries to play mediator and keep the tempers down. Denise isn't really saying too much.

So I sit back down at the table "Ok, are you really, really willing to hear it?", and I run through all that I know again. This time it's Denise. "What do you think happened?"

"I don't bloody know, ok? All I can tell you is that what I explained to you, that's what happened. That's what I know so far. Otherwise I'm a mess. I'm having dreams about this old lady in this big black hat and I can't see her face and she's sitting on the end of my bed and I don't know who she is and I get this feeling that I'm scared of her."

"Oh what," sneers Fiona, "so are you saying that a Kehua [ghost] did this to your sons?"

And I'm like "no, I'm not saying that! I'm telling you what's going on for me. I'm telling you that these are some of the dreams I'm having, now that the boys have passed. And you're trying to tell me to recall what happened with them and I'm trying to tell you, in between my dreams, in between answering all these people's questions, in between asking Chris what has happened, and Banjo what has happened, I am like this. And this is what's going on for me."

Then Robert stands up and goes "Yeah well don't bloody talk to her like that Fiona, I can tell you that I've been spending the last six weeks with Macsyna at her house in Courtenay Cres in Mangere, and she did everything for those boys. She cared for them and she'd call out to Chris 'Chris can you help me please?' and he would not, hardly ever help. So don't point your finger at our sister because it definitely wasn't her."

That just sparked off Fiona again, and by this time I've had enough. "F*** off and get out of this house or I'll throw you out. You're not welcome here. Take your shitty ass attitude and get the hell out. Don't want you here."

"Yeah, well, you're a bunch of f***ing murderers and f*** you," swore Fiona at me. "You're a suicide, you're just a stale suicide like your f***ing useless mother. A whore!"

She just starts hard out on a rampage and attack. I remembered thinking 'you cold, cruel person.' It was really gutting, sitting there, looking at my older sister. Knowing very well and remembering her while I was three, four years old. The very one who used to slap me around. Slap my brothers and sisters around. Always be really, really angry if my father would make her look after us. And she resented it, resented us, didn't really like it. Now she was beating me up again.

That was the final straw for me. I heard from her every day after that with threats of "Yeah, you f***ing watch it. When you get thrown in jail, don't ever f***ing call me your sister, you're a disgrace to our name. You're a disgrace to our father's name. You f***ing wait till you go to jail, I'm going to make sure that you're taken care of you f***ing bitch...we've got some connections in the Black Power and they're going to come and get you."

Finally, after these daily abuse sessions, I answered back. "You gutless coward bully, bitch. You're sending all these people to do your dirty work, but it's you that's angry. You're the one that thinks that you need to be taking vengeance on me for my sons. You come here and you come do your dirty work yourself. Don't send other people, gang members at that. Are they happy with you spreading their name all over the place?"

And she goes "ah f*** up, you're just a suicide." She just kept on nailing me with my mother's death. Kept calling me a stale suicide and kept telling me "Just kill yourself man. Just kill yourself. Save us all the hassle. Just kill yourself, wipe yourself out, man, do the world a favour. You don't deserve to live anymore."[105]

At the time I was angry, although hurt more than anything else. There's my older sister being that sort of example for me. The only thing that's changed now in 2011 is that I don't hate her anymore. I don't feel those feelings of hatred towards her cold-hearted attitude. Now I just feel sorry for her. I really, really do. If I could have anything else for her, I would just have compassion. If she just doesn't see that there's something wrong with that, then I really do feel sorry for her.

Two sisters of Macsyna King came forward to TV3's Campbell Live, telling the network Macsyna had confessed the name of the killer to them at a family meeting. They named Chris Kahui as the killer, although the network bleeped it out. Fiona was nine years older than Macsyna, and her older brother Robert later told the Weekend Herald Fiona's disgust at the so-called tight 12 was "rich" considering how Fiona had treated Macsyna and the younger children during their childhoods. Fiona later became a witness for the Kahui defence and urged a reinvestigation of Macsyna.

It created much fodder for the tabloids, but Fiona King's 15-minutes-of-fame moment also had the effect of making the Kahui clan more suspicious of King. Newspapers started being fed negative things about King that appeared to be part of a Kahui clan PR blitz, and tensions began to reach boiling point.

---

105 Fiona King also got into a very personal spat with her half sister Emily around this time culminating in a text war. The Kahui defence lawyers accused Emily of sending threatening texts to Fiona regarding the twins murders. Emily freely admitted sending the texts, which included messages like: "I am going to find you and murder you, you mother f*****. You wait right between your mongrel eyes bitch, I'm coming". However Emily denied it was to do with the murders. Instead, she was responding to taunts from Fiona: "I do not remember the exact texts but it was along the lines of insulting myself, my family, even sent me texts saying things like 'I'm going to take your husband, he needs a real woman, he needs to come to me' and things like that. So I responded in kind and yes, it was not a nice thing but it was not anything to do with the twins. It was a personal matter between me and her." See cross-examination of Emily Hepi, Coroner's Inquest 2010

CHAPTER EIGHTEEN

Confronting Chris

I went around the neighbourhood where Banjo and Chris and Mona had moved to after we had moved out. So the twins were buried and it was leading up to when Chris got arrested. I went around to their neighbourhood and I went in to the neighbours' homes, "So how's it going? Do you know who I am?"

They were all like "Yeah, we know who you are."

I wanted to know what the Kahuis had been up to, whether they were still boozing all the time, a whole range of things. Then I knocked on the Kahuis' door. I purposely did it in the middle of the day. Tuesday when they got paid so they had money. They'd just purchased alcohol and I knew it, because they're like clockwork. People of habit. Turned up while they're on the piss. "You f***ing did it," I said to Chris.

"No I didn't."

"Yes you did. That's why you lied to me, that's why you don't know what happened there." I really did, just went hard. I accused each of them personally. The reactions I got, my brother Stu went "If you really believe that, I will go down to the police station now and say so. So just tell me that you think that now and I will go."

"Go on," I challenged him, "go down there and go do it then."

The idiot did, but I just needed to know that if I pushed him that much, would he be willing to do that. Stu hates the police. I know he has an inbuilt, severe pet hate for them. Like, really, really hates them. So this was a big ask.

Then I get a call from Detective Sergeant Colin Higson, the detective in charge at the time. He seemed bemused. "I've got your brother Stuart down here who's saying he's got to come down here and confess to killing the twins because you believe so."

And I went "Did he?"

"Yeah, he's sitting right in front of me."

"Oh yep. He didn't, I know he didn't, he's just proving a point to me so can you let him go?"

"What are you up to?"

"I just have to know, you know, have to take some drastic measures just to find out and just to know."

I did the same to Mona at one point. She went right off, "Oh, bullshit! Those twins aren't even my brother's, you slept around on him. You might have gone through all this Chris and they're not even yours."

"Whatever," I said, "but I'm confronting you, but you know, and probably had a solid hand in what happened with my twins. And you know damn well."

"So? F*** off!" she snapped at me. So she never ever denied it to me and I thought 'you....'

She proceeded to tell me, "Nah, you're all shit and I'm going to punch your f***ing head in."

I just laughed and picked her up with pretty much one hand, I was going to give her a good hiding as best as I could, but Stuart interjected and picked me up and carried me out. Fair enough. There I am, attacking his woman and he stood up for her.

For the record, yes, I'd slept with other men when Chris broke up with me after Shayne's birth, but we did get DNA confirmation, the twins were his, and I knew they were.

Stories emerged from within Team Kahui that Macsyna got drunk and sexually promiscuous at her twins tangi, and was hitting on one of Chris' female relatives…

There were only a few of his female relatives. When I say a few, I mean Eva, and Mona, and the others were friends of Tracey's family. Adele turned up for a time. And then left. They were the only female relatives of Chris' there. The others I sort of knew because I had seen them around Clendon and Manurewa. It's a small community and if you show up there all the time, you see the faces.

At the end of the night, the only ones still standing were myself, Chris' cousin Colin, another ugly cousin of his and his missus. Their relationship is, they're first cousins, but they've had three children together. So that's Chris' other female relative there. and I would rather kiss a frog any day of the week for the rest of my life than kiss that lady. Ugly as sin. I mean ugly like Shrek's Fiona is prettier than this lady. So nah, not going to happen, and I'm definitely not into females.

Chris' lawyer had taken a crack at me on this. She initially tried it with a depositions hearing. Something came up there. My lawyer, Marie, comes out and asks me questions and so do the crown lawyers. They just ask me about specific things like "at any time did you have a full on relationship with Chris' little [name suppressed]?" that was about the closest in relation to that sort of line of questions. That was the closest that I got to it.

And my answer to them was "What the f***? You've *got* to be kidding me. Seriously."[106]

And they just both said "we'll just leave it at that. You answer it how you answered us, just answer it like that."

So that was the first sort of thing that triggered that. When we went to trial she put it to me, she said "I put it to you that you did not care about your sons immediately after you buried them. And that's true, isn't it?"

I went "Nah." I answered, "No, nah. That's not true. That's a lie."

"Well I put it to you that you had just buried your sons and were at a party and you were angry with Chris weren't you?"

Couldn't deny that. "Yeah, I was angry at a number of things, I was at angry at him."

Then she carried on and said "I put it to you that you were acting promiscuous and floundering yourself around from person to person and trying to have a sexual" – I forget her word – "with one of Chris' female relatives. Didn't you?"

And I said "No."

I think it ended with, she said "I put it to you that you're lying."

These were questions being put to King directly by Kahui's lawyer. There were no smoking-gun witnesses presented. As a piece of legal theatre

106 Kahui's young female relative later went on to claim to Chris' defence lawyer that one of Macsyna's sisters had made a drunken confession at a party in 2010 that she (the sister) killed the twins, supposedly when the sister and the younger girl were sleeping in a room "together". The sister, a married mother with children, denied ever sleeping in a room with the girl and denied killing the twins. The girl refused to make a statement to police saying she would only talk to defence lawyers, and even her relative Mona Kahui told police that the girl was just "talking strange" and not making sense.

to a crammed public gallery and media bench, it was an Oscar-winning performance, reinforcing every secret prejudice the jurors had about King. Slut. Skank. Ho. As a piece of character assassination, it was masterful. By raising these issues in cross-examination and making Macsyna deny them, Smith was painting King as a denier, so that when the jury weighed up Macsyna's answer to the inevitable, "Did you murder your babies?" question, it was just another worthless denial from a worthless mother.

Game, set, match. Slow clap.

When Kahui was found not guilty, one of his lawyers, Michele Wilkinson-Smith told reporters she was really unhappy about police building up this image of an uncooperative "tight 12". Without a trace of irony she stated:

"It's just not true. Who didn't cooperate, who didn't give a statement? Everybody gave a statement and numerous statements. Chris Kahui gave three."[107]

In Chris Kahui's case, multiple statements were a sign of stories changing. The accused was a self-confessed false witness. The police knew that, Crown lawyers knew that – openly calling him a liar – Kahui's lawyers knew that, but it went sailing over the heads of the jury and the media.

When newspapers reported why the trial had fallen over, King was the eminence grise:

"King was a convicted fraudster, car thief and burglar, and a domineering, violent bully. She was promiscuous; the jury heard that there had been question marks over the paternity of the twins, but not that King had also had sexual relationships with both Chris Kahui's father, Banjo, and with one of Chris's female relatives.

"King was a mother who had suffered the loss of two babies, yet it was hard to feel any sympathy for her. The twins had sustained injuries – multiple fractured ribs, and in Chris's case, a head injury – weeks before the fatal wounds were inflicted. As their principal caregiver, King had either never noticed, or never sought help for them.

"There were allegations (which she denied) that she had threatened those who assisted the police inquiry. At a function following the twins' tangi, she made a drunken mess of herself, hit on a female guest, and was asked to leave, prompting Kahui to angrily accuse her of not caring about the babies' deaths; the defence alleged she was found outside shortly afterwards kissing Kahui's teenage brother (King denied this too)."[108]

Yet the newspaper reports had missed the subtleties of the trial. King

107 "Kahui lawyers attack police attitude", NZ Herald, 28 May 2008
108 "Sins of the fathers and mothers", Sunday Star-Times, 25 May 2008

had never noticed what even seasoned doctors had failed to pick up. To say she had "never sought help" for the twins was simply untrue – according to the Crown she was the only one of the parents to consistently get medical attention for the twins or Shayne.

Did she really lose control at the tangi to the extent suggested, or was this just more Kahui spin? King liked to drown her sorrows, yes, but the rest?

I look at that and I laugh in disbelief. For me it's like a brick on top of a brick on top of a brick. I know bullshit is bullshit. Like a sin is a sin is a sin. It was a bit hurtful for me, especially the idea that I'd had sex with old Banjo, but the allegation that really annoyed me was the teenage brother thing.

I just think, 'I'm the target, that's ok, but implicating the younger teenage boy, you sail really close to the lines, lawyer or not.'

You know, this boy, he hardly ever talked much, he did like to be around Chris and I. When were at the tangi after-party, he came up to me on the front lawn and said, "I've got to go home now. I'm sorry for you Max." And he gave me a hug and a kiss goodbye. Adele was there, she knows what happened, and so was Tane, who was up the side path. So that's what the lawyer's talking about with kissing the teenage brother. I think, 'how you make what you printed from that is despicable. It really is despicable.' I understand having shots at me and yes, she's doing her job as a lawyer and defending Chris. Just don't agree. Not like that. Why involve an innocent child? Teenager, but still a child.

At Kahui's trial, party guest Rebecca Rangi testified that Macsyna had refused to go home with Chris Kahui, prompting him to lash out and loudly accuse her, "You don't give a F about our babies being dead". Macsyna, of course, had no intention of joining Chris, and she told Rebecca Rangi that she'd prefer to stay and drink. There was no mention in Rangi's evidence of hitting on female partygoers or kissing Chris' younger brother inappropriately.

After their death there were some things that I just refused to justify or dignify, even though I had people in my face about it. I refused to do it. I just wasn't going to do it. And that was one of them. At first that did hurt me for a while. I was angry as, every time I heard it I'd go off "F*** these f***ing assholes!" and I rang APN media and asked to speak to the head person that prints all this rubbish, and I went "How the hell do you justify all the crap that's being printed about me?"

"Who am I speaking to?"

"I'm Macsyna King."

"Well how do we know that you're not just any old person?"

"Because I'm telling you that I'm not. And I'd just like to know where you get off printing all that stuff."

And they're like "We're just printing what we were told."

"So if somebody tells you anything, you'll just say you'll hold that person accountable?"

"Yeah."

"And you can pretty much write what you like?"

"Yeah."

So I just went "Yeah, nah."

From that point I made a decision to just zip it. I refused after that. Anything to do with media, I was just absolutely anti.

Coroner's Inquest, 5 October 2010, Kahui's lawyer Chris Wilkinson-Smith speaking: "I think, your Honour, there needs to be a distinction drawn between 'blackening character' and simply revealing aspects of a person's past that is true. Now if there are aspects in my cross-examination that Ms King does not accept and there in fact turns out to be no evidence to support, then maybe your Honour wants to take steps that that aspect that has not been accepted, which would be a slur – and an unsubstantiated slur – perhaps those unsubstantiated matters should not leave this courtroom.

"However, if I am simply putting to this witness matters which… appeared in a New Zealand Herald article all about Ms King's background. She took no steps to ask for a correction, I assume, and I have a good faith foundation that the reporter responsible, that they are accurate, because if they were untrue they would be defamatory."

It was the ultimate circular argument. Having been tried by the media, Macsyna King found Chris Kahui's lawyers using the media feast as an excuse to call her a killer. The media then used the court reports of the lawyers' questions to beat King around the ears again. Little wonder you haven't heard Macsyna King speaking to a journalist until now…

We had Mihingarangi Forbes and Martin Cooper, who's now attached to the Maori Party, come over, maybe three days after the boys had gone. I turned up at Emily's address in Papakura, and it's dark and it's night and I don't know what day it is, but anyway I walk in and I open up the lounge door and there's Mihi Forbes and there's Martin Cooper. I recognised her face and I knew her name as soon as she introduced herself, she said "Kia ora." She put out her hand and I just looked at her, looked at him, looked at my sister and went "What the hell are these assholes doing here? What the hell are they doing in our house? How could you let them in here?"

"Well they came to ask you something, they want to know if you did it."

I looked at Emily, darkly. "If I did what? Just say it."

And she goes "Did you-" and my sister's going at me, she's really giving it a go! And she's going "Did you kill the boys, did you kill the twins, did you do anything to put them in hospital and cause their death, did you?"

That's it, she's all on for young and old. "You effing bitch!" we're having a full on argument. Swearing. "You know damn well I didn't, I wasn't even there. I turned up with them at the hospital. You bloody know that! You know I'd never do that! You know!

"These f***ers," I swore at the TV reporters, "they don't know, actually get the hell out of the house!" I was booting them out of the house and swearing.

"Well they came for answers!" complained Ems.

"I don't care to answer them! But I can't believe that you're doing it!"

I was just beside myself. Again. Martin Cooper, he just stood up and walked outside. Mihingarangi Forbes just stood there and got out her notepad and I went, "You write anything and you print it, I'll do to you what you do to me. I'll hound you, I'll find out what your children's names are, I'll follow you around at work and see if you like it. Do something with yourself and get the hell out."

My behaviour was appalling, and Mihi, I'm sorry. I just let Mihi have it, and she was just sitting there, hadn't said boo to me apart from "kia ora". My sister, she just outright laid it on me, I just let loose. I was angry, I was mourning the loss of my boys. I figured the TV crew had probably wound up Emily and she in turn wound me up. The processional effect. In that small time before I unleashed, I sensed as much. I was looking to get some of it off my chest at the same time, I really was. I was happy to swear. It was a form of getting some of this frustration and anger and this whole not knowing about certain areas about what happened with the boys, crap, out of me. Verbal mouthiness was my strongest outlet at the time. Anybody who was a willing victim, I was keen as.

CHAPTER NINETEEN

Afterburn: The Scandals Of Macsyna King

When Chris Kahui was acquitted of murder in 2008, one of the lines his legal team used to devastating effect was reference to Macsyna King's "P habit". The Longman Dictionary defines "habit" as "something you do regularly". The clear implication when lawyers were asking witnesses about King's "P habit" is that here was a mother addicted to methamphetamine. A crack-head, in colloquial terms, out for her next fix and that's it. If that was the case, Chris Kahui told the court he never saw it, "I did not know she was smoking P at all, yes. At any time."[109]

Macsyna King had snorted speed once – long before dating Chris – and damaged her nose in the process. She told the court, and me as well, that she also only ever tried P once …

As you know I was in hospital with the twins prior to their birth and Chris' cousin Adele, she was in there with her son. She kept me company and we formed a bit of a bond of sorts. They were discharged a week before I delivered the boys, but Adele still came back to visit me, every second day, often bringing me a kai from home that she'd cooked.

Then I had the twins and when I got out, she was around our house a lot. Every second day or so. Stuart and Mona, they'd drink a fair bit at Courtenay Cres. They used to drink all over the show at the house, out the front, out the back, whatever. Down there in the kitchen with the closed door at nights. I'd often bail them up about it. "We've got our boys here, you've got your girl here, and it's just not cool."

---

109 Cross examination of Chris Kahui, Coroner's Inquest, 2010

Sometimes Adele would pop around and help me out with Shayne and the twins. One particular day, she was there when I had a disagreement with Chris. "Please could you help me feed the twins?"

"Nah," said Chris.

"Please can you help me Chris?"

"Nah man, you do it! I don't know how to handle them, I'm too scared."

He'd always have some excuse, but at the end of the day it still fell on me, the other parent. So I was juggling my Shayne and the twins and on this day Emily had also dropped off little Ellen, who was born a day after the twins. So I had Shayne and Ellen and my boys. It was a bit much. The difficulty was feeding the twins because they had to sit upright while feeding.

Adele goes "Man, I don't know how you do it and you still manage to stay happy and you don't even get on the piss with those fullas. All you do is clean, clean, clean. I think you should make these fullas help you."

I shrugged. "At the end of the day, it's me that's got a problem with it, so I'll clean it. I'll do it."

"You know what?" said Adele after a moment, "I know what you need. You need to have a try of some P. Me, you and Chantelle (Chris' transsexual brother William), we should just have, like, a half a night to ourselves at my house, we'll go away from here."

It was just a suggestion from Adele. She didn't force me to do it. "Please, Macsyna, I need a break. You need a break. Chris can stay here and babysit the kids. I'll pay Eva and Mona $20 to watch my two." Who were a lot older. I thought about it for a moment, and my 'dumb idea' warning light which had pretty much been non-functional for ten years was evidently still on the blink. Yeah, I thought, Mona and Stu were at home to help Chris too. And Adele's mother, that's right, Mary. Aunty Mary. She was there.

"So ok?"

I just thought "Yeah. Yeah ok. Why not?"

I hear there are housewives in Remuera and Parnell who use P. We must have looked like the Mangere housewives branch. "Well I can tell you I don't actually know how to smoke it," I said. "I know how much it costs, it's like a hundred bucks a turn."

"Nah, sweet as," goes Adele, "it's just like cigarettes, you smoke cigarettes, you should be sweet."

Which brought us to the next problem. "Where do you get it?" "I dunno."

We look at each other blankly, then William pipes up, "I know where to get it. So can I come with you's? I'm keen." It wasn't really my call, and Adele was keen, so we all just in unison went "Oh, ok, yep."

Then it came to the issue of dollars and Adele goes, "I don't get paid till tomorrow."

And William goes "Yeah, same."

They're looking at me. "Have you got any money?" I nodded. "You shout us, we'll pay you back tomorrow." So as it happened, I paid for it. William and I went for a ride.

Adele gave the kids dessert and cleaned the dishes and cleaned the house and made beds in the lounge for her two children. Eva and Elvis, Chris' brother and sister were there. Chris was home, we let everybody know we're going to have a bit of a hoo haa at Adele's house. I talked to Chris about it, he was sweet. He didn't even care, he had a Playstation game to play, and he had enough help to help him with the twins. Stu and Mona were sweet to help Chris.

We drove there in my car, and found Adele's house in a bit of a mess and bitterly cold. She lit the fire and put the heater on and closed all the curtains up, to get the house really warm. William and I, we first went to this place in Papatoetoe, but there was no-one there so we forged on to the next of William's haunts, a massage parlour in Manukau, We went upstairs and William goes "Let me do all the talking, just don't say anything."

The guy/girl that serves us talks to William, they engage in secret whispers for a moment, then William hands over some money and away this thing goes. Comes back out and gives William a kiss and slips it in the back of William's skirt pocket and off we go. That's how smooth the transaction was.

When we got back to Adele's, she pulls out her pipe – she's got a special case for it and she's got pipe cleaners and all of that jazz. I just remember immediately going, "That's organised! Done this before, obviously!"

She just shovels the whole bag into the pipe, burns it, melts it and we all just keep passing it around until there was absolutely nothing left. Suddenly, it was like invasion of the pixies from one of those children's stories where they come in at night and do things. We all just got this major cleaning spree bug. In the morning there was this big old ugly blanket and all of Adele's crappy broken things that she'd been hoarding were all out on this sheet, all tied up. The house was sparkling.

So yes, the drug is highly illegal and it is dangerous. I went out with a gang member who used it. It has broken families. My experience with it this time was a once-off. We were the only three participants. No children.

Of course it was going to come up in court, and none of us could lie about it. I don't have any regrets. That's what happened. I've said it through High Court and it's all I can keep saying. I never touched P again, despite people calling it a "habit". This happened only a week or so before the twins were injured, and after that my life changed. So, no, I've not touched it again.

It got called up in court and I'm sitting there and I'm answering the question honestly, as I was told. All the while in the back of my mind I know very well that here, after this, they're dealing with this matter now, but I wouldn't be surprised if telling the truth about trying P is going to come back and bite me in the ass. I'll just have to face the music, should that come. There's not a lot I can do about it and I don't look forward to it, but I've owned it and I have to live with that.

There's another aspect to this that people probably don't understand. I'd been around a motorcycle gang member who had used P, and my sister's husband had gang affiliations and had been convicted of involvement with the methamphetamine industry. I found his knowledge, his involvement with all those things beneficial to me. Why? Because I'd had bad experience with people and situations involving alcohol, meth or weed, and I wanted to know more about it. I could ask him a question, "Bro, I tried it, I did, I tried it and I was hungry and it says that you want to stay awake. Well I was hungry and then I slept for like nearly 14 hours. What's that?"

He would give always an unbiased and true understanding of the effects based on his own knowledge and experiences. He would explain, "This is addiction. This is how a habit starts."

He gets out a pen and paper, he was that intent about teaching us. He would write on this bit of paper. He goes "Ok, this is how a habit starts." And he writes the letter A. "This is how a habit starts. And the A, think of it as an apple or think of it as a whatever, and then you think about it and you're like 'well I'd like to know more.' And then it becomes two letters." And he writes an H in front of the A. "So now that one singular thought has had another thought on top of it, so it's a little stronger and now you're thinking about it." Then he adds a B on and he explains "So now the curiosity has kicked in and it's added to that initial first A and that second thought which was the H and now you've got a B there and you've got a half a habit. And then, the last part is you start deciding that you like this whole something about it, and then you just choose your substance of choice. Drugs, alcohol, whatever. Gossiping, hating on people." And he writes the word 'it.' and writes it beside the habit. But he writes it all, you know, A, then Ha, then Hab, then Habi, then Habit. All staggered like that. And clearly, he explained "It starts small, and then it gets bigger, and as the word goes down the page, you're sinking deeper into the habit hole."

And we're like "Oh! Yeah."

There has been speculation in the public mind that Macsyna King was continually out partying instead of looking after her twins. King denies it, and gets unlikely support from Chris Kahui's sister Mona who told the inquest, "she never really went out much. She never went for too long, usually."[110] As the newspaper editors wrote, Macsyna was also "a convicted fraudster, car thief and burglar". Did that mean she was a professional hardened criminal, or simply a victim of her own foolish choices…

The first criminal charge came out of my relationship with Gerald, back in Napier ten years ago. I was owed some money, a little bit more than $2000. Gerald knew the money was coming in and was angry that I'd turned to drink and was being unreliable. I think his actual words to me were, "Well you f***ed me over and you've mucked me around, I'm going to take your money off you. I've got some money saved of my own and I'm going to buy me this car."

He sent me off to the bank to get a bank cheque covering the amount I'd just received and his top-up, and asked me to place it as a deposit on a brand new Ford XR6 in his name. When I picked up the bank cheque I remember taking ten seconds of my time and going 'damn, I actually don't want a debt on my name for hp on

---

a car that's not even going to be mine.' So I scribbled some extra zero's on the bank cheque.

It was a forgery on my part, and the car dealer didn't even check it out. The original value of the cheque was something like $3500, and I altered it to $35,000. I never changed the wording, I only added the zero's on the end. Which makes it null and void. There was no way that that was going to be ok, and I knew that. The car dealer was just really happy because that was a decent down payment. Gerald gets the car and decides to try his luck even more. "I'm going to get you to go and sell some of your artwork that your brother and sister have given you," he said, referring to my cousins who have custody of Shayne and Tina now.

That wasn't going to happen any time soon, that artwork was from family. "Stuff you man," I thought. Say goodbye to your car. Gerald had no idea what I was about to do, but I walked into the Westpac bank in Napier and I said to them "Look, I came in here yesterday and got a bank cheque." The teller remembered me. "I want to confess to changing and forging your bank cheque."

It's not often that happens. She called in her manager and I explained to him what I'd done.

"I changed the value of one of your bank cheques. I don't want you to just get this cheque back and give the car dealer crap, because it wasn't his doing, it was mine. I added the zero's on the end. The bank cheque is null and void and I know it. My partner now, he wants my money, but he's just pissed me off and I'm not keen, so I'm handing myself in."

The bank manager calls the police, who come in, arrest me, take me down to the Napier police station. They gave me diversion and 50 hours of community work. The car was repossessed and Gerald was none too pleased.

So that's the fraud charge.

The car thief and burglary stem from a different incident that happened in Auckland in early 2004. One charge was stealing a car, and the other was being a party to burglary. What happened was actually quite amusing, in the grim way you can look back at things and laugh. At the time I wasn't so forgiving. One of my friends from Clendon in South Auckland, a guy named Corey, used to supply weed and we'd go over to Banjo's house and smoke it with Banjo. Anyway, Corey turns up one night and goes "Want to come for a ride?"

"Yep. Where are we going?"

He goes, "Anywhere you want."

"Bullshit."

"Yeah, nah, anywhere you want."

"OK. Lets' go to Cambridge."

So Corey gets his mate and I get my mate, Angel, and the four of us are bandidos in a stolen car, although I didn't immediately realise the car had been nicked. Halfway down the highway I nudged Corey, "Who did this car come from?"

And he's like "Mmm."

"Mmm what, whose is this car?"

"Yeah."

"Yeah what?"

"Yeah."

"F***, is it stolen?"

"Yeah."

"Oh man. Come on man!"

By this time we were way past Meremere.

"Dude, turn around."

"I can't," he said. "It's been stolen from Auckland but we've got a bit of time if we get out and I'll just steal us another car, we'll come right back."

"You stupid boy!"

But it was too late, I was in the car. There wasn't anything I could do, so I just resigned myself to whatever the night brought. "Oh well, I'm only a passenger in the car. Doesn't matter," I told myself. Turns out it did. Corey drove this stolen Subaru all the way from Auckland to Tokoroa, where he hooked up with another friend who I'll call 'Wanda'. She turns out to be in a stolen four wheel drive, but the guy she'd nicked it from had gone up to hospital in Auckland and didn't even realise his car was missing. Wanda knew the man's granddaughter and sussed out how to get into his house.

So this 4WD was stolen, but not hot.

"I'll swap you!" said Corey excitedly, offering the Subaru in trade. It's a deal, and we all jump in the truck for the trip back to Auckland. I wasn't the world's best navigator and we ended up running out of fuel in Morrinsville in the middle of the night. Corey can't get the engine to fire so it's "abandon ship".

"Well let's go and get some more gas."

"It's a diesel."

"Oh, you idiot."

Angel and I are left to twiddle our thumbs in Morrinsville while Corey and his mate, Dog, go sniffing around – I presumed for diesel but I was wrong. Turns out they broke into a tow yard, then into the tow office, and stole the keys to a Caldina. It didn't look in great condition.

"Jump in," said Corey, "I've just got to go and see another mate."

At two in the morning?

He finds his mate's place, is in there for five minutes while the three of us are still in the car outside. When he comes out he whispers through the window, "We're just going to go next door and get the keys for this Holden."

"We already got a stolen car," I complained, why the hell do you want another one?"

We start arguing and he's like "Shut up man!" so he goes next door. Eventually he can't find the keys, so he hotwires it. Now we're all sitting in this white Commodore. Driving out of Morrinsville on the main north road there's this one liquor store. He parks the car by the railroad, tells Angel and me, "just wait here", and signals Dog.

"Bro, we'll just get us a few liquors."

I'm just beside myself. 'Shit'. So we're sitting there and next thing we hear, there's this "psssh", then all I hear is the clinking of bottles. Dog and Corey come running out and they've got their pants and their jumpers and their hoodies and all their pockets are loaded with bottles and they're running in zig zags and shielding their faces like a right pair of amateur commandoes. It's the middle of the bloody night. But anyway, they come running for the car. Next thing, there's this bright as light appears and I knew it wasn't the Star of Bethlehem because it was moving too fast. The constabulary were obviously on the way. It was like one of those big searchlights that sit on boats. Strong as, moving towards us rapidly.

By this time Corey has clambered and clinked into the driver's seat. He goes to put his foot on the gas and stalls the car; it won't restart. "Every man for himself!" he yelps as he makes a run for it, stripping off the jacket full of bottles, sprinting for the railway line that runs beside the road. The road part's fine, but to either side of the railroad, there's blackberry bush and gorse. Must have been a difficult choice, but Corey tries to leap over the blackberry bush and falls straight into it.

Idiot. It was really stupid. I just sat there, refusing to run. The other chick, Angel, she tried to escape and Dog, he tried to run. I just sat there. 'Nah. I'm going to just wear it because it's the best thing to do. This is stupid.'

The police car screams to a halt, officer leaps out with his dog. "Come out of the bush. Or I'm going to let the dogs go."

There's not so much as a squeak from Dog and Corey who've both ended up in the briar patch together. They won't come out of the bush, so in the dog goes and suddenly all you hear is this chomp and "Aaaahhh, get your dog out!"

Officer calls the dog back and out they come and they've got branch sticking there and gash there and bush all over them. Dog comes out and the blackberry is absolutely stuck to his pants, he gives it a wrench and the vine just slices his shorts apart, and suddenly he's standing there in the nuddy. This is the most awesome failed burglary I've ever seen.

"You're a classic idiot," I couldn't help pissing myself with laughter.

The officer's going to Dog, "Don't you move," but when I start cracking up the policeman starts cracking up too. "You pack of absolute bunnies," he chuckles. "You know, it's almost embarrassing for me to have to arrest you and write this report out. I'm sorry for you."

Then he turned to me. "You're just as bad. You look like you didn't want to do something so stupid, so that tells me it was the three of them, you probably had the most sense but you didn't really because you jumped into the car. How'd you wind up with these clowns?"

I just shook my head. Corey, Dog and Angel were all looking sheepish and I wanted to look staunch.

"I don't feel like talking to you man."

The drive back to Hamilton for processing was only interrupted by police radio traffic – "You're never going to believe this, but..." Eventually he delivers us, still pissing himself laughing, to the Hamilton team. The two boys are put in the caged rooms for questioning, while Angel and I are in adjacent standard rooms with table and chairs each.

I can hear them talking to me, and they're going "We think those two guys were the instigators, we think you two girls came along for the ride and pretty much that's it. Is that right? Here's what you can do. You can cooperate with us and we can be a little bit more lenient towards you and help this process go through fast, because you've pretty much got a clear record, bar one diversion for altering a document."

I was in my own thoughts, however, thinking 'how the hell am I getting so stupid?' I retraced my steps back to the two choices I'd made that night. "Yep, I'll come for a ride." And "yep, I'm only a passenger, this is alright." Not till the consequences are right in my face do I realise, 'dumb move, dickhead. You're the dickhead Max. Not them. You.'

Despite the officer's kind offer, I refused. Good cop walks out the door, and bad cop comes in. "Well, your three good friends are all saying that you're the master mind, and this is all your idea."

"Oh, go get stuffed," I responded, which, in police talk, is called 'failing the attitude test'. The officer just looks at me, clearly thinking, 'just how dumb is this girl?' "Well, if you're calling me a liar, that's your call. Here's their statement. That's their signature. Read it."

"Nah. Not playing."

"Well, they're saying that it's you, so we've got three witnesses that say it was you, and we can go ahead and go to court and say that it was you."

"I want a lawyer."

"Lawyers don't make house calls at three o'clock in the morning, sorry. So you'll have to enjoy the cell." They didn't put me in the cell, though, they just left me in that interview room. It wasn't a locked door, they just left me there.

The next day we were transferred from the police station over to the court's holding cells and we all got to see a duty solicitor. The charges were car theft and being a party to burglary. Mine was a woman who comes out and she goes, "look, here's how simple it is. If you say that you did it, all four of you get off, you get a smack on the hand because you don't have a history. There'll be no defended hearing and you'll pretty much get dealt with on the spot. If you defend it and say that you're innocent, then you're going to have to come back to Hamilton, there's going to be dramas, according to you you're unemployed. You can't afford it, so just make it easy on yourself."

It seemed easy, but I would be admitting to crimes I'd never intended to commit and which had been someone else's stupid idea. "I don't know."

"If you do admit to it," said this Maori lawyer who'd been listening, "that stays on your record for good and you can't do anything about it Max."

"Shit, man. I don't want to be in this mess. I want to go now."

And he goes "Yeah, but it's better if you put up with it and do what you need to do and get this cleared up. Because if you're just an accessory by being there, that's relatively minor. But being a party to burglary is a serious charge, Max."

If I hadn't been so staunch the night before, I'd probably have been facing an accessory after the fact misdemeanour, but that train had already left the station and now I was up for Burglary proper.

Corey was putting pressure on me to take the rap. "If I get this charge, I won't get out on bail." Dog and Angel were also fearful, as they'd already been prosecuted for fraud, theft, burglary and assault with weapons. Their grand scheme was that I should own up to being the mastermind like they'd said in their statements, and take the hit essentially as a first time offender. "If you just say it was you, and we get out on bail," said Corey, "then we'll get out on the run and we'll go and live together."

I just looked at him sideways. "Yeah, nah."

But I agreed to admit the charge, and sure enough we all got bail. I shook myself loose of those "friends" and ended up doing a couple of months in Arohata Womens' Prison.

So that was the burglary charge. I found out a bit later that Corey, when I'd taken him with me to another one of my friend's homes, went back into that house later and stole a car belonging to my friend's dad. So this was a definite case of picking the wrong friends and not listening to alarm bells. My self-worth had taken a serious knock over the years and I didn't really care enough about me or who I mixed with, as you will have seen from my time with Johnny from Highway 61. That's not an excuse, but it is an observation, and it's only by re-examining our mistakes that we learn from them.

CHAPTER TWENTY

New Revelations

Why did the trial of Chris Kahui for the double murder of his sons end in a not guilty verdict after a record one minute deliberation by the jury? Obviously, the character assassination of Macsyna King played a key role – defence lawyer Lorraine Smith repeatedly told the jury, "Macsyna did it" or words to that effect.

The cellphone call controversy played right into the defence team's hands, allowing Kahui's lawyers to trumpet, "That is completely new, the fact that there is an admitted return trip by them on the evening half an hour before one of the babies stopped breathing", whilst ignoring the inconvenient truth that the call went through a different cellsite than the one covering the homes where the twins were.

"It places her in Mangere, the very place where the twins are," thundered Lorraine Smith, again, conveniently ignoring that it actually placed Macsyna several kilometres away, in an area covered by a different cellsite, one that covered the Southwestern motorway that you drive past Mangere on.

At the 2010 inquest, this theory developed further. Even the defence team by now realised there was no way on God's earth that Emily and Macsyna could have travelled from Papakura at 6.58 pm and arrived 25km away at Courtenay Crescent, Mangere with time to sneak into the house and throttle the kids, unseen by her brother Stuart in the lounge, then sneak out again before Chris arrived home at 7.20pm. So they came up with Plan B, that Emily had left Papakura on her own at 6.58pm and travelled to West Auckland, while Macsyna had left earlier, borrowing Emily's car, and returned to Mangere separately.[111]

---

111 See page 119 for a comprehensive debunking of this theory. If Macsyna was not with Emily, how did she remember going with Emily to drop off baby Ellen at the Takanini office, when others five years later had forgotten? Macsyna's version fits the cellphone sequence. If she and her sister and brother-in-law had cooked up a story together, Emily and Pou would have been singing the same

Problem with this theory? No one heard or saw Macsyna drive up, park the car or walk in. According to Kahui's lawyers at the inquest, having done her dastardly deed Macsyna rings a person unknown – not Emily – and that person rings Emily's husband, who in turn rings Emily at 7.38pm in Avondale and tells her to go back and collect Macsyna.

Missing links? No Vodafone evidence that Macsyna's cellphone was used. No evidence of a call from Macsyna to Emily's husband (and why not simply ring Emily direct, rather than risk dragging an extra person into the conspiracy?) No evidence of Emily's car being left behind at Courtenay Crescent.

Further, under cross-examination at the inquest Mona Kahui said the reason she and Banjo went driving to find Macsyna after the breathing incident, was because they couldn't ring her – she could see Macsyna's phone was plugged into a wall charger on the kitchen bench at Courtenay Cres.[112]

Kahui's defence lawyer Chris Wilkinson-Smith felt it was all too convenient that only Emily, her husband and Macsyna could testify about the 19.54 cellphone call from the motorway:[113]

MR WILKINSON-SMITH: "You have had another two years to think about what happened and you knew that you were going to be a witness at this inquest – – "

EMILY: "And my answer has not changed."

MR WILKINSON-SMITH: "You cannot think of anybody, apart from your husband and your sister, that can support your explanation, can you?"

EMILY: "No."

COUNSEL ASSISTING THE CORONER, MR MORRIS: "Sir, I wonder what the value of that sort of question is? If two people are involved in a conversation, there is only ever going to be two people that can support that conversation...I am just again, sir, anxious to ensure that the point is made and not laboured for the half hour that it has been."

CORONER: "Yes. It is a case of res ipsa loquitur, the facts speak for

---

song instead of no longer remembering the detail. And if Macsyna was with Emily at Takanini around 7.15pm, she could not have been in Mangere.

112 This was a case of mistaken cellphone identity. There were several similar cellphones in the house. Macsyna told the inquest she had hers with her, and indeed there are active calls on Macsyna's mobile the morning after while she was still in Papakura, so it cannot have been hers on the bench. However, Emily had told the court she hadn't seen Macsyna with her phone when they went to Ginta's. The defence claimed Macsyna must have grabbed the phone at the same time she snuck back to kill the babies. Macsyna says the truth is simpler: "I'm pretty sure I didn't have it with me when we went to Ginta's but that's because I think I had left it back at Emily's house and forgotten to take it with me. So yeah, the phone was definitely there when I woke up." – Interview with author, 2011

113 Cross-examination of Emily Hepi, Coroner's Inquest, 2010

themselves, as Mr Morris says. Unless there was some electronic eavesdropper, the answer is obvious, is it not?"

The Cellphone Conspiracy ranks right up there with the Moon Landing Conspiracy.

Ironically, this whole red-herring could have been cleared up at the time of the murders if detectives had taken what should have been the routine step of asking Telecom and Vodafone to track the mobile phones of key family members.

What do I mean? Well, police subpoenaed the phone call records, which is all well and good, but they didn't ask for another folder of information that would have answered every question about the movements of Macsyna King and Emily Hepi on the night: location records.

Every mobile phone is in touch with its phone network 24/7 if it is switched on. If you leave your mobile beside a clock radio on your bedside, you might sometimes hear random interference and clicking every half hour or so, even if there are no calls or text messages being sent. That's because your phone and the network are "handshaking" – telling each other where they are and which cell-tower is providing the best signal.

Thus, to get a true picture of a person's movements, phone call records are not enough – police could have obtained the cellular location records to fill in the knowledge gaps between the phone calls. As Emily's phone moved through its journey that Monday night, it was continually passing through different cellsites, handshaking each as it entered and left the coverage zone while the car was moving. Telecom and Vodafone would have recorded this in their network files, regardless of whether or not calls were being made.

At the moment in NZ, this information is held only for 24 to 48 hours, as it forms part of the engineering data used by the networks to keep track of the performance or faults on their cellsites. In the UK, this ability to track mobile phones in real time based purely on their location data has been commercialised and is accessible to the public.

For police it could be a useful tool if cellphone companies can store the data for, say, 14 days, but that would require a legislative change and confirmation from the networks that they can output the data in a form police could recognise and use (separating out the location handshakes from the wider engineering data being collected).

Days at the inquest were taken up debating cellphone calls, and those days cost money.

The other major piece of the defence case was on timing. The prosecution's medical experts argued the breathing incident was so severe that the trauma that caused it must have happened only minutes earlier. The defence expert argued the fatal blows could have been inflicted "four to six hours" before breathing stopped. That meant the injury had to have been administered, at the earliest, by 3pm – hours after Macsyna had left the house, and two hours after April Saunders had fed the babies and reported they were perfectly normal in their behaviour.

So even on the defence case, Chris Kahui had a problem. Unless the defence could make their argument – however unlikely – that Macsyna King had secretly snuck back and bashed the babies without anyone seeing her.

The best laid plans of the defence lawyers came crashing down at the inquest, however, in an exchange that went unreported by the media (you read it here first!). Chris Kahui was being cross-examined by Macsyna's lawyer Marie Dyhrberg about the moment he became aware Cru was having breathing difficulties. Have a look at how he describes baby Chris at that moment:[114]

> **MS DYHRBERG:** Now, when you were holding Chris, just before Mona picked up Cru and noticed that his face was changing colour, how was Chris when you were holding him?
>
> **MR KAHUI:** He was fine.
>
> **MS DYHRBERG:** And in fact – – -
>
> **MR KAHUI:** He was fine.
>
> **MS DYHRBERG:** – – – would you say he was good, he was just looking around?
>
> **MS DYHRBERG:** Would you agree with that?
>
> **MR KAHUI:** Yes.

If baby Chris really was "fine…good…just looking around" then the whole cellphone "Macsyna snuck back at 7pm to beat the babies and that's why Cru was lifeless" claim flies out the window: Chris has just shot down his own legal team's carefully constructed conspiracy theory.

Of course, baby Chris cannot have been "fine" because he had similar head injuries to Cru, worse in fact in terms of the tearing injuries. In my opinion Chris Kahui's latest claim that baby Chris was "fine" is another in a long list of untrue statements. In a sense Kahui picked up a double-edged sword. By saying Chris was normal he destroys the cellphone beating theory. But by saying Chris was normal when obviously he wasn't, he clearly adds to suspicion already surrounding him. The medical experts

---

114 Cross-examination of Chris Kahui, Coroner's Inquest, 2010

have testified that in hindsight it is now certain baby Chris cannot have been "normal" at that moment.

In reality, international studies have shown 42% of babies with inflicted head trauma are dead in less than two hours after the attack[115], and certainly well on their way, with "apnoea, irregular respiration and cyanosis" setting in, often within minutes.[116]

"The whole case was about timing," Crown Prosecutor Simon Moore later told the Sunday Star-Times. "What we said was that every one of the paediatricians and pathologists said if we can identify a time when the twins were last normal you will know the injuries were inflicted after that. Where they tended to disagree was whether the evidence that they were feeding normally could be relied on. That ended up being a more critical issue that the issue of the timing of the CPR event and the linking of that to the infliction of the injuries."

April Saunders had fed baby Cru for 15 minutes on the afternoon of Monday June 12. She testified that he'd had a hungry cry, alert eyes and drank well, that he was perfectly normal. Chris likewise fed baby Chris – his sister Mona said she saw Chris carry a full bottle into baby Chris, and come out with an empty bottle a little while later.[117] Chris Kahui admits this, and also says the babies acted perfectly "normal" when they settled them down again between 1 and 2pm.

Defence expert witness and forensic paediatrician Dr Terry Donald is the one who argued a baby with traumatic head injuries might still feed normally – albeit he admitted the baby would not act normally. The baby could feed, he told the court, because a primitive sucking reflex might allow the child to drink. Other experts disagree, but Donald used the example of babies born without brains, just a brain stem, who still have a primitive sucking reflex.

That may be a different issue, however. Researchers have found that when children are born without proper brains in the first place, brain activity can sometimes be found in brain stems because those pathways have been created during fetal development. However, where the child has a normal brain then loses capacity through injury, it's not certain that an injured brain can suddenly teach other parts instantly to pick up the slack.

If I can make the analogy, you have a 50mb file on your computer that you save to two memory sticks. One stick is only 60mb and is almost filled

115 "Neuropathology of inflicted head injury in children", Geddes et al, Brain 2001, 124, 1290-1298
116 "Shaken baby syndrome", I Blumenthal, Postgrad Med J 2002; 78:732-735
117 Evidence of Mona Kahui, Coroner's Inquest, 2011

up with the one file, the other memory stick is 2 gigabytes. Then one day your two gig memory stick is accidentally wiped to US Defence Department standards. The information you stored on it is gone, forever. It's the same with the brain – information already allocated to the bigger storage area and then lost is lost. The smaller memory stick still has the info.

The classic case is that of a 44 year old French office worker who, in 2007, underwent an MRI scan for a problem he'd been having, and medics were stunned to find the man had virtually no brain.[118] His skull was empty. Yet he'd lived a perfectly normal life since birth, because what little brain he had was sufficient. But again, could you take a normal person, remove 95% of their brain and expect them to have a meaningful life? No.

The presence of a primitive sucking reflex, however, doesn't mean the brain injured baby can follow that up by swallowing. Most experts agree sucked milk would spill straight back out of the mouth. There were no reports of the babies drooling by the time they got to hospital, and the experts in court debated the significance of that. However if the twins were severely dehydrated by this point saliva production would already have been minimised and no drooling would be expected.

A recent German study on head injury consequences in infants leaves little doubt that the trauma and the symptoms like apnoea – or breath-holding – in serious cases, are usually immediately connected:[119]

"Even if a long-lasting episode of apnea is not immediately fatal, the resulting hypoxia [lack of oxygen] causes cerebral edema [swelling] with increased intracranial pressure and thus reduced cerebral blood flow, leading to a vicious circle of increasing cerebral hypoxia. The end result in such cases – depending on the delay before initiation of emergency treatment – is either protracted brain death or prolonged survival with serious deficits.

"For forensic purposes…impairment of cerebral function, or symptoms, begin immediately after the shaking event. In other words, a shaken infant who displays severe neurological symptoms at a later stage is unlikely not to have shown signs of injury straight after shaking. Furthermore, the accounts given by many confessed perpetrators describe occurrence of the symptoms immediately following non-trivial shaking."

If the breathing event witnessed at the Kahui house on the Monday night was the first event, immediately after the children were injured, then the fitting and convulsing requiring resuscitation when they got to

118 http://www.physorg.com/news104143971.html
119 "Shaken Baby Syndrome", Matschke et al, Dtsch Arztebl Int. 2009 March; 106(13): 211–217

Middlemore Hospital 17 hours later was the manifestation of "severe neurological symptoms at a later stage" referred to above. There had been no need for further resuscitations in the intervening period, unless they have never been disclosed.

There are exceptions to every rule, but by their very nature they are rare, which is why they are exceptions. Starship child abuse expert Patrick Kelly, for example, told the court that a substantial head injury trauma of the kind suffered by the twins would certainly lead them into a coma within minutes. Yet there is the strange case in medical records of a nine month old baby boy who fell backwards off a bed and smashed his head on a concrete floor. After a cuddle he was deemed OK, and acted perfectly normally for the next three days, feeding, laughing and playing. Until he was found dead in his bed. The baby's grandmother, mother and babysitter all verified the normal behaviour, but an autopsy revealed substantial fatal brain trauma and swelling.[120]

Such cases are so rare they make the medical journals, and the chances of twins suffering identical trauma and each lasting that long are infinitesimally small. The mere fact that both Chris and Cru suffered trauma, and entered comas, and then died within 14 hours of each other shows both were following classic neurological damage timelines and courses originating with injuries inflicted at the same time. As Crown Prosecutor Simon Moore said at the start of Kahui's trial, "There's no way the injuries to either twin, let alone both, were caused by accident…There was nothing the miracles of modern science could do. They were going to die. It was just a question of when."[121]

Chris Kahui's sister Mona claims Macsyna had also talked of a previous apnoea episode and how you just gave the babies "a gentle shake" if that happened.[122] King absolutely denies this. Was this a Kahui cover-up, a misunderstanding, or the truth? I'll reveal the right answer shortly, but let's examine the options.

It could have been a misunderstanding – Macsyna King and Chris Kahui were aware of an incident in the neo-natal ward shortly before the babies were sent home when one had a brief apnoea episode as a newborn.

That condition is known as Apnoea of Prematurity, or AOP, and is relatively common in premature babies.

---

120 "Delayed Sudden Death in an Infant Following an Accidental Fall: A Case Report With Review of the Literature", Denton, Scott MD; Mileusnic, Darinka MD, PhD, American Journal of Forensic Medicine & Pathology: December 2003 – Volume 24 – Issue 4 – p 371
121 Opening submissions of Simon Moore, Queen vs Kahui, 2008
122 Evidence of Mona King, Coroner's Inquest, 2011

"In a premature baby, the part of the central nervous system (brain and spinal cord) that controls breathing is not yet mature enough to allow non-stop breathing. This causes large bursts of breath followed by periods of shallow breathing or stopped breathing. The medical term for this is apnea of prematurity, or AOP," reports the US medical website Kidshealth.[123]

"Apnea of prematurity is fairly common in preemies. Doctors usually diagnose the condition before the mother and baby are discharged from the hospital, and the apnea usually goes away on its own as the infant matures. Once apnea of prematurity goes away, it does not come back. But no doubt about it − it's frightening while it's happening.

"Apnea is a medical term that means a baby has stopped breathing. Most experts define apnea of prematurity as a condition in which premature infants stop breathing for 15 to 20 seconds during sleep.

"Generally, babies who are born at less than 35 weeks' gestation have periods when they stop breathing or their heart rates drop. (The medical name for a slowed heart rate is bradycardia.) These breathing abnormalities may begin after 2 days of life and last for up to 2 to 3 months after the birth. The lower the infant's weight and level of prematurity at birth, the more likely he or she will have AOP."

Kidshealth advises that if the hospital is aware of an infant suffering apnoea, it should provide a breathing monitor for the parents to take home, as well as provide training to the parents in CPR should an emergency arise. Middlemore has admitted training Macsyna King and Chris Kahui in CPR, but told the court apnoea was never raised.[124] Chris received explicit instructions to call an ambulance on 111 in the event of any breathing emergency, just five days before the breathing emergency.

The symptoms of Apnoea of Prematurity will sound familiar to readers:

"Those with AOP have drops in heart rate below 80 beats per minute, which causes them to become pale or bluish. They may also appear limp and their breathing may be noisy. They then either start breathing again by themselves or require help to resume breathing."

You'll recall that Mona Kahui saw her brother stroking Cru's arm when first told about the baby's failure to breathe. Now read the advice from KidsHealth:

"If a baby doesn't begin to breathe again within 15 seconds, a nurse will rub the baby's back, arms, or legs to stimulate the breathing. Most

---

123 http://kidshealth.org/parent/medical/lungs/aop.html Peer-reviewed by Dr Michael Spear, Professor of Pediatrics, Thomas Jefferson University, Philadelphia
124 Evidence of Amanda Retter, Queen vs Kahui, 2008

of the time, babies with apnea of prematurity spells will begin breathing again on their own with this kind of stimulation."

If that doesn't work, immediate medical attention is required.

According to international data, 85% of premature babies born before 34 weeks' gestation suffer apnoea of prematurity, so the chances of the Kahui twins having this condition were extremely high.

According to Dr Michael Spear, a pediatrics professor and head of a neo-natal intensive care unit in the US, who peer-reviewed that information, all hospitals should have full records on file of the breathing episodes of premature neonates, as recorded by hospital monitoring equipment. If Middlemore knew of an apnoea episode/s in the neo-natal ward and failed to provide follow-up assistance, that could be a matter for fresh investigation.

To see just how significant this was, I asked Macsyna King to describe exactly what happened in the Middlemore apnoea incident. She told me she wasn't there, but it was later described to her by another mother on the ward who witnessed it, and eventually by the medical staff involved. She believes the incident happened only one or two weeks before the babies were discharged home...

It was Cru who had the apnoea attack. There were four babies in the neonatal ward at the time and some other mothers were visiting when it happened. Cru and Chris were side by side. At the time Cru held his breath there was a couple in there and the beepers went off. There was another lady who had been in the ward with me during my stay at Middlemore and she was in the room when this happened.

A nurse went to attend to Cru because the beepers went off, and she was really going for it. I was told she'd been trying to resuscitate him for about a minute, then she hit the panic button, the red button, for doctors' backup. A full team came in and they kept going, but she had already been administering the CPR and she kept up the compressions while the doctors were assisting her.

The nurse just kept on going and she pulled Cru out of his apnoea attack. Watching them were the other parents in the ward and this woman who was in Middlemore with me. I was told that after they got his heart going they got him breathing again and they stabilized him, and put him back on the CPAP machine, the respirator. They reconnected it for him, changed all the tubes and cords, put new ones in, they did a pretty thorough job from what I was told.

Once it was all done, they all told me the nurse who'd performed CPR on baby Cru was really shaken by it, she was in tears. The nurse came and talked to me about it after I found out, came with a doctor, and held my hand and told me, "Yeah, he gave me a real fright, but we got it back under control, and I'm just glad that you are here to spend some time with him." I felt indebted to her.[125]

It's not clear whether this dangerous episode was due to Apnoea of Prematurity or a malfunction in Cru's life support equipment, but having experienced apnoea as a prem, the hospital was on notice to properly advise the parents and – according to international best practice – ensure the babies had monitoring equipment on them when they went home. Did this happen, were the parents advised that Cru and Chris could have apnoea attacks up to three or four months old?

The hospital never told me it could happen again. They never told me the babies were still at risk, they just explained what apnoea is. They explained to me that it wasn't completely understood what caused apnoea. One nurse said she'd read in a journal that apnoea may be related to Sudden Infant Death Syndrome. Was I told that it might continue to affect the twins, or that it might happen again? No! No I wasn't, they just explained what apnoea is, that baby simply holds his breath and his oxygen levels drop.

Although a doctor came with the nurse, the doctor didn't introduce themselves to me or explain, "Look, this is what's happened to Cru, this is how severe it can be, these are the effects", no, they never said that. I never got any of that, none of it.

They didn't give me any monitors to take home, but I have to confess I stole a piece of hospital equipment – well, borrowed because it would have gone back, but I didn't ask permission. It was a machine that attaches to the baby's finger and reads their blood oxygen levels. This was how the nurses had always kept track of the babies' oxygen and I wanted to make sure when we went home that I could keep an eye on it.

But the hospital never warned me to look out for apnoea, and they never gave me a CPAP machine like the one they use in hospital to help them breathe.

---

125 I interviewed Macsyna about this incident twice, some time apart. The facts, including a detailed description of the attending nurse, did not change.

The hospital would not have handed out a CPAP breathing machine for home use, but in the United States they would have sent Macsyna home with a specialized apnoea monitor from the neonatal intensive care unit, as the KidsHealth site explains:[126]

"Before your baby leaves the hospital, the NICU staff will thoroughly review the monitor with you and give you detailed instructions on how and when to use it, as well as how to respond to an alarm. Parents and caregivers will also be trained in infant CPR, even though it's unlikely they'll ever have to use it.

"If your baby isn't breathing or his or her face seems pale or bluish, follow the instructions given to you by the NICU staff. Usually, your response will involve some gentle stimulation techniques and, if these don't work, starting CPR and calling 911. Remember, never shake your baby to wake him or her.

"It can be very stressful to have a baby at home on an apnea monitor. Some parents find themselves watching the monitor, afraid even to take a shower or run to the mailbox. This usually becomes easier with time. If you're feeling this way, it can help to share your feelings with the NICU staff. They may be able to reassure you and even put you in touch with other parents of preemies who have gone through the same thing."

When the hospital was telling me what apnoea was and how they didn't know why it happened, but that it had a direct impact on the babies' oxygen levels, I just resolved to make sure I had the equipment at my fingertips. What was I going to do if it happened to me? The hospital had all these alarms and machines, and I had nothing. The oxygen reader was something I could fit in my bag, so when we took them home I brought it with me. And when the twins came down with their chest infection, that's how I knew to take them to the hospital – I noticed the oxygen levels in their blood had dropped, it was Chris because he was the smaller of the two twins and we'd had a visit from the Plunket nurse. I'd told her I'd seen some clear fluid coming from Chris' nose and the nurse said he might be coming down with a cold or flu and just to keep an eye on it. So I hooked up the oxygen monitor to Chris' finger, and by that night the levels had dropped to about 4 or 5 on the readout. Lucky I checked, because I took them to hospital and they were admitted

126 http://kidshealth.org/parent/medical/lungs/aop.html Peer-reviewed by Dr Michael Spear, Professor of Pediatrics, Thomas Jefferson University, Philadelphia

for two days and two nights. So it came in handy, it really did.[127]

So yeah, I used to hook up the boys' fingers from time to time and I'd enter the oxygen readings in their Plunket books, which the police have, and the police took the machine back too.

It is now evident, and will be if and when Middlemore discloses Cru Kahui's full medical records, that baby Cru suffered an event serious enough to require CPR in the neonatal intensive care unit.

The information you are reading here has never been discussed this deeply in court or at the inquest. I know – I have the transcripts. It would not have helped the Crown, as they were reliant on expert witnesses from Middlemore Hospital, and it would not have been welcomed by the defence whose strategy was to accept abuse but name Macsyna King as the abuser. This evidence fell between the cracks and disappeared. Until now.

What raises massive questions is that Middlemore Hospital appears not to have disclosed this incident to authorities. Lindsay Mildenhall, a neonatal paediatrician at Middlemore where this incident occurred, told the court trial in 2008 that despite the twins being premature there were no health issues. Mildenhall was specifically asked whether apnoea, known to be common in prem babies, was an issue and he told the court it was not an issue with these twins.[128]

His evidence to the 2010 inquest was the same, and he was questioned about this by Counsel Assisting the Coroner, Chris Morris:[129]

MR MORRIS: Now, again, if you need to, by all means refer to the clinical notes, but did either of the twins have any history of apnoea whilst at the hospital?

DR MILDENHALL: There were two admissions; the newborn admissions and the subsequent admission from bronchiolitis. During neither of those admissions did they display any signs of apnoea, although during the newborn admission there was some prophylactic [preventive] treatment for that condition, which was withdrawn at around the 34 week mark.

MR MORRIS: And they were discharged in which week?

---

127 Sister Emily and her husband Pou were staying with Macsyna at this time. Pou told the inquest he remembered discussions about a twin not breathing. Macsyna believes it was probably related to the oxygen monitor she had hooked up to the twins. She is adamant there were no apnoea incidents after the twins came home, and Mona, Stuart and Chris have all testified the same.
128 Evidence of Lindsay Mildenhall, neonatal paediatrician, Queen vs Kahui, 2008
129 Cross-examination of Lindsay Mildenhall, Coroner's Inquest, 2010

DR MILDENHALL: They were discharged at – no, I have made an error. It was at 32 weeks that the medication was discontinued and they were discharged at 35 weeks and six days.

MR MORRIS: And was that in respect of both twins or one?

DR MILDENHALL: Both twins.

DR MILDENHALL: There was never any apnoea events with these twins throughout their whole course.

MR MORRIS: And they were on apnoea monitors throughout?

DR MILDENHALL: For the initial period, and then it is our process to withdraw them at around the 34 week mark because they are no longer necessary.

MR MORRIS: And was that prophylactic treatment in the form of caffeine?

DR MILDENHALL: It was.

MR MORRIS: So as far as the hospital records are concerned and your discharge, they had no history of apnoea whatsoever?

DR MILDENHALL: None whatsoever.

CORONER: Does that mean that the phenomenon of apnoea of prematurity had effectively been excluded?

DR MILDENHALL: It had been excluded, Mr Evans. But it can recur if there are intercurrent illnesses, or sometimes it is – it reasserts itself after an immunisation.

CORONER: Right.

DR MILDENHALL: These babies were challenged with both those things and never showed any signs of apnoea.

This leaves us with a clear conflict of evidence. Macsyna is adamant she was briefed by both the nurse who revived Cru, and a friend on the ward who personally witnessed the incident. But the hospital says "it never happened". Surely the objective reader will believe the hospital over Macsyna?

But that's not where this ends. Support for Macsyna's version of events is found in testimony Chris Kahui himself gave to the inquest – it came as a shock to his own lawyer:

MR KAHUI: I just remember Macsyna telling me about the text, that one of the kids had – the alarms went off and one of the kids must have stopped breathing and the nurses freaking out.

CORONER: Well, this was never put to Macsyna King by you, Mr Wilkinson-Smith.

MR WILKINSON-SMITH: Well, I am just asking about it now. I mean, it was asked whether he was aware of any breathing problems in the past – – –

CORONER: Well, you should have put it to Macsyna King, because he says that he was told this by Macsyna.

MR WILKINSON-SMITH: Well, he is just telling us now, sir. I am not sure what he is going to tell us about this, sir. But he should – I have asked him did he know about any breathing episodes and he is telling us about this one. I will ask him about any other breathing episodes because it arises out of cross examination and obviously the Court will be interested as to whether he had knowledge that the babies did sometimes stop breathing and how serious that might therefore be.

What Chris Kahui went on to reveal is legal dynamite. I am including it all because to my mind it proves Middlemore has not accurately reported the twins' medical histories to police – and that is extremely serious:

MR KAHUI: There was one time up at the hospital. One of the ladies from – when the twins were in the incubators one of the ladies texted us and said that one of the twins had stopped breathing up at the hospital. So me and Macsyna went up to the hospital. I am not too sure how far, how long ago that was when they came out.

MR WILKINSON-SMITH: Was this before they were discharged to go home?

MR KAHUI: Yes.

MR WILKINSON-SMITH: You need to tell, just explain, somebody texted you?

MR KAHUI: One of the women that was in the actual hospital with Macsyna before she – this is when she had to stay up at the hospital too with the twins. She had – – –

MR WILKINSON-SMITH: Okay, and was this – was that when Macsyna first had the – given birth or did she have another stay for a few days just before they were discharged home?

MR KAHUI: Yes, I think it was just before they were discharged to come home, yes.

MR WILKINSON-SMITH: Okay, so it – the text – was received and you understood the alarms went off because one of the twins had stopped breathing?

MR KAHUI: Yes.

MR WILKINSON-SMITH: And what did you and Macsyna do when you got the text?

MR KAHUI: We went up to the hospital to see what was going on.

MR WILKINSON-SMITH: And how were the twins when you did get up to hospital?

MR KAHUI: I am not too sure which twin stopped breathing, but they were fine – not fine, but – I think he had come to and everybody was sort of – still on the verge of freaking out too, yep.

MR WILKINSON-SMITH: Okay. So, any other occasions where you were aware that one or other the twins had a breathing problem?

MR KAHUI: No, just that.

MR WILKINSON-SMITH: Now obviously at the hospital it sounds like they have got equipment that sets off an alarm if a baby stops breathing. You just tell us whether there was any discussion about getting some sort of alarm at home.

MR KAHUI: Yes, there was. I think we had a heart meter for the twins, but it was only one of them. But I think we had to – that was the hospital's and we gave it back to them.

MR WILKINSON-SMITH: So, – yeah, sorry your Honour.

CORONER: Did you say "a heart meter"?

MR KAHUI: Yeah, like it takes the pulse of the babies, yeah.

MR WILKINSON-SMITH: Sir, I would quite like to just explore this a little further – – –

CORONER: Yes, well this is something, of course, that maybe explored.

MR WILKINSON-SMITH: So they had – the hospital had given you and Macsyna some equipment?

MR KAHUI: Yes.

MR WILKINSON-SMITH: So just tell us how that equipment worked, was it something in the cot or how does it work?

MR KAHUI: It is a little machine and it has got a wire coming off it that you strap to the finger and it takes a pulse and it reads it, and you can hear the pulse of the babies.

MR WILKINSON-SMITH: Okay. And that was given to you and Macsyna to take home?

MR KAHUI: Yes.

MR WILKINSON-SMITH: Was that device ever setup at home?

MR KAHUI: Yes, it was, yes.

MR WILKINSON-SMITH: And was there one for both babies or just – – –

MR KAHUI: Just one.

MR WILKINSON-SMITH: So it could only monitor one baby?

MR KAHUI: Yes.

MR WILKINSON-SMITH: And was there one of the twins that it was sup-posed to be used for or?

MR KAHUI: No, it was – I think we were just trying it, yeah. We were just seeing how it worked and stuff like that, yeah.

MR WILKINSON-SMITH: Okay. So how long was it actually used at the home?

MR KAHUI: I think we only used it a few times.

MR WILKINSON-SMITH: Okay. So, if we think about when they first came home after discharge, how long after that were you using the heart monitor?

MR KAHUI: I think we were using it straightaway, once they came home.

MR WILKINSON-SMITH: So why did you stop using it?

MR KAHUI: I thought there was no need for it because – – –

MR WILKINSON-SMITH: So apart from the heart rate monitor, were there any other electronic monitors for either breathing or heart monitor that you used?

MR KAHUI: No. Just those.

MR WILKINSON-SMITH: So no pads under the mattress? You know about those devices that can tell you whether a baby stops breathing and sets off an alarm? You did not have one of those?

MR KAHUI: No, we did not. No.

MR WILKINSON-SMITH: And you did not borrow anything from family members in terms of monitors for small babies?

MR KAHUI: No.

So here's what we know. Both Macsyna King and Chris Kahui are telling identical stories about a CPR resuscitation of a twin by Middlemore hospital. Both remember going up to the hospital and being briefed on it, and that everyone up there was still "freaked out". Yet Middlemore's most senior witness swore on oath there had been no incidents.

Question: did someone in Middlemore alter the medical records before Dr Mildenhall was able to review them for the court case? Did someone in Middlemore know the hospital may have caused brain damage to baby Cru while he was in their care, and quietly erased all records of it? I attach no blame to Mildenhall who has an excellent reputation, but the possibility of an underling covering something up without their superiors' knowledge does exist.

Here's some more evidence to consider. Nurse Amanda Retter is sent to the twins' home to give Macsyna and Chris training in CPR. Yet she explicitly tells the court that an apnoea incident was never discussed as part of that briefing.[130] As a frontline nurse, she should have been aware of the breathing failure in hospital, but clearly the information had not been passed to her either.

---

130 Evidence of Amanda Retter, Queen vs Kahui, 2008

Question 2: If for the sake of argument Middlemore Hospital has falsified its records or failed to keep proper records, then is it possible that baby Chris also had an apnoea attack and Middlemore have covered it up? Think about it for a moment. Cru had an attack, and he was the largest and most developed of the two babies. Chris was the runt – even more likely to suffer apnoea. Assume the alarm goes off in the middle of the night, no visitors (independent observers) are in the intensive care unit. A hospital team resuscitates Chris, just as they resuscitated Cru. Nobody else will ever find out. Eighty-five percent of prem babies suffer Apnoea of Prematurity. The chance of Chris not having an attack while in Middlemore's care is actually extremely slim. Were I a betting man, I'd put a substantial sum of money on it. But there's no record of Cru's attack, which we know happened. And there's nothing on Chris either.

What do we know about Apnoea of Prematurity? We know it doesn't just happen once:

"AOP can happen once a day or many times a day. Doctors will closely evaluate your infant to make sure the apnea isn't due to another condition, such as infection."[131]

"The baby may have only one or two episodes a day, or as many as a dozen," reports a Canadian health site. "As the baby's brain matures, the condition disappears, usually with no more episodes when the baby's breathing centre has fully matured, usually around 40 weeks' gestational age."[132]

We should be seeing records from Middlemore showing numerous apnoea events for both prem twins. Instead, nothing. And the hospital testified in court there was never an event, which would make these prem babies miracle twins given that 85% of prems have apnoea of prematurity. The law of averages dictates that at least one of these babies must have had AOP at some point, but the hospital has no documentation.

Middlemore says it gave the babies caffeine as a preventive so that AOP did not develop, but the prestigious Cochrane Collaboration on medical research published a study early this year saying caffeine doesn't work as a preventive. "The results of this review do not support the use of prophylactic caffeine for preterm infants at risk of apnoea...There were no meaningful differences between the caffeine and placebo groups in

---

131 http://kidshealth.org/parent/medical/lungs/aop.html Peer-reviewed by Dr Michael Spear, Professor of Pediatrics, Thomas Jefferson University, Philadelphia
132 http://www.aboutkidshealth.ca/En/ResourceCentres/PrematureBabies/ AboutPrematureBabies/OtherConditions/Pages/Apnea-of-Prematurity.aspx written by Andrew James, BSc, MBChB, FRACP, FRCPC, Aideen Moore, MD, FRCPC, MRCPI, MHSc

the number of infants with apnoea, bradycardia, hypoxaemic episodes."[133]

So just because Middlemore had the twins on caffeine doesn't mean they didn't suffer apnoea events – it simply might mean Middlemore was overconfident and no longer looking for apnoea events. Or maybe the resuscitation of baby Cru was put down to an equipment malfunction, rather than apnoea.

Again, for the sake of the argument, you would not falsify the records for one baby but leave the other baby's records intact. If engaging in a cover-up you would erase all trace across both twins. They were discharged at a gestational age of only 35 weeks – still five weeks prem, weighing just over 2kg each. Relative to normal newborns they were still tiny (and in fact stunted weight gain is a known side-effect of caffeine treatment). Under US AOP guidelines, they would not be out of the danger zone until 52 weeks post conception. When they were fatally injured they were only 41 weeks, still well shy of being totally clear of AOP – but the hospital is on record as claiming these twins were not at risk.

Were they injured previously by nurses performing CPR? Is that how their tiny premature ribs got cracked? Is Middlemore Hospital covering up? Did the hospital effectively set King & Kahui up to take the rap if something ever went wrong with their twins?

Question 3: If the hospital has falsified records in this case, has it done so in other cases, or is this a one-off? Or does the hospital simply not document apnoea or CPR resuscitations – pushing this not into the realm of conspiracy but systemic cock-up?

This is extremely significant information, but before leaping to any conclusions about this, a note of caution: both twins suffered brain damage and death, dying within hours of each other. Even if we accept both twins had an apnoea condition (which now appears highly likely), the laws of random probability still don't appear to make it likely that disaster strikes simultaneously in two babies, even if they are identical twins. Somebody must still have injured them, even if they didn't expect to cause the harm they did.

Here's why: any minor brain haemorrhaging or other damage caused by the resuscitation attempts in the Middlemore hospital neonatal unit could have left the babies' brains more vulnerable to damage from any further trauma in the home. Numerous medical studies have confirmed that a brain already recovering from a subdural or subarachnoid haemorrhage

133 "Prophylactic methylxanthine for prevention of apnoea in preterm infants (Review)", Henderson-Smart DJ, De Paoli AG, The Cochrane Library, 2011, Issue 1

is more prone to reopening the wounds at a lower force threshold than what caused the first trauma.

If the hospital failed to alert the parents about the condition, or possible haemorrhaging the twins may have suffered during any apnoea resuscitations, then the parents would not be aware that Chris and Cru were even more in danger from any rough handling than their status as prem babies already suggested.

Which brings us back to the original question: is Mona Kahui's claim that Macsyna told her the babies sometimes hold their breath, and to "just give them a gentle shake", a credible reference to an apnoea event in the home, or a misunderstanding based on Macsyna telling her about the hospital apnoea event at some point? It's worth noting that Mona's memory of who told her that may have been contaminated, as she admitted to the inquest that she had been reading about babies holding their breath before it happened. "I had read a bit about it."[134] Under questioning from the coroner Mona said she couldn't be sure exactly what Macsyna had said.

I've said it to Mona's face in front of my brother, my sisters Emily and Ellen, and other people who were there: "What exactly did you say in regards to the twins and breathing?". And she goes, "I remember you saying that the twins hold their breath sometimes".

"No, I didn't say that Mona, I've never said that to you. I've told you about the incident they had in the hospital!"

"Oh, well I told the police that you sometimes said to give the babies a gentle shake if they hold their breath."

"Well, Mona, there's Emily, there's Stuart and there's Ellen. I've told all of them how to look after children. Look at them and ask them if I've ever taught them to do that! I've always taught them to never ever shake a baby. If there's something obstructing their mouth you carefully open their mouth and look, you don't try and shake it because you can seriously harm the baby. You never ever do that."

Mona just shrugged and said, "Well I'm sure that you did say that, so tough." I said it in court, and I said it to her, I would never ever tell anybody to shake a child.

The implication from Kahui's defence lawyers, additionally, was not that the twins suffered from a pre-existing medical condition, but that any pre-

134 Evidence of Mona Kahui, Coroner's Inquest, 2011

vious apnoea was proof of previous abuse. So could Macsyna's alleged comment to the Kahuis genuinely have referred to an abusive apnoea episode previously? Could one of the babies have suffered apnoea on an earlier occasion as a result of non-accidental head injury and then had a complete recovery for several weeks? A reading of the medical studies suggests that if the apnoea resulted from a bang or shake, then probably not, and certainly not if the child was not immediately hospitalised. At the stage when apnoea sets in as a response to head injury, she's usually all downhill from that point because it is part of a chain reaction, as one study notes:

"Apnoea was significantly associated with hypoxic [lack of oxygen] ischaemic [stroke-like] brain damage. Severe symptoms at presentation, apnoea, and diffuse brain swelling/hypoxic ischaemic damage were significantly associated with a poor prognosis. Eighty five per cent of cases had associated injuries consistent with a diagnosis of non-accidental injury."[135]

Another study warns that apnoea is probably the most damaging thing a baby can suffer, not something casually experienced and waved off with "a gentle shake".

"We conclude that trauma-induced apnea causes cerebral hypoxia and/or ischemia which is more fundamental to outcome [survival or death] than the mechanism of injury (shaken vs. shaken with impact), subdural hemorrhage, subarachnoid hemorrhage, diffuse axonal injury, parenchymal shear, or brain contusion."[136]

The Mayo Clinic reports:

"The prehospital phase of head injury, also called the critical phase, consists of trauma-induced apnea and stress catecholamine release. This immediate period after head injury remains poorly summarized in the literature and essentially ignored with respect to treatment…Apnea induced by head injury produces hypoxia, hypercarbia, and subsequent cardiac failure and hypotension, which, along with substantially elevated catecholamine values, promote secondary mechanisms of organ injury. Treatment for this immediate period after head injury requires a rapid response to the scene of trauma and development of treatment options that can be instituted at the scene of injury."[137]

Which, of course, wasn't done for baby Cru, whose father Chris refused

---

135 "Apnoea and brain swelling in non-accidental head injury," Kemp et al, Archives of Disease in Childhood, 2003;88:472-476 doi:10.1136/adc.88.6.472
136 "Role of apnea in nonaccidental head injury", Johnson et al, Pediatr Neurosurg. 1995;23(6):305-10.
137 "The neglected prehospital phase of head injury: apnea and catecholamine surge", Atkinson, J., Mayo Clinic Proceedings 2000 Jan;75(1):37-47.

to call an ambulance despite having completed a CPR course at Middle-more Hospital where he and Macsyna were advised to always call an ambulance in the event of any CPR emergency.

The New York Medical Examiner's Office conducted a peer-reviewed study of its own, and records:

"Concussion or injury of the cervical spinal cord and/or brainstem may result in apnoea and other cardiopulmonary dysfunction. If the apnoea is prolonged, the infant may sustain ischemic brain injury because of cardiac compromise and hypoperfusion. Both diffuse traumatic axonal injury and cerebral ischemia eventually may result in swelling of the brain. In either of these scenarios, one would not expect an infant to have a lucid interval (ie, act healthy and then suddenly become unresponsive). If these mechanisms are in action, the neurologic decline would occur immediately following the injury."[138]

On this basis, the claim that Macsyna had casually related a previous apnoea episode to the Kahuis seems highly unlikely – firstly an apnoea event would have sparked an ambulance call given Macsyna's hospital experience, and that didn't happen, and secondly the medics see apnoea as primary evidence of traumatic brain injury and the start of a rapid slide into brain death. Given that all witnesses agreed the babies were happy and normal right up to the day of the fatal injuries, and had been given a "thorough" examination by a doctor only a week earlier, [139] the claim of an earlier apnoea event linked to King by the Kahuis can probably be swiftly discounted. Apnoea of Prematurity reduces in frequency as babies age, and it appears the twins endured their traumatic episodes in hospital, not at home.

The NYME study sheds new light also on one of the controversies of the medical evidence at trial. Despite any conclusive evidence that the twins actually impacted with anything (no skull fractures, no fresh relevant bruising), the Crown ran the argument that the injuries were "consistent with impact" – as indeed they are. But as defence expert witness Terry Donald argued, an impact injury instead of shaking raised the possibility of a longer timeframe for the twins to have been injured and slowly drift into decline, including apnoea, as their brains started to swell – this gave the defence enough time to possibly implicate Macsyna.

Terry Donald, in fact, stated that without evidence of significant damage

---

138 "Fatal Head Injury in Children Younger Than 2 Years in New York City and an Overview of the Shaken Baby Syndrome", Gill et al. Archives of Pathology & Laboratory Medicine: April 2009, Vol. 133, No. 4, pp. 619-627
139 Evidence of Dr Gopinth Nayar, Queen vs Kahui, 2008

to the cervical spinal cord and brain stem, you wouldn't expect the baby to suffer an apnoea event initially. Crown witnesses of course argued the primary injury would have set off the apnoea episode quickly.

The New York Medical Examiner's Office says this is a controversy at the heart of the child abuse debate globally:

"There is controversy in the field of forensic pathology as to whether the Shaken Baby Syndrome (SBS) exists; that is, can an infant be shaken to death without a head impact? Two popular forensic pathology textbooks have different opinions. In one textbook, the authors state that there is no conclusive evidence that the entity exists. These authors agree that the findings are traumatic but state that the injuries are due to impacts and not to shaking. [140] In deaths in which there is no evidence of impact on the scalp or the skull, they state that the "absence of trauma does not preclude impact." In the other textbook, a balanced discussion is given of the issues involved and asks why it is necessary to conclude that an impact must have occurred when there is no evidence of a bruise in the scalp and the caregiver gives a history of shaking without impact. [141]

"In 2001, the American Academy of Pediatrics' Committee on Child Abuse and Neglect reported that SBS results from extreme, rotational, cranial acceleration induced by violent shaking or shaking and impact.[142] Two popular pediatric textbooks use the terms nonaccidental injury or intentional head trauma to describe head injuries in children. One notes that "some so-called 'shaken babies' have some evidence of injuries due to impact."[143] Therefore, "because it is often difficult to be certain whether intracranial bleeding is due to shaking and/or impact, the term shaken baby has been replaced with shaken baby/impact syndrome."

"In 2001, the National Association of Medical Examiners published a position paper on fatal, abusive head injuries in infants and young children and sidestepped the issue of the SBS. Their original charge was to produce a position paper on the shaken baby syndrome. Instead, "because the term shaken baby has taken on such controversy,"[144] they decided only to address the topic of abusive head injury in infants and young children.

140 DiMaio, V. and D. DiMaio . Forensic Pathology. 2nd ed. Boca Raton, Fla: CRC Press; 2001:565.
141 Spitz and Fisher's Medicolegal Investigation of Death. 4th ed. Springfield, Ill: Charles C Thomas Publisher Ltd; 2006.
142 American Academy of Pediatrics Committee on Child Abuse and Neglect. Shaken baby syndrome: rotational cranial injuries – technical report. Pediatrics 2001. 108:206–210.
143 Rudolph, C. ed. Rudolph's Pediatrics. Dallas, Tex: McGraw-Hill; 2003. (p465)
144 Case, M. E. , M. A. Graham , T. C. Handy , J. M. Jentzen , and J. A. Monteleone . for the National Association of Medical Examiners Ad Hoc Committee on Shaken Baby Syndrome. Position paper on fatal abusive head injuries in infants and young children. Am J Forensic Med Pathol 2001. 22:112–122.

Recent reports in the neurology[145] and neurosurgical[146] fields have also addressed this controversy.

"Although this controversy exists, the actual injury is not in dispute," stresses the NYME study. "There is little disagreement that these deaths are due to trauma. Those who do not accept the SBS believe that these internal head injuries are due to an impact of the head (not shaking alone). A problem with this approach occurs, however, in infants who die with these same internal findings and circumstances but do not have any impact site at autopsy. The offered explanation is that there was an impact but that it occurred against a soft surface and so it left no impact-site injury. The confessions of caregivers who state they only shook the child are disregarded, and perpetrators are assumed to be more likely to admit to shaking than to "slamming [the child's] head against an object or throwing [the child] across a room like a football."[147]

"According to this argument, if there is no evidence of impact, the child's head presumably must have impacted on a soft surface when the child was slammed or thrown across the room. Others, however, question how an infant who is impacted forcefully enough against any surface to result in a subdural hematoma, retinal hemorrhage, or axonal injury can escape having some evidence of a scalp impact.[148] In these instances, violent shaking (without impact) explains the absence of an impact site."

So that's what the NYME wanted to discover: is there evidence that impact like injuries can result simply from a shake, and is such a shake capable of causing an immediate breathing episode even if the shaking injuries are not obvious?

Gill et al found that even a moderate shake could damage nerve roots in an area of the brain and spinal cord stem controlling cardio-pulmonary function – the heart and lungs. In this way you could have a child with no visible skull impact point (which neither of the twins had), and who had not been shaken enough to cause obvious whiplash damage to the spinal cord, but who nonetheless collapsed into apnoea rapidly.

"Violent shaking (without impact) that causes cardiopulmonary abnormalities (eg, apnoea, bradycardia, hypotension) may result in hypoxic-

145 Defino, T. As studies emerge, debate still surrounds shaken baby syndrome. Neurol Today 2004. 4:1,17,21.

146 Uscinski, R. H. , L. E. Thibault , and A. K. Ommaya . Rotational injury. J Neurosurg 2004. 100:574–575. author reply 575.

147 DiMaio, V. and D. DiMaio . Forensic Pathology. 2nd ed. Boca Raton, Fla: CRC Press; 2001:565. p360

148 Alexander, R. , Y. Sato , W. Smith , and T. Bennett . Incidence of impact trauma with cranial injuries ascribed to shaking. Am J Dis Child 1990. 144:724–726.

ischemic cerebral injury if the compromise is prolonged. Instead of the brain swelling occurring as a secondary effect...it is due to a primary hypoxic-ischemic event from the trauma-induced cardiopulmonary pathology. Of our 10 infants without an impact, all but 2 had ischemic injury."

As did Cru, and to a lesser extent Chris. And the twins had retinal haemorrhages, which are usually caused by shaking, rather than impact, and sometimes by CPR – particularly in the case of premature babies.[149]

Although the autopsy of the twins found no haemorrhage around the cervical spinal cord, it did find evidence of axonal injury, and pathologist Jane Vuletic told the court this would be consistent with "stretching" of the upper part of the spinal cord. [150] That, says the NYME, could be the smoking gun because of its effect on "nerve roots":

"These roots have been found to be [only] 10% as strong as the nerve and relatively little applied force may produce obvious damage in the nerve roots. Therefore, nerve roots may be more susceptible to damage by tensile forces, such as from spinal flexion-induced deformations of the spinal cord within the spinal canal."

So to wrap up the defence case on apnoea and Macsyna King, a charitable interpretation is that Mona Kahui misunderstood the reference to the hospital apnoea incident and assumed it related to more recent events. It cannot be a referral to a real apnoea event caused by violence a week or two earlier because violence big enough to cause apnoea would most likely have set off a chain reaction at that point. It is not likely to have referred to an apnoea of prematurity event because if Macsyna had experienced one of those she would have called an ambulance – she had after all stolen an oxygen monitor because of fear that the hospital event might repeat.

For five years, Macsyna King has lived under suspicion of covering up a previous apnoea event with this alleged comment. For five years, Kahui's defence lawyers capitalised on it, especially at trial. I've taken you through the possibilities surrounding previous apnoea for a reason, but I can now report what emerged under cross-examination of Mona Kahui at the inquest in June this year. Kahui was reminded of what she had originally told the police the week the twins died:

---

149 "Bilateral Retinal Hemorrhages in a Preterm Infant With Retinopathy of Prematurity Immediately Following Cardiopulmonary Resuscitation", Polito et al, Archives of Opthalmology *Arch Ophthalmol.* 2001;119:913-914

150 New research has sounded a note of caution in reliance on axonal injury as proof of abuse. Researchers have found that infants dying of documented natural causes also show signs of axonal injury, meaning that although it can be caused by trauma, it can also happen naturally. See "Spinal nerve root β-APP staining in infants is not a reliable indicator of trauma", Squier et al, Forensic Sci Int. 2011 May 25

"About two weeks after the twins got home Maxine told me that she had to watch Chris because he holds his wind...when his wind comes up he sort of gets a fright and swallows when his wind tries – y'know, and that's what causes him to hold his breath... She said if it happens you shake his shoulder and he should become right. She told me it had happened once before and he came right after a gentle shake, only enough to wake him up." [151]

Astounding, it wasn't a random apnoea event King had been referring to at all, it was a baby burp after feeding, bringing up wind!

Even Coroner Garry Evans appeared stunned the explanation was that simple, "So that's what she really said to you is that right?" [152]

"Yes," admitted Mona.

"Right."

Another example of the kind of word games and innuendo defence lawyers were prepared to run surfaced again at the inquest when one of the defence team posed a question to expert witnesses, "Are the babies not suspiciously settled after the mother leaves the house?"

Yet when Mona Kahui gave evidence she was asked by that very same lawyer for Chris Kahui:[153]

"During that afternoon before you went to the hospital, do you recall the twins being difficult to settle or crying a lot?"

"Yeah," replied Mona, "I think when April went to feed one or both of the twins."

"So when April went to feed one of the twins, one or both of the twins were unsettled then?" asked Kahui's lawyer.

"I think it was the twin that she was feeding was crying," said Mona.

How can a defence lawyer get front page headlines alleging the twins were "suspiciously settled" after their mum left the house, and in hours be posing to another witness that the twins were "unsettled"?

Another argument the Kahui defence ran to implicate Macsyna King is that she bathed her babies before taking them to the doctor and must have noticed they were unconscious. For the defence, this was important in order to build their picture of the secret abuser who'd known all along. King has consistently denied bathing them, and no witness says they saw her doing this. The closest the defence gets is a statement from Macsyna's brother Stuart that he thought she was bathing the twins because

151 Statements of Mona Kahui to police on June 13 and June 20, 2006
152 Cross examination of Mona Kahui, Coroner's Inquest, 2011
153 Ibid

he heard water running. However, this may have been when King was washing down baby Shayne in the nursery after finding him in a dirty state when she returned.

Stuart may also have confused the bathing with the same period on the Monday morning, when Macsyna had returned and bathed the twins.

The defence team made much in both the trial and later inquest of a phone call that Emily and Macsyna made to Stuart on 2 August 2006, while their brother was giving a lengthy video statement to police.

MR WILKINSON-SMITH: So Emily and Macsyna made it clear they did not want you speaking to the Police, were there any other family members, made it clear to you that you should not speak with the Police?[154]

MR S KING: No.

A simpler explanation for Macsyna's phone call emerged only in further cross-examination:

"Did Emily and Macsyna say in effect they did not want you talking because they did not want you there without your lawyer?" asked lawyer Marie Dyhrberg.

" Yes," confirmed Stuart King.

" Yes. But you were happy to talk without the lawyer?"

" Yes, yes."

" And we can see that from the video," concluded Dyhrberg.

Finally, the defence made much of what they described as a former boyfriend of King's, now a prison inmate requiring segregation, Eru Tuari. In his most famous outing, Tuari told the recent inquest he'd heard Macsyna once say, "Chris didn't do it – I did it," before she then punched the wall. Miraculously, Tuari just happened to have his phone video camera switched to record at the exact moment that she said this. Or so he told police. When they checked his phone they found no evidence of any such recording, and when Tuari was cross-examined at the inquest he admitted he couldn't be sure what he heard, either.[155]

"You're not all that careful about telling the truth are you?", Tuari was asked. "I'm not too careful about anything, to be honest," he admitted.

A littler later, his honesty was again questioned: "Now, earlier today I asked you about this, how careful are you with the truth Mr Tuari?"

"Um, past experience not very good to be honest."

Quite.

154 Cross-examination of Stuart King, Coroner's Inquest, 2010
155 Cross-examination of Eru Tuari, Coroner's Inquest, 2011

CHAPTER TWENTY-ONE

Alternative Theories

With a case like this, there has been enormous speculation about who or what caused the injuries, and I want to briefly cover some of those issues off for both the sake of completeness but also for the benefit of furthering understanding of what is, and what might not be, child abuse.

For all the 46,000 Facebook boycotters who assumed they knew it all, read this and know that nothing is ever as simple as a 300 word newspaper report claims it is.

The case against Chris Kahui seemed straightforward enough, with all the talk of fractured skulls, massive haemorrhages, broken ribs, a broken thigh bone, rolling eyes and brain damage. As you've seen, however, the police failed to make a conviction stick and Chris Kahui can never be retried – even if he admitted guilt in front of a nationwide audience on TV tonight.

What may come as a surprise is that some of those injuries traditionally hailed as proof of child abuse are in fact disputed by medical experts, and a great debate is raging internationally on whether prosecutors have allowed themselves to be conned into thinking all children found injured without explanation have been abused.

In June this year, the Journal of Primary Healthcare published a debate between two leading paediatricians.[156] Waney Squier, a consultant paedi-atric neuropathologist at John Radcliffe Hospital in Oxford, Britain, made this stunning statement that most readers will never have heard:

"The first problem with the [shaken baby] hypothesis is empirical: in nearly 40 years, no one has ever witnessed shaking to cause the collapse of a well baby. The only three witnessed cases in the world literature were babies who had already collapsed."[157]

---

156 http://www.rnzcgp.org.nz/assets/documents/Publications/JPHC/June-2011/JPHCB2ByesJune2011.pdf
157 "Case analysis of brain-injured admittedly shaken infants: 54 cases, 1969-2001", Leestma J, Am

In other words, despite all the alleged child abuse cases, no one has actually independently witnessed a fatal shaking of a healthy baby anywhere in the world. Surprising, no?

Central to the shaken baby concept is what medics call "the triad" – three symptoms believed to prove child abuse. One is retinal haemorrhage, or bleeding behind the eyes. Two is subdural haemorrhage of which you've already read about. Three is encephalopathy, or brain injury leading to an altered mental state. That's "the triad".

Squier makes the point that a number of new studies are finding shaking or whiplash simply doesn't account for the kind of injuries we are seeing, in the form of subdural haemorrhaging or retinal haemorrhaging: "In one real life example, a baby who suffered serious neck injury in a 70mph [nearly 120km/h] crash had no SDH or RH[158], confirming the vulnerability of the infant neck and raising the question: if 70mph whiplash does not produce the triad, how can the 'single firm shake' do so, as frequently cited in court?"

The force of a car slamming into a wall at 120km/h seriously damaged the baby's neck, and must certainly have flexed the spinal cord where it enters the brainstem, stretching the nerve roots referred to in a previous chapter, but no haemorrhaging resulted.

But what about the subdural and subarachnoid haemorrhaging you've read so much about in the last few chapters, which was testified at the Kahui trial as proof of inflicted injury? Squier's journal article reports that "subdural and retinal bleeds are seen in about half of asymptomatic neonates". Half of newborns? As Squier writes, with such widespread brain bleeding in newborns, "the hypothesis that these bleeds are caused by shaking and are immediately symptomatic cannot be supported."

We have all been led to believe by media reports of battered children and court cases that these brain injuries also certainly are caused by abuse, but Squier writes, "Even the staunchest supporters of shaking agree that there is a multitude of causes…including trauma, birth defects, metabolic or genetic conditions, cardio-respiratory arrest, seizures, ruptured aneurysms, infection, stroke and sinovenous thrombosis."

In other words, before we work ourselves up into absolute certainty about apparent child abuse cases, it's actually really important to rule out other possibilities first.

J Forensic Med Pathol., 2005 Sep:26(3):199-212. See also "Axonal injury and the neuropathology of shaken baby syndrome", Shannon et al, Acta Neuropathol (Berl) 1998 Jun:95(6):625-31
158 "Unusual cervical spine injury in a 1 year old", Winter et al, Injury, 2003; 34(4):316-9

Squier writes that apparent signs of head trauma – such as brain swelling injuries and haemorrhages – can sometimes be caused by apnoea events on their own. "The most obvious, and the most frequently overlooked, distinctive feature of many triad babies is an extended period of hypoxia (lack of oxygen) prior to resuscitation and ventilation, frequently with a 'downtime' of over 30 minutes. This period of hypoxia damages vascular endothelium; subsequent reperfusion and the pressure surges of resuscitation and ventilation can be expected to produce the triad. The association of these factors with retinal haemorrhaging has already been demonstrated."[159]

In plain English? If baby suffers an apnoea attack when no one is in the room and no alarm is connected, his brain is deprived of oxygen, sometimes for very long times. That lack of oxygen kills brain cells, just as it does in adults. The brain starts to puff up because of the traumatic damage caused by a lack of air and a drop in blood flow. As it swells it can tear itself from its foundations, so to speak, and begin to cause haemorrhages both inside the brain and behind the retinas of the eyes – usually regarded as telltale symptoms of violent child abuse, along with the altered mental state resulting from a brain that had no oxygen for too long. In other words, the triad.

Canadian forensic pathologist Evan Matshes has recently published groundbreaking research throwing existing ideas about triad injuries out the window. [160] He's found that a whiplash injury to a baby from shaking may not in itself cause a brain haemorrhage, but that it appears to paralyse the nerve roots in the neck that control baby's breathing diaphragm. In other words, a shake brings on a near immediate breathing difficulty leading to apnoea and resulting hypoxia, which then causes the brain to literally explode as detailed above.

As a mechanism, it seems a much more likely description of what happened to Chris and Cru Kahui than police claims that they were "slammed" against a solid object – given there were no obvious impact points found at autopsy. But if a shake is what ultimately killed baby Chris and Cru, then the effect must have been immediate under Matshes' scenario – the shake cuts the nerves that control breathing, and the implication of that

<hr>

159 "Retinal and optic nerve sheath haemorrhages are not pathognomonic of abusive head injury", Matshes E, Presentation G1 (Pathobiology) American Academy of Forensic Sciences, Seattle, 2010: p272
160 "Retinal and optic nerve sheath haemorrhages are not pathognomonic of abusive head injury", Matshes E, Presentation G1 (Pathobiology) American Academy of Forensic Sciences, Seattle, 2010: p272

is obvious. There would be no wait of four to six hours for symptoms to emerge. Again, the cellphone location debate would be irrelevant.

But because these triad injuries can now be linked to a breathing episode, either natural apnoea or inflicted by shaking, it means police and medical experts need to pay closer attention at autopsy or in intensive care to what may be the extended range of natural causes for apnoea.

Middlemore Hospital's Dr Lindsay Mildenhall, for example, told the inquest that natural apnoea attacks can be triggered by prematurity, and re-triggered by infections – if baby gets a virus or bacterial problem it can bring on apnoea. Mildenhall added that there is one more event capable of triggering apnoea: immunisation.

Here are the specific words Mildenhall used: "It can reoccur if there are intercurrent illnesses, or sometimes it is – it reasserts itself after an immunisation. These babies were challenged with both those things and never showed any signs of apnoea."[161]

Except, we now know Mildenhall was wrong. Both Macsyna and Chris have separately stated there was an apnoea incident just before the babies were discharged home from the hospital, and here's the twist: that timeframe fits with the twins receiving their six week vaccines.

Is that why some nameless person in Middlemore apparently altered the twins medical records so there is no hint of an apnoea event? Because it might otherwise have been seen as an adverse vaccine reaction? It is unfounded speculation on my part, but plausible given Mildenhall's acknowledgement that apnoea is a side-effect of vaccination and I am still unable to think of many other good reasons for the resuscitation of baby Cru not to appear in the official records.

Internationally, debate has been raging in medical circles about whether some natural conditions are being misdiagnosed as child abuse. In 2004 the New Zealand Medical Journal published a letter from American scientist Alan Clemetson, a professor emeritus at Tulane University School of Medicine in New Orleans. Clemetson suspects a childhood disease of a century ago, scurvy, is still present but being misdiagnosed by modern doctors who are not used to seeing it.

"Has infantile scurvy, or Barlow's disease, really disappeared? Or is it now diagnosed as 'shaken baby syndrome' without any evidence that the infant was ever shaken?" he asks in the letter. "If so, we may be missing the mark in infant care and subjecting parents to a grave injustice."

---

161 Evidence of Dr Lindsay Mildenhall, paediatrician, Coroner's Inquest, 2010

Clemetson published a peer-reviewed medical study on the problem in 2004 and goes on to remind his colleagues that the symptoms of Barlow's disease mimic the so-called "triad" injuries:

"In the first, 75 years of the 20th century, Barlow's disease – with bruises, broken bones and sores that would not heal – was a well recognised condition in the Western world." The problem was a lack of vitamin C, causing scurvy in infants.

Scurvy weakens the walls of blood vessels, making them much more prone to haemorrhaging. The weakness of the capillaries "is the result of elevated blood histamine levels, which occur with even mild ascorbate (vitamin C) depletion." Those raised blood histamine levels can ultimately cause both retinal and subdural haemorrhages, as well as general bruising – all classic signs of abuse.

If a baby isn't getting enough vitamin C, causing its histamine levels to rise, and then doctors come along with immunisations, the baby's body generates further histamines in response to the vaccination. "Any further production of histamine by vaccinations, infections and other stresses can give rise to toxic histminaemia, which could be fatal," warns Clemetson in the NZ Medical Journal.

"Not so long ago we gave infants one, two or three inoculations at one time," reports the study in the Journal of American Physicians and Surgeons, "but now infants often receive six inoculations together at eight weeks of age. This challenge may be too great for some infants with borderline vitamin C depletion due to an upper respiratory infection or other illness."[162]

The twins, you may recall, had been hospitalised for two days with a bronchial infection and were still being treated for it when they died.

Eerily, the 2004 study warned: "To reduce the risk of Barlow's disease, we should consider the following: 1) Postponing inoculations for infants who are premature or ailing in any way, even with an upper respiratory infection; 2) reconsidering the wisdom of giving as many as six inoculants, all at once, to infants at eight weeks of age; and 3) administering 500mg of vitamin C powder or crystals, in fruit juice, to infants before inoculation; and 4) giving an additional ascorbic acid by injection to any infant showing a severe reaction such as convulsions or a high-pitched cry.

"We should not start by asking, 'Was the baby shaken?', but rather, 'Were the capillaries of the retina and venules of the bridging veins strong enough to withstand normal handling?'"

---

162 "Is it 'Shaken Baby' or Barlow's Disease variant?", Clemetson, C Alan B, Journal of American Physicians and Surgeons, Vol 9, No. 3, Fall 2004

The idea of injecting or supplementing babies with vitamin C at the same time as they get vaccinations emerged from the work of Australian doctor, Archie Kalokerinos, who was horrified that one in every two aboriginal babies were dying.

In his book, Every Second Child, Dr Kalokerinos documents what led him to try vitamin C supplements to help babies survive vaccination:[163]

"One research worker in the laboratory had been immunizing animals against diseases like tetanus and Diptheria. His experience showed that after being immunized, some of the animals died suddenly within 24 hours. These deaths had been attributed to anaphylaxis. Authorities the world over had decided that this was so (it is a severe allergic reaction). I suggested that vitamin C deficiency was the cause. The animals involved did not make their own. Like primates they required it in their diet. To discover the truth only required a simple experiment…

"The result was definite, unquestionable and final. Half of a group of animals were supplemented with vitamin C before being immunised. None died. The un-supplemented half continued to die at rates equal to those found in previous experiments.

"The importance of this discovery can hardly be stressed. In Australia and all over the world, infants were being immunised. Those whose vitamin C status was low were at risk. Here, at last, was experimental evidence that supported my claims that stepping up immunisation campaigns among Aboriginal infants increased the death rate."

Sixteen years ago, Kalokerinos told an anti-vaccination group who were interviewing him that practices of his medical colleagues in the name of immunisation were nothing short of barbaric:

"I found that they were visiting the reservations, the outlying camps of Aborigines in the desert, and if for some reason a mother didn't want her child to be vaccinated they would simply grab the child and forcibly vaccinate it. I saw them chasing them on foot, and chasing them in Landrovers and grabbing the kids and vaccinating them.

"Now, a lot of these kids were terribly sick. They were malnourished and everything else. And if they survived the first vaccine, in a few weeks they would come back with booster shots. And then with more and more, and then they would come around with polio shots and so forth. It is a wonder that any kid survived really, not that the death rate had just doubled. It is a wonder that any one survived."[164]

---

163 "Every Second Child", by Dr A Kalokerinos, MD, p139
164 Interview, June 1995, http://users.telenet.be/vaccine.damage.prevention/kalokerinosEng

He says he was called to help with a vaccine-related problem in Italy soon after.

"In 1977-78 there was an epidemic of a very peculiar disease in Naples, Italy. They called it the dark disease of Naples where infants and children would suddenly become unconscious without any special reason and autopsies would not really reveal a cause. Now this was just the sort of trouble I saw amongst Aborigines. So, to make a long story short, I went over with a "60 Minutes" television team, and we found that two thirds of the infants and children had upper respiratory tract infections, but one third of them had just been recently vaccinated with triple antigen including whooping cough vaccine. So my advice to the Italian doctors was to give the children vitamin C intravenously and to stop using the whooping cough vaccine. This terrible, strange disorder has never recurred since! So there was a connection."

But there's another aspect to infant scurvy/Barlow's disease worth mentioning: bone fractures. The scurvy affects collagen development which in turn creates "some complex bone pathologies that, to the uninitiated, look like trauma-induced fractures."

So here we have a naturally occurring medical condition, known primarily to affect infants, where vitamin C levels have dropped allowing blood histamine levels to climb, weakening blood vessel walls and in some cases causing haemorrhages, fractures and bruising.

And here's the kicker: hospitals and autopsies are not routinely testing blood for vitamin C or histamine levels. That means children in New Zealand could be dying of a medical condition that bears all the hallmarks of child abuse, but isn't, and the real diagnosis is missed because forensic and medical experts are not testing for it.

In a 2006 study[165], scientists examined the case of a mother who had vomited heavily virtually every day of her pregnancy and who had failed to keep down most of her food and the pregnancy supplements she was taking. The baby, like the Kahui twins, was formula fed and was not taking any extra vitamin C supplements. The baby was given multiple vaccinations at eight weeks, and hospitalised within six days of the immunisation after beginning to refuse food and vomiting. On the 11th day after vaccination, during a feed, the baby "collapsed, stopped breathing, and went floppy". Emergency teams estimated the baby had been hypoxic for about 6-8 minutes. CPR was attempted but the infant later died.

---

165 "Vaccines, apparent life threatening events, Barlow's disease and questions about 'Shaken Baby Syndrome", Innis, M, Journal of American Physicians and Surgeons, Vol 11, No. 1, Spring 2006

Radiology found a subdural haemorrhage, "12 'fractures' involving all four limbs, and seven rib 'fractures' of varying ages. These findings were confirmed at post-mortem," reports the study. The post-mortem also found evidence in the ribs of "scorbutic rosary", which is listed as a "typical feature" of scurvy.

Despite the scurvy pointers, the paediatricians were convinced this had to be classic case of child abuse on repeated occasions, because of the varying ages of the fractures and haemorrhages.

The study notes that heating infant formula before feeding baby usually destroys the vitamin C content in formula, meaning the baby will become vitamin C deficient.

Again, a plea was made for hospitals to mandatorily test for vitamin C and histamine levels in all cases of suspected infant child abuse, saying "infantile scurvy, while uncommon in affluent countries, should neverthe-less by routinely excluded before a diagnosis of Shaken Baby Syndrome is made."

The author of that study, Michael Innis, somewhat sarcastically asked how parents were supposed to know what might have caused injuries that they honestly have no knowledge of, and raised another vitamin deficiency as a highly technical example:[166]

"As regards fractures and bruises found on a child, suspicion falls on the carer if no explanation can be offered. It is absurd to demand an explana-tion. How can you expect them to say: 'You know doctor, there are several vitamin K dependent proteins in the body which require to be carboxylated by the enzyme gamma-glutamyl carboxylase before they become functional. Without vitamin K these proteins, some of which control haemostasis and prevent bruising, and others which control mineralisation of bone and pre-vent fractures, cease to be carboxlyated and hence bruises and fractures are likely to occur anywhere…That is my explanation doctor for the bruises and the fracture. I hope you can understand it and don't report me to the police or social services. They may take my baby away and kill my dreams."

"Currently the [medical] profession, in general," writes Innis, "seems to imagine that scurvy disappeared with the sailing ships. They are unable to comprehend it has resurfaced in the form of infantile scurvy due to their unrestrained enthusiasm for vaccinating children in unfavourable circumstances."[167]

166 "Vitamin K deficiency disease misdiagnosed as SBS", Innis, M, letter to the editor, British Medical Journal, 28 September 2008
167 "Iatrogenic misadventure", Innis, M, letter to the editor, British Medical Journal, 5 April 2003

It's a matter of public record that the Kahui twins received their first multiple immunisations at a time when they were still effectively five weeks premature – it was like sticking the needles into the womb of a pregnant woman at 35 weeks and saying, "she'll be right".

Middlemore Hospital is on record as saying this was a "challenge" for apnoea that the twins passed with flying colours. Except we now have evidence that they didn't, because of the undocumented collapse of Cru at this time in the hospital requiring immediate resuscitation by a crisis team.

Even so, those vaccinations and that apnoea collapse happened around six weeks before the twins died. During that time they'd been normal in the eyes of everyone – medic or family – who had seen them. I'm not a doctor, so take this with a grain of salt, but it would be difficult, in my opinion, to link the vaccines to their deaths six weeks later. By all accounts there had been no further apnoea incidents at home that their parents were aware of.

Now that we know of the hospital apnoea attack, and at least one of the twins evidently failing the vaccine "challenge", for the sake of completeness we need to consider the other "challenge" mentioned by the Middlemore paediatrician: recurrent illness.

The twins had an ongoing chest infection known as bronchiolitis for which they had been readmitted to hospital for a couple of days in mid-May, 2006. "It is a condition of children less than one year of age particularly," Dr Lindsay Mildenhall told Kahui's trial in 2008, "and it is almost always of viral origin. These babies have been particularly predisposed to this because of their prematurity. A function of that is that they miss out on a lot of immune information transferred from the mother in the latter period of pregnancy."[168]

"Is it an indication of want of care within the environment that they've been living in?" asked Crown Prosecutor Simon Moore. "Not necessarily," said Mildenhall.

But there may have been other infections. The autopsy on baby Cru established that when he died he was suffering from acute colitis, which is inflammation of the large bowel, and he also had developed peritonitis. Unfortunately, Starship Hospital failed to take blood cultures that would have revealed whether the colitis was caused by infection (probable) or physical assault (possible, but less likely given the absence of any obvious impact or bruising).

168 Evidence of Dr Lindsay Mildenhall, paediatrician, Queen vs Kahui, 2008

Baby Chris had diabetes insipidus, which results in rapid dehydration. It can be a congenital disorder (although given that they were identical twins you would expect them both to have it), or it can come about as a result of head injury.

There is a condition known as "endotoxic shock", or septic shock, where infections effectively overwhelm the body and it begins shutting down. A side effect of endotoxic shock can be adrenal insufficiency, which has the same effect as diabetes insipidus.[169]

Endotoxic shock can be a result of infection, in which case high doses of vitamin C have sometimes been found to bring recovery[170], or the shock can be a symptom of physical trauma – abuse. The twins were not running high fevers when first brought to Middlemore on June 13, but the flip side of that is that if their immune systems were not functioning properly the fever response might not have been present.

Without proper blood tests of the twins to determine whether any of the above alternative explanations of "child abuse" were present, we cannot truly know whether the injuries were natural or inflicted, or a combination of both. The possibility exists that illness had weakened them whereupon injuries were easier to inflict. It might be that tissue or bone samples are still held that could answer some of these questions.

I still believe the twins died of inflicted injury, however, and I have some points that might be plausible. I'm not a doctor, I'm a journalist, but in the course of researching this book I've read a lot of medical papers and transcripts of evidence, and I believe two possible scenarios are these:

SCENARIO ONE: Both Chris and Cru Kahui suffered one or more apnoea attacks at Middlemore Hospital's neonatal intensive care unit, consistent with Apnoea of Prematurity. Both twins at some point have required CPR to bring them around. Given their tiny size – at between 29 weeks and 35 weeks gestation during their hospital stay (still five weeks premature on discharge) – CPR performed by adults could have fractured their tiny brittle ribs and caused historic haemorrhaging. The hospital, for reasons so far undisclosed, has apparently failed to declare evidence of these events in the children's official medical file.

The hospital has failed in its duty to advise the parents that their children

169 "Effect of Treatment With Low Doses of Hydrocortisone and Fludrocortisone on Mortality in Patients With Septic Shock", Annane et al, JAMA. 2002;288(7):862-871. doi: 10.1001/jama.288.7.862
170 "Mechanism of action of vitamin C in sepsis: Ascorbate modulates redox signaling in endothelium", John X. Wilson, BioFactors, Vol 35, issue 1, Jan/Feb 2009 DOI: 10.1002/biof.7

may have been harmed, and failed to provide monitoring equipment to prevent any further apnoea events at home. The hospital has failed to warn the parents that their babies are particularly at risk from any further knock to the head or shake, more so than they would normally be.

The twins' broken ribs would have healed sufficiently in hospital during the week or so before they were discharged not to cause any further discomfort when they were handled at home, which is why all witnesses described them as placid babies – they were not in pain. This actually is the most credible explanation for the failure of home care nurses and doctors to detect any rib pain – the wounds must have already stopped hurting and that can only be because they happened in hospital and were healing.

The timing fits – both Macsyna and Chris remember the incident happening probably in the last week of April or first week of May, just before the twins were discharged. They both attended the hospital immediately they received a text from Macsyna's friend, so given the hospital's claim that they didn't visit very often, this date should be easy to isolate.

The so-called historic injuries were entirely caused within the hospital but not recorded and not disclosed – possibly not even noticed – in an apparent butt-covering exercise that left parents or caregivers in the gun if anything subsequently happened.

On the night of June 12, as a result of an argument in the house about the babies, someone has gone into the room in frustration and picked them up roughly or deliberately hurt them, causing fresh trauma in what is actually the first genuine incident of child abuse the twins have faced. Because of their already fragile state, the damage to the twins from their handling was more acute than would normally have been the case, resulting in coma and death as their old wounds were re-opened.

In failing to make full and frank disclosure of the twins medical history the hospital has perverted the course of justice and wasted police time and money.

In my view only traumatic injury inflicted on both children at the same time is fully consistent with their dual slide simultaneously into unconsciousness and death within hours of each other. A pathological (disease) cause could cover both children, but I am not convinced that the effects could be virtually simultaneous unless both children were suffering from an acute infection that the hospitals failed to test for. I am however a lay person and the intricacies of that debate are above my pay grade.

Regardless, an entirely natural cause does not explain why witnesses have lied to police on key aspects of the case.

SCENARIO TWO: Baby Cru has suffered an unrecorded apnoea attack and CPR event while in the neonatal unit, but not been injured by it, and all subsequent injuries were the result of abuse.

Somewhere between those two scenarios, I suspect, lies the truth.

These then are a range of alternative causes of the injuries normally caused by traumatic child abuse. I mention them for the sake of completeness, not because I find them overly convincing in the Kahui case. For reasons already expressed, you could argue some of the above where you were dealing with one child. But trauma striking two infants simultaneously is different.

As we move towards a conclusion in this investigation, now is the time to hear from the man who never testified at his trial – Chris Kahui.

CHAPTER TWENTY-TWO

The Self-Destruction Of Chris Kahui

The elephant in the room that was ignored by the jury in 2008 is the honesty of Chris Kahui. The man never testified at his trial, never spoke. His lawyers ensured he was dressed well, clean-shaven and baby-faced. But he never faced the hard questions he was later asked at the inquest, and the jury that acquitted him in one minute might not have been so hasty if they'd had a chance to hear him facing the music.

For example, although his lawyers had been at pains to try and say Chris had not directly blamed his baby son Shayne for the injuries to the twins, during cross examination at the inquest he was reminded what he had said in one of his police video statements:

"No, it was just when he was on the ... when I put them on the couch he was standing on them. He did not mean to, so I took him off."

"So you say that you saw Shayne standing on them?"

"Yeah, when they were on the couch," claimed Kahui to police.

Eyeballing him on the witness stand, Macsyna King's lawyer Marie Dyhrberg asked, "so, do you agree that what you said there is, you are saying you actually saw Shayne standing on the twins while they are on the couch?"

"Yes, that is what I said," confirmed Kahui on oath, directly contradicting his sworn statement to the inquest.

"[But] you have just said that, 'No, you actually did not see that'," pounced Dyhrberg, "so having looked at that, can you now tell us: Did you see Shayne in the nursery standing on the twins while they were on the couch? "

"No, I could – – -"

"No?"

"No."

"So what you said to the Police then that is wrong?"

" Yep," said Kahui on the witness stand.

"What you said there on page 48 – what you said to the Police about seeing Shayne standing on the twins, is that wrong what you said?"

"Yeah, I got that wrong."

"You go further and you are talking about Shayne being on the couch when the twins are on the couch and are you now saying that is wrong, what you said to the Police?"

" Yeah, I think he was on the floor crawling, yeah," replied Kahui.

So not only had Chris Kahui changed his story about feeding times, he had changed his story about seeing his son on the couch, standing on the twins.

He was caught on more discrepancies, such as the suggestion all the way through his statement to the inquest that he'd been absent looking after his mother most of the time after the twins came home, and Macsyna had been the main caregiver. The implication of this, when taken with the so-called historic injuries, is that the mother must have had the opportunity to inflict those. Additionally, it allowed defence lawyers to argue that the mother should have noticed the signs of abuse, whereas the father had so little to do with the twins, how would he know?

MS DYHRBERG: Yes, if you look at this statement, you were really trying to say, "Hey, look, Macsyna really did it all, I hardly did anything to do with the twins."

CORONER: Do you think someone reading that statement might get that impression – that idea, that Ms Dyhrberg is suggesting?

MR KAHUI: If you really looked into it like that, yes.

MS DYHRBERG: Because I will just – just point to just a few parts, because where you say there on page 1: "I spent almost everyday at hospital with mum and I slept there a lot as well. Looking back I left Macsyna to do everything for the twins. She was alone in the house with them and my eldest son, Shayne, who was only just one, almost everyday." So would you agree that what you are saying there is, you really were not around and the only one who was was Macsyna in terms of looking after the twins, would you agree with that?

MR KAHUI: It looks like that, yes.

MS DYHRBERG: And did you deliberately put that in this statement because you wanted this Inquest to believe Macsyna is the one who – could only have been the one who hurt the children first – – –

MR KAHUI: No.

MS DYHRBERG: – – -you deliberately wanted to set out that impression, did you not?

MR KAHUI: No, it was not, no.

MS DYHRBERG: But it is not right, is it?

MR KAHUI: No, it is not, no.

MS DYHRBERG: In your statement to the Police, the three video statements, you did tell them that you had quite a role in looking after the twins, did you not?

MR KAHUI: Yes, I did.

MS DYHRBERG: And Shayne?

MR KAHUI: Yes.

MS DYHRBERG: You knew precisely what was in this statement and you agreed that this was the statement that should come to this Court, that is true is it not?

CORONER: Is that true?

MR KAHUI: I just read it roughly through, sir, and signed it.

CORONER: No, is it true what Ms Dyhrberg was putting to you or was it untrue? Put the question again, Ms Dyhrberg?

MS DYHRBERG: When you said that you read this roughly, that simply is not true, is it?

MR KAHUI: Yes, it is true.

MS DYHRBERG: And when you said in this hearing that you were careless about some of your answers, that is simply not true, is it?

MR KAHUI: I think I was being a bit careless, yes.

MS DYHRBERG: In fact, Mr Kahui, you knew exactly everything that was in this statement and understood it, did you not?

MR KAHUI: No.

MS DYHRBERG: Did you not care that you made a truthful statement for this Court?

MR KAHUI: I did care. Yes, I did.

MS DYHRBERG: So you say you did care but you just read it roughly?

MR KAHUI: Yes.

CORONER: Did you think that it was okay, knowing this document was to be produced to a Court of law, just to read it roughly, it being a very important matter to you?

MR KAHUI: I think I did not go over it more than I should have, like I did not understand it as – – –

CORONER: Did you know this – I am sorry, you did not go over it as much as?

MR KAHUI: As I should have.

CORONER: As much as you should have.

MR KAHUI: Yes. No.

CORONER: Did you know this was a very important document and that it contained evidence that was different to that which was given in the criminal court?

MR KAHUI: I did not actually read all my statements and stuff, or go over my videos, so.

CORONER: You see, in the fourth line on page one of that statement you say "there are some matters which I wish to add". Do you see that, page one, fourth line down?

MR KAHUI: Yes.

CORONER: "There are some matters which I wish to add".

MR KAHUI: Yes.

CORONER: But when one reads this statement there are all kinds of changes, are there not, in relation to what you had said earlier to police?

MR KAHUI: Yes.

CORONER: You know that?

MR KAHUI: Yes.

CORONER: The statement does not say "There are some matters that I wish to change", does it?

MR KAHUI: No, there is not, no.

CORONER: If you knew that the document contained a lot of changes from what you have said earlier, would you not have wanted the document to be accurate?

MR KAHUI: Yes, as accurate as can be, yes.

CORONER: And would that not mean that you had to pay special care in reading it to make sure it was accurate?

MR KAHUI: Yes, it would have.

CORONER: It had been read to you by your solicitors you say.

MR KAHUI: Yes.

CORONER: When it was read to you did you find anything that was read to you that was wrong?

MR KAHUI: At the time I did not think it was wrong, no.

Kahui was in the unusual position of not being able to wriggle out of testifying to the inquest. Ordinarily, he could have chosen not to answer questions on the grounds of self-incrimination, but because he had already been found not-guilty of murder he can never be charged with that again, even if the evidence points overwhelmingly towards his guilt. And because Kahui is as free as a bird and can never be charged, he had no option but to front up to the inquest and speak. And the police lawyers had no intention of letting him off lightly. They too wanted answers about his misleading statements:

MR MOUNT [Counsel for Police]: Those words, "I left Macsyna to do everything for the twins" are wrong?

MR KAHUI: Yes.

MR MOUNT: You have told us already you did not write this statement.

MR KAHUI: Yes.

MR MOUNT: It was written out by your lawyers.

MR KAHUI: Yes.

CORONER: Did you tell them what to put in it, yes or no?

MR KAHUI: No.

CORONER: You did not?

MR KAHUI: No, I did not.

MR WILKINSON-SMITH: Well sir – – -

CORONER: Yes.

MR WILKINSON-SMITH: Obviously we are now getting into the area of lawyer/client privilege.

CORONER: I know we are.

MR WILKINSON-SMITH: If my learned friend is going to suggest that this is simply something that has been made up by his lawyers, that will unfortunately mean I will have to withdraw – that is quite a strategy, sir, and I really wonder whether that needs to be explored, and that is the difficulty. I would have thought it would be abundantly obvious that this is the result of lots and lots of discussions and this is a document that has then been prepared and Mr Kahui has gone through. He has told us he made some changes, but I really wonder at the utility of that line of cross-examination and the problem it can create if Mr Mount is trying to – if it means this becomes an issue it would mean that Mr Kahui, all his defence team and myself would have to withdraw, and I think that would be, given that we seem to be the only ones that are willing to explore any theory other than that Chris Kahui did this, would be very detrimental.

So I just really wonder why my learned friend is pushing on this. There are other ways of doing it. He could simply say "Well that is not accurate, is it?" and Mr Kahui can accept that. But if he is going to stray into client and lawyer discussions, I doubt we have got anything to hide, but I think the Code of Conduct would mean I would have to withdraw, and that would be very disappointing given that that would also apply to Ms Smith and to Ms Wilkinson-Smith, because Mr Mount's questions would be creating a conflict.

Of course, Mr Mount is in a similar position – there would be areas we could go into which might create a conflict for him, and we need, and it would only be, you know, we should try and avoid that unless it becomes something central.

CORONER: Yes. Thank you, Mr Wilkinson-Smith. Mr Mount, what do you say about that?

MR MOUNT: Sir, this is a very important document. The witness has signed it as true and correct. It fundamentally and dramatically changes his position from what he has said earlier on at least one key issue – probably the main issue in the trial. In my submission it must be appropriate to ask Mr Kahui whether in fact this is his statement or whether it has been written for him by someone else.

Imagine a jury's reaction if they had witnessed that exchange. The lawyers agreed to find a different way to ask the questions, but the point had been made, and at the centre of it remained the biggest question of all: how honest is Chris Kahui?

In my view, Chris Kahui's lawyers had a clear agenda – they would call it 'strategy'. During trial it was obvious they wanted blame shifted to Macsyna King, and during the inquest that was equally their aim. But again you have to ask the question, would a sensible jury have found Kahui not guilty after one minute's deliberation, if he had been forced to take the witness stand at trial?

The Coroner, for one, could be forgiven for thinking Chris Kahui could not actually lie straight in bed, literally.

CORONER: Is it appropriate to put a baby, who has just had an episode like Cru had, back into bed as though nothing had happened?

MR KAHUI: No.

CORONER: Is it all right to do that?

MR KAHUI: No.

CORONER: No. What time did you look at the twins on the Tuesday morning when you awoke?

MR KAHUI: I do not know the exact time, but I got up to see if they – if his breathing was okay.

CORONER: I am sorry, when you got – did you say when you got off to sleep Cru's breathing was okay?

MR KAHUI: No, when I woke up in the morning.

CORONER: Sorry, when you woke up in the morning his breathing – – –

MR KAHUI: I checked it, yes, I checked to see if he was breathing okay.

CORONER: Right. Did you sleep on the sofa in the room in which Cru lay?

MR KAHUI: Yes, I did.

CORONER: And did you go to sleep?

MR KAHUI: Yes.

CORONER: All right. Now, at page 3 of the statement that you produced to the Court you say that you slept on the sofa so that you could hear if Cru's breathing got worse again.

MR KAHUI: Yes.

CORONER: If you were asleep how could you hear whether Cru had stopped breathing or not?

MR KAHUI: I was like – I was like trying to get up every so often to check if he was – like if he was still breathing and stuff.

CORONER: Well, how often did you get up?

MR KAHUI: I tried to stay up most of the night.

CORONER: Well, you have told me you went to sleep.

MR KAHUI: Yes.

CORONER: Now, what is the – just think very carefully, you have told me that you tried to get up to listen to his breathing, but you say you went to sleep. How often did you get up?

MR KAHUI: I stayed up most of the night, just to keep an eye on his breathing and then I just lay there and nod off and then wake up and just keep checking him.

CORONER: But a baby's breathing is so faint you would actually need to be looking at its little face to see whether it is breathing, would you not?

MR KAHUI: Yes, I would, yes, and I would get up and check that.

CORONER: But, you see, how could you be checking the faint breathing of a baby by simply getting up from time to time to see if it is still breathing?

MR KAHUI: Just get off the couch and check them.

There was no evidence from any witness that Chris Kahui was sleep deprived on the day Macsyna took the twins to hospital. If he had truly stayed up all night – despite saying in his statement that he slept – then he would have been awake since at least 9am the previous day. By the time he was interviewed on video by police on Tuesday evening, he would have been awake at least 33 hours. He showed no signs of such deprivation in the video.

Often when it looked like Chris Kahui was sailing into dangerous waters, he was frequently rescued by his lawyer, prompting a stern rebuke from Coroner Garry Evans.

"You see, I get the distinct impression, rightly or wrongly, Mr Wilkinson-Smith, that you are pressing this Court in a manner that may constrict my questioning."

But Chris Kahui's most dangerous moments came when he was questioned about when the babies actually fed. This issue is crucial, because the act of not just sucking but actually drinking, and how the children responded during the feeds, allows forensic experts to time the attack. If babies were drinking properly and alert, the trauma must have occurred after that time.

For the sake of the conspiracy theorists who won't believe the evidence unless they see it with their own eyes, I intend to quote this portion of Kahui's cross-examination almost verbatim. It is extremely important testimony and this will be the only easily accessible document to the public that contains this much of the inquest transcript.

At the inquest, Kahui was reminded what he had told detectives the night the twins went to hospital.

MR MOUNT: You told the police that night that after Macsyna left on the Monday everything was okay?

MR KAHUI: Yes.

MR MOUNT: And that is true?

MR KAHUI: Yes.

MR MOUNT: That the boys were fine?

MR KAHUI: Yes.

Kahui was then asked whether he had fed the twins at 5pm, as per their schedule and expected wake-up routine.

MR MOUNT: You did tell the Police that you fed the boys at about 5 o'clock?

MR KAHUI: Yes, I did.

Remember, he was making this statement only 24 hours later. The events of the previous afternoon should have been absolutely fresh in his mind, and Kahui agreed they would have been.

MR KAHUI: Yes.

MR MOUNT: Yes. And you knew it was important to tell the Police everything you knew?

MR KAHUI: Yes.

MR MOUNT: Because you knew that the Police wanted to know all of the details about what had happened to the twins.

MR KAHUI: Yes.

MR MOUNT: And you were trying to help the Police as much as you could and tell the truth.

MR KAHUI: Yes.

MR MOUNT: So what you told the Police about feeding at 5 o'clock now that is correct, is it not?

MR KAHUI: I do not remember.

MR MOUNT: I understand you might not remember now, but in this interview you are just remembering what happened a little over 24 hours earlier, so we really have to go off what you told the Police, do we not?

MR KAHUI: Yes.

MR MOUNT: Is there any reason why you would have told the Police something wrong?

MR KAHUI: I just do not think I got the – I mean, I am not accurate on those times.

MR MOUNT: Okay. Let us not worry about whether it was 5 o'clock or whatever time. You definitely fed them again after that feed where April fed Cru, right? And before the CPR?

CORONER: Is that correct?

MR KAHUI: I am not too sure, sir. No.

MR MOUNT: Can you think of any reason why you would have told the Police something wrong?

MR KAHUI: No. No, sorry.

MR MOUNT: So when you think about it wrong, even if you got the time 5 or 6 o'clock wrong, it is correct that you did feed them again after – – –

MR WILKINSON-SMITH: Well, sir, he has asked that three times, he has said he does not know, and I am worried my learned friend is trying to make it sound like a submission.

CORONER: No, he is not making it sound like a submission, he is trying to get to the truth.

MR WILKINSON-SMITH: Well, the answer is he does not know. He has said that three times, and in my submission he has given his answer on that and three times is – to ask it twice might be arguably objectionable, but asking it three times and to get the same answer, I do not think – it does not necessitate to be asked for a fourth time.

CORONER: The witness is not an ordinary witness and there may be a need for an extraordinarily different approach. Carry on, Mr Mount, but bear in mind what has just been said by Mr Wilkinson-Smith.

MR MOUNT: Perhaps I will approach you in this way. Feeding the twins was a big job?

MR KAHUI: Yes.

MR MOUNT: I think you said it could take an hour?

MR KAHUI: Yes.

MR MOUNT: For one person to feed both twins would take even longer than an hour?

MR KAHUI: Yes, it would.

MR MOUNT: Feeding the twins was probably the number one most important thing you had to do when you were looking after them?

MR KAHUI: Yes.

MR MOUNT: When the Police officer was talking to you, she was very interested in what had happened with feeding?

MR KAHUI: Yes.

MR MOUNT: After you told her that you fed the twins at about five o'clock, she went back and she confirmed it a second time with you?

MR KAHUI: Sorry?

MR MOUNT: We have just seen in that second clip that the Police Officer went back and confirmed with you, this is the reference at page 7, confirmed with you that you had fed them about five o'clock?

MR KAHUI: Yes.

MR MOUNT: You were not trying to lie to her, were you?

MR KAHUI: No, I was not trying to lie to her, no.

MR MOUNT: So would you accept that what you told the Police that day must be right?

MR KAHUI: Well – I do not know if it was exactly that time, so.

MR MOUNT: I appreciate you might not remember now whether it was exactly five o'clock or exactly what time on the clock it was, would you accept that you did feed them some time between Macsyna leaving the house and CPR?

MR KAHUI: I could have.

MR MOUNT: You could have?

CORONER: Mr Kahui, as time goes on, our memories get dimmer, they start to fade – our memories of events, do they not?

MR KAHUI: Yes, they do.

CORONER: You can remember events best during the few days after the event and then as time goes on you might not remember them so well, do you think that is true?

MR KAHUI: Yes.

CORONER: Would you agree that what you told the Police in the interview, the day after the event, would be likely to be true, that is that you fed the babies about five o'clock?

MR KAHUI: Yes, it could be true, I am not certain that it was at that time, yes.

CORONER: I know you are not certain now, but would you have told the Police that you fed the babies about five o'clock unless you were certain of that or unless you remembered it?

MR KAHUI: I would have, yes, I think I was just going off my head.

CORONER: Going off your -?

MR KAHUI: Like off my – from the time I had actually remembered feeding them to that time, yes.

CORONER: You mean from the time that April last fed them?

MR KAHUI: Yes.

CORONER: What, on a six-hours basis?

MR KAHUI: Yes, I would have been going from that. I do not exactly know – I know I said it in there, I do not actually know if I did feed them at that time.

CORONER: You do not know whether you did?

MR KAHUI: I do not remember, yes.

CORONER: But at the interview you said you did, did you not?

MR KAHUI: Yes, I did.

CORONER: And you agree that your memory would have been better for events then than it would be now?

MR KAHUI: Yes.

The cross examination doesn't capture the full flavour of just how far Chris had taken his feeding story. In one of his police video interviews, he not only states that they fed at 5pm on the Monday, but that they also fed "normally" at 11pm before quietly going to sleep. In his first two video interviews, Chris also claims he fed the twins on the Tuesday morning after the breathing incident, and that Cru – who'd been unconscious the night before – took ¾ of his usual feed. These are pretty explicit comments, and he made them within 24 hours of the events in question. At the inquest this had all changed…

MR MOUNT: The CPR event when Cru stopped breathing was about 9 o'clock or somewhere between 8.30 and 9 o'clock?

MR KAHUI: Yes.

MR MOUNT: Now, that was not a normal feed, was it?

MR KAHUI: No, it was not.

MR MOUNT: It was about nine hours after the feed before Macsyna left?

MR KAHUI: Yes.

MR MOUNT: You would not have waited nine hours before feeding the boys again?

MR KAHUI: I am not too sure.

CORONER: Well, would you have waited for nine hours before feeding the babies again? You just told me that you were keeping up the six hourly cycle.

MR KAHUI: Mm.

CORONER: All right?

MR KAHUI: Yes.

MR MOUNT: So if we forget about the exact time on the clock, it is true that about six hours after the earlier feed you did feed the twins again?

MR KAHUI: I might have. I cannot be sure.

MR MOUNT: You might have but you cannot be sure?

MR KAHUI: Yes.

MR MOUNT: We know that you talked to the police again on the 21st of June. Now, for this interview you had your lawyer there?

MR KAHUI: Yes.

MR MOUNT: Now, you knew that the police were investigating the death of the twins?

MR KAHUI: Yes.

MR MOUNT: You knew that it was very important to be accurate with the police?

MR KAHUI: Yes.

MR MOUNT: You must have gone back over all of those events of the Monday very carefully in your mind.

MR KAHUI: Yes.

MR MOUNT: Trying to think what happened.

MR KAHUI: Yes.

MR MOUNT: So with this [second police] interview you again told the police that you personally fed the twins at about 6 o'clock.

MR KAHUI: Mm.

MR MOUNT: So you agree that is what you told the police?

MR KAHUI: Yes.

MR MOUNT: And you had had time to think about it?

MR KAHUI: Yes.

MR MOUNT: So if they had not fed at around 6 o'clock that would have been unusual.

MR KAHUI: Yes, it would have – yes.

MR MOUNT: That is something that would have been a warning sign for you, as a parent, that there was something wrong with the twins.

MR KAHUI: Yes.

MR MOUNT: Especially both of them, because one of them might get a little sick or not be ready to feed, right? For both of them to miss a 6 o'clock feed that would be something really unusual, would it not?

MR KAHUI: Yes.

MR MOUNT: If the twins had not fed around 6 o'clock you would have told the Police that.

MR KAHUI: Yes.

MR MOUNT: You would have said to the Police in the very first interview because you would have remembered that it was just the day before.

MR KAHUI: Yes.

MR MOUNT: The whole point of that interview was to find out if there had been anything unusual with the twins.

MR KAHUI: Yes.

MR MOUNT: That could help explain how they got injured.

MR KAHUI: Yes.

MR MOUNT: You would have thought to yourself, "Yes" or something very unusual happened they did not feed.

MR KAHUI: Yes.

MR MOUNT: And if for some reason you had missed it out of the first interview, then going back over it in your mind you would have remembered by the second interview, "There is something I did not tell you. The twins did not feed about 6 o'clock."

MR KAHUI: Yes.

MR MOUNT: What you told them then in the first and second interviews, when you think about it now, that must be right.

MR KAHUI: It could have happened, yes.

CORONER: I beg your pardon?

MR KAHUI: It could have happened, yes.

CORONER: It could have happened?

MR KAHUI: Yes.

MR MOUNT: Three months later on the 3rd of October you had another interview with the Police, right?

MR KAHUI: Yes.

MR MOUNT: Now, again, you had your lawyer, Lorraine Smith with you?

MR KAHUI: Yes.

MR MOUNT: And you knew what you had told the Police before and this was your chance to correct any mistakes.

MR KAHUI: Yes.

MR MOUNT: And in fact during that interview you did take care to correct some mistakes.

MR KAHUI: Yes.

MR MOUNT: I am going to show what you said in that third interview about the twins feeding again, okay – and, your Honour, this is a third interview, pages 61 to 63.

(Video played to the Court)

MR MOUNT: Of course, that was three months later, so you were a bit vague about the time, were you not?

MR KAHUI: Yes.

MR MOUNT: You told the Police that there was another feed after April and Shane had gone?

MR KAHUI: Yes.

MR MOUNT: And before CPR?

MR KAHUI: Yes.

MR MOUNT: Now that was correct, what you told the Police?

MR KAHUI: To my knowledge.

MR MOUNT: Correct to the best of your knowledge?

MR KAHUI: Yes.

MR MOUNT: If you had made a mistake about the twins feeding again, you could have corrected that?

MR KAHUI: Yes.

MR MOUNT: You said to the Police in this interview that that feed went good?

MR KAHUI: Yes.

MR MOUNT: Just like normal?

MR KAHUI: Yes.

MR MOUNT: And you said something similar to the Police in the first interview on the 13th of June?

MR KAHUI: Yes.

MR MOUNT: The third question and answer from the bottom, I will just read it to you to remind you, Mr Kahui. Question: "Okay, what about the next feed they had, the one after April, how did that go?" Answer: "It went good." Question: "Went good?" Answer: "Yeah, just like normal." Question: "Both of them fed normally?" Answer: "Yeah, that was – I think I gave that one in the cot, fed them in the cot, yeah." And that is what you said. And looking back now, that could be right?

MR KAHUI: Yes.

MR MOUNT: So do you accept that – when you look at all three of your Police interviews, you have said pretty much the same thing?

MR KAHUI: Yes, pretty much, yes.

MR MOUNT: Now, I want you to have a look at the – sorry, before I, I will just confirm again, and now that you think about it, what you told the Police those three times, to the best of your knowledge is correct?

MR KAHUI: Could be correct, yes.

MR MOUNT: Could be correct. Now, just have a look at the Inquest statement that you have got in front of you, the one prepared for this hearing, can you just read from the top of page two what it says in the statement now.

MR KAHUI: Sorry?

MR MOUNT: Just read it out from the top of page two.

CORONER: Yes, let him read it.

MR KAHUI: "I now know that this is really important to know exactly when the last feed normally and (INDISTINCT 4.54). When I first spoke to the Police I didn't realise that it mattered and that much then – oh, when they were fed. I did not, did not know or want the police to think that I was a bad father and over the two nights Macsyna was away I had pretty much tried to keep to their feeding routine, which is every six hours. But looking back, the boys did not feed when they usually would have after Macsyna left on the day of the power cut.

"I cannot now remember exactly when they fed, but I think that what I said in the last police interview must be correct, that is the babies were fed before Macsyna left around lunch time. I was expecting Macsyna back for their next feed. I do not think baby Chris cried or fed at all after Macsyna left. Baby Cru did cry and that is when April Saunders gave him the rest of the feed that he did not finish. I did not make a fresh bottle, so it would have just been what was left over from his feed before Macsyna left".

"The babies did not wake up or cry at all during the afternoon. If they had, everyone in the house would have heard them. It was not a big house".

MR MOUNT: That is completely different from what you told the police, is it not?

MR KAHUI: Yes.

MR MOUNT: What is written down in that statement is not true, is it?

CORONER: What is the answer? What was the answer to that question?

MR KAHUI: I have not answered it yet. No, this is quite, you know.

CORONER: Just take your time. What Mr Mount is saying is that what is written down in that statement that you have just read out is untrue. That is, it is different to what you told the police.

MR KAHUI: It is different to what I told the police, because this is about like how I was feeling.

MR MOUNT: Yes, well this statement is saying that the last feed that baby Chris ever had in his life was before Macsyna King left the house.

MR KAHUI: Could you – – –

MR MOUNT: Yes. You see the sentence "I don't think baby Chris cried or fed at all after Macsyna left", do you see that there?

MR KAHUI: Yes.

MR MOUNT: Well, that is not true, is it?

MR KAHUI: Well, that is what I thought....because I am not sure if they did feed after.

MR MOUNT: Okay, all right. So are you just saying in this statement that now, four years later, you cannot really remember?

MR KAHUI: Yes.

MR MOUNT: Yes. So we really need to go off what you told the Police, do we not?

MR KAHUI: Yes.

MR MOUNT: That is more accurate than this statement, is it not?

MR KAHUI: Yes.

MR MOUNT: Yes. You see at the top of page 2 it says, "I know now it is really important to know exactly when they last fed normally." Of course, you knew when you were talking to the Police that it was really important to explain to the Police when the twins were normal.

MR KAHUI: Yes.

MR MOUNT: Now you are not saying that you told lies to the Police, are you?

MR KAHUI: No.

MR MOUNT: You were being as honest and accurate as you could be with the Police.

MR KAHUI: Yes.

MR MOUNT: And if baby Chris had not fed at all after Macsyna left the house that is something you would have told the Police.

MR KAHUI: Yes.

MR MOUNT: Because at 9 o'clock that night, roughly when the CPR incident happened, that would have been nine hours since Chris had had a feed.

MR KAHUI: Yes, it would have.

MR MOUNT: And if one of your sons had not fed for nine hours you would have thought there was something seriously wrong.

MR KAHUI: Yes, I would have.

MR MOUNT: You would have taken him to the hospital?

MR KAHUI: Yes.

MR MOUNT: Yes. Or called an ambulance?

MR KAHUI: Yes.

MR MOUNT: Or called a doctor.

MR KAHUI: Yes.

MR MOUNT: And the same for Cru if he had not fed for nine hours you would have thought there was something seriously wrong.

MR KAHUI: Yes.

MR MOUNT: And got some medical help for him.

MR KAHUI: Yes.

MR MOUNT: The next day – the Tuesday – you went to Dr Nayar with Macsyna?

MR KAHUI: Yes.

MR MOUNT: That was around about 1 o'clock in the afternoon?

MR KAHUI: Yes.

MR MOUNT: Dr Nayar asked some questions about why you were bringing the twins in?

MR KAHUI: Yes.

MR MOUNT: It is the first thing the doctor always does, is it not? Ask, you know, "what is going on with this baby?"

MR KAHUI: Yes.

MR MOUNT: You did not say to him, "this baby has not or both of these babies have not fed for 25 hours"?

MR KAHUI: No, I did not.

CORONER: No, you did not?

MR KAHUI: I did not tell him that – the doctor.

MR MOUNT: So if what is written down in this statement was true, well then the babies had not fed for 25 hours when you went to Dr Nayar, right?

MR KAHUI: Yes.

MR MOUNT: Now that is something you would have told the doctor if that was true.

MR KAHUI: Yes.

MR MOUNT: But that would have been a serious situation if they had not fed for more than 24 hours.

MR KAHUI: Yes.

MR MOUNT: One other thing that you said in that third interview was that – and I will give, your Honour, the reference – it was page 29 of the transcript, that there was nothing wrong with the twins before the CPR event.

MR KAHUI: Yes.

MR MOUNT: You remember telling the Police that?

MR KAHUI: Yes.

MR MOUNT: And that is right, is it not? There was nothing wrong with them before the CPR event?

MR KAHUI: Yes.

MR MOUNT: And what you meant by nothing wrong with them was that they were completely normal?

MR KAHUI: Yes.

MR MOUNT: Up until then.

MR KAHUI: Yes.

MR MOUNT: They had been doing all of the things that you would expect as a father they would do?

MR KAHUI: Yes.

MR MOUNT: Because if you had noticed anything unusual before then you would have done something about it?

MR KAHUI: Yes.

CORONER: Mr Kahui, why is there a completely different version in your statement? A different story to what you told the Police – why is it?

MR KAHUI: Because I am not too sure if I did feed them after Macsyna had left the house. I was not too sure if I did or if I did not.

CORONER: But it goes further than that, it says you did not feed Chris again. You see, completely the opposite of what you told the Police. Why is that? Because you have told us that you wanted to be honest with the Police and that what you have told the Police was correct to the best of your knowledge, not once, not twice, but thrice – three times you gave the same evidence to the Police, and now I am told something quite different and I want to know what the reason for that is, you see?

And that is what Mr Mount has been trying to discover, the reason for our finding in this statement a different story to that which you had always told before. Can you give any explanation?

Is there an explanation? Or is there no explanation?

MR KAHUI: No, there is not.

CORONER: There is no explanation, is that correct?

MR KAHUI: Yes.

CORONER: All right. Mr Mount?

MR MOUNT: You know now that this statement is completely different from what you have ever said before?

MR KAHUI: Yes.

MR MOUNT: Did you realise how completely different it is when you signed it?

MR KAHUI: No, I did not.

So after five years, what do we now know? We know Chris Kahui took the witness stand at the inquest and effectively self-destructed, helped in a major way by yet another changed statement apparently designed to pin as much blame as possible on Macsyna King.

The defence was relying on three main planks. Historic injuries at a time when they claimed Chris had little or no involvement with the babies meant the mother could have done it. Yet the historic injuries largely disappeared at autopsy, and those that remained may have other causes, or could have been caused by the killer at an earlier time. Secondly, the cellphone controversy – if true – gave her opportunity (if you ignore the timings). Thirdly, the Eru Tuari 'evidence' of the alleged "I did it" statement. You've now seen and heard all this evidence tested, and you've seen Chris Kahui speak in depth for the first time.

You can make up your own mind as to whether the transcript shows someone who didn't understand the questions, or whether in fact he understood only too well the questions and where they were leading.

Clearly, Chris Kahui was lawyered-up, and clearly his lawyers had done an excellent job of blackening Macsyna King, but to my mind this transcript shows Kahui and his lawyers caught in the headlights over this. As counsel for the police stated, this was perhaps the most important issue at trial, yet Kahui was asking the Coroner to believe that he could not remember feeding the twins for an hour at a time, only 24 hours after the event.

There's your "wall of silence". Right there.

We still don't know exactly when the babies last fed normally, but we do know Kahui made claims early in the police investigation, perhaps before he knew the significance of feeding times, that the twins fed normally at 5-6pm on the Monday, and in fact were normal right up to the CPR incident, and we know he claimed that they fed normally after the CPR incident. We know the latter statement simply cannot have been true.

CHAPTER TWENTY-THREE

Wider Policy Issues

The debate over the Kahui case has been a touchstone for the whole field of child abuse. The failure to gain a conviction has polarised the community, and allowed social workers and other health professionals to wax lyrical about the entire range of possibilities. The mythical story of the "tight 12" and the "wall of silence" have been used to pass laws that force people to answer questions about child abuse – even though there was no "wall of silence"!

As you have now seen from reading the evidence in this book, there was no forensic trail going cold while police waited for the family to hold their tangi. Nothing significant was actually held back, except for the answer to the obvious question: who did it?

The presumption seems to have been that someone in the family knew who the killer was, which ignores the possibility that only the killer may actually know, only the killer may have been in the room.

"They all should be thrown in jail until they talk," muttered one Facebook boycotter before contradicting himself, "and why is this Macsyna King woman being allowed to tell her story?"

The logic of some of our fellow New Zealanders is truly a delight to behold, sometimes.

As you've now seen, who did not talk? There is not a single person in the Kahui/King families who would be caught by the new child abuse right to silence abolition – everyone gave statements. But as Coroner Garry Evans remarked wryly, the real question is how much weight you give some of those statements.

That's the problem with child abuse. It is such an emotionally charged subject that it's easy to get politicians to enact knee-jerk law changes to make it look like they are doing something, when in reality the law changes achieve very little.

In the Kahui case, there is one aspect where Macsyna King was strongly criticised in retrospect, and it left CYFS wondering if it should have done more. While Macsyna was "rooming in" with the twins before their discharge, social worker Manaaki Poto witnessed what she later told the court was a distressing incident.

In the middle of Macsyna King giving Chris Kahui a tongue lashing for not bringing the baby wipes fast enough, Poto felt King placed one of the twins into his cot too roughly. She didn't drop him or do anything stupid, she just seemed to do the task "aggressively". It didn't cause the baby to cry or become upset, but Poto felt it was an inappropriate way of handling someone so small.

Rather than note it officially, she chose to approach King and gently rebuke her as a Maori woman to another Maori woman, and explain that it wasn't the right way to handle a baby.

Understandably, when news broke that the babies appeared to have suffered fatal child abuse, Manaaki Poto was beside herself with regrets for not reporting the incident to CYFS, and her own "what if?" questions have haunted her so much she no longer works with neonates.

How significant was it, however?

Starship paediatrician Dr Patrick Kelly told the inquest that in his view a notification to CYFS would have made no practical difference at all in the Kahui case – because the family was already under considerable surveillance from home nurses and social workers.

The then Children's Commissioner John Angus agreed that Manaaki Poto should probably stop beating herself up about it:

"I think that the most likely outcome of a referral to, and this is speculating, of course, would have been support for the sorts of support services that were put in place, but they are the nurse who visited and the family support programme that was visiting and the referrals to other family support programmes that were being made."

I've mentioned previously in this book that Starship has an attitude – according to one GP practice – that "all parents should be treated as liars". The Children's Commissioner apparently agrees:

"I think good practice requires that to sit alongside a very questioning attitude to what parents tell you about their own behaviour, and I am speaking very generally here, but parents who are abusing their children are deny, deny, deny. Parents who are abusing alcohol and drugs, people who are abusing alcohol and drugs deny, deny, deny, and I think that social work that is strongly focused on the interests of the child has to take that pattern of denial into account."

The problem with the New Zealand Government's army of social workers is, however, that one would also expect innocent parents to "deny, deny, deny". How many innocent families will be subjected to official investigations merely because they "deny, deny, deny" smoking dope, drinking too much or beating their children? And how much resource will be wasted chasing up the innocent instead of finding a better method of identifying the guilty?

Call me old fashioned, but assuming someone's guilt simply because they deny it is close to witch-dunking.

Chris Kahui's lawyer Michele Wilkinson-Smith wanted to know whether the Government could do more to encourage struggling parents to get help, but Angus wasn't so sure when he realised the implications:

MRS WILKINSON-SMITH: Now, if we could encourage people to report the first incident to go to someone and say "I have shaken my baby", of course, the fact that there are likely to be criminal charges would be a disincentive to seeking that help as matter of logic?

DR ANGUS: Yes. The common pattern is to deny it.

MRS WILKINSON-SMITH: Yes, for fear of the consequences no doubt?

DR ANGUS: No doubt.

MRS WILKINSON-SMITH: So looking at all possibilities for preventing this type of fatality, one possibility is to encourage people if you have done it once, get help now and take a supportive and educational approach at that point rather than an immediately punitive approach.

DR ANGUS: Yes, I think there would need to be a case by case call about how best to keep a child safe from future injuries, and that would be a difficult judgement.

The inquest heard about other initiatives designed to check up on families, such as a warning flag for children who are taken to a hospital more than three times in one year.

Angus was questioned about one of Macsyna King's comments at the inquest, when she suggested that social workers would be more useful if they provided "time out" assistance – essentially a government sanctioned babysitting service who could step in for a few hours if a parent needed a break.

"Well first I need to acknowledge that she would be in a good position to make that assessment, having the care of these infant twins and knowing that medical interventions that had to be made to help in the pregnancy and after they were born. So she would be in a good position to judge that, let me say first. And secondly, I think that that sort of extra help would have assisted in their development in that period of time."

But there was also evidence that the Government and Counties Manukau District Health Board had failed the Kahui twins, by not telling the parents that they were entitled to 200 hours of home help because they had newborn twins and an older child to look after. What a difference that piece of information could have made in those crucial first weeks of the twins' lives.

A lawyer for CYFS wanted to know an answer to that as well:

"It seems, Mr Angus, that there were a number of things in place – the babies were engaging with Plunket, there were home help nurses available who were seeing the babies, but in this case that has not prevented this tragedy. So I wonder whether when at risk families are identified this concept of providing respite care might be as useful as having nurses visiting?"

"I would say it might well be as useful or more useful in a supporting or improving the likelihood of the good development of these twins in terms of their health and wellbeing," agreed Angus, who nonetheless pointed out that with no conviction and therefore no definite explanation for abusive behaviour, it would be difficult to speculate further on what might have prevented the tragedy.

Angus confirmed there have been studies trying to predict risk factors for violent child abuse, but it remains "very difficult to predict on an individual case basis that child maltreatment will occur, and in particular gross acts of physical abuse."

The studies, he said, have confirmed what authorities already know... that children under the age of six months are the most vulnerable, and that there is "a pattern of non-biological parents often being the perpetrators of the grossest assaults on young children."

The "industry" that has built up around the child abuse phenomenon clearly sees scope for more work. Submissions to the coronial inquest included that lawyers and/or specialist child advocates should be appointed at taxpayer expense to represent the interests of the dead children in any prosecution or inquiry.[171] Given that the clients are dead, one wonders whether that is truly the best use of taxpayer funds in combating child abuse, or whether more money at the coal face might be a better idea.

Children's Commissioner John Angus told the inquest CYFS received in excess of 110,000 notifications in 2009, a continuation of a huge increase

---

171 Submissions of Family Help Trust to Coronial Inquest

in notifications in the wake of the anti-smacking law and the publicity surrounding the Kahui case. Angus confirmed tip-offs ranged from physical
abuse down to behavioural issues, and also an apparent increase in the
number of parents screaming at their kids now that smacking is off the
agenda:

"Young children's needs are being neglected – their physical needs
for supervision and good care, and often their emotional needs for an
emotional climate in the house that is not dominated by fear and anxiety,
on the part of those caring for them – their mothers usually."

CHAPTER TWENTY-FOUR

Omega

CORONER: What do you say about the suggestion or allegation in the High Court that responsibility for the injuries lay with you?

MS KING: I am absolutely not responsible for my sons being hurt and then eventually dying. Emotionally and mentally it is not very nice to hear and take in – process and go forward in my day knowing that that has been put to me, and I still maintain to this day I would not – I never have, nor will I ever, ever have done that to my sons.

It's been asked, "why speak up now?" There's this idea that I've stayed silent for five years, said nothing. Well, I've said nothing publicly because I lost trust in the news media. They were happy to sell papers based on my sons' deaths, but they didn't care about whether what they were printing was true or just rumours.

In fact, I haven't been silent for five years by choice. As a police witness in the trial of my former partner Chris Kahui, it was made clear to me that my side of the story was sub judice – that I could not really speak up until the end of the proceedings, so as not to prejudice a fair trial.

I wrote an eight page letter to Chris, but wasn't allowed to send it. My lawyer and police all said that anything I said to Chris could be used in court to his benefit, because all his lawyers needed to do was create reasonable doubt, and I was the target of the defence lawyers. I was told just to stay quiet, to bite my lip. We've taken it upon ourselves to find the perpetrator or find out what's happened. This is the system of our world. Like it or not, I'm a part of it. Can't really do much about it except tell the truth, cooperate whether it is good for me, or not.

When the trial ended in 2008, I found I wasn't ready to speak publicly – I had issues with my past that I was still working through, which you've read in this book but which I wasn't mentally ready to confront back then. The decision was taken out of my hands when it was announced that I would be required to testify to the inquest, and that's only just ended. Throughout these five years, as a primary police witness, I have been assisting police. After testifying at the inquest and with no further proceedings in sight, I felt it was finally time to tell the whole story as I knew it, including the parts that were not relevant to the court case.

I've also been spending these years picking up the pieces of my life, and that's been hard. I could barely eat and I would barely sleep for a while after their deaths. I was at a size ten and then went down to a size eight when I began working. And now I'm at a healthy 14 and a half (well, really 16 or 14 depending on the retailer). So I experienced that.

Through trial after trial after trial, I have learned that there's another reserve of resilience and strength that I never realised existed.

The Facebook "Boycott Macsyna" page was a full-on attack – my family have just stopped looking at Facebook. It was like the days of old when people were stoned to death, just because one person would say they were guilty and the rest of the crowd would get in on it. That's how the Facebook thing felt. If I don't look, it's sweet. If I look then I find an overloaded inbox full of hate. Has it died down? No. Do I look any more? No, I can't. They really hurt my son who's living with us, he's had a real hard time with it.

You know that old saying, "they're only words" or "words can't hurt you"? Well, they can. I used to believe that words could only hurt if it was the truth, but words hurt regardless, I have discovered. Words can hurt you if you have feelings. If it hadn't been for the earlier troubles and trials I had been through, I don't think I would have been strong enough to handle it.

You can't expect other people to understand where you are coming from – even if you tell them the honest truth about what you saw. I'm speaking my truth, it's the way I remember it as it happened to me. I've explained it as best I can, but it's not going to be good enough for everybody. I can't keep looking over my shoulder, stepping back into a past life that I can't live again, or back track or take back. I have to make efforts to keep going, because I still have four children who live.

Every now and again they ask me questions about life, and I'm a perfect example of things you should not do. Does that help my children? Yes it does.

As much as I could, I tried to be self-sufficient. I don't think that I was greedy in regards to being dependent and being on the benefit. I have always tried to give more than I needed to, to help balance things out. Food and board is one thing, but being with my family, especially after the boys had passed for the last four to five years, was really hard on my sister's relationship, because her husband is ex Black Power. Still affiliated with them.

He still has that sort of mindset. "You put my name to shame. I look ratshit with the bros," at times that would come up with Ems. Then other times he would stand by me faithfully and tell me "I don't care what these people think, even my own brothers in my club, I know you and I don't believe for a second that you would ever do that to your children, let alone mine. Otherwise I'd never let you anywhere near my daughter or my wife, or me for that matter.

"I wouldn't have anything to do with you. I'd probably do something nasty to you. Like take you for a ride and accidentally forget where I left you. Concussed, knocked out, tied up, don't know. But yep. If I really thought you were, or even half thought you were, I'd be likely to do something like that."

So there were those sorts of things going on and in that period of time when the boys passed in 2006, there was hardly any income. None of us were on any sort of income support benefits at that time. Although the media says, yeah we were, what they talk about is the period leading up to it, or the period before we found paid work. How it's been portrayed is pretty inaccurate.

Sometimes people have confronted me, attacked me, yelling out, "You're just a f***ing scumbag of this earth, you're a dole-bludging, useless, no-hoping…"

I would absolutely go right off my face and front them right back. "Up yours, you don't know shit! I've worked harder than you would ever know!" And I could still do it to this day. Unfortunately, my name makes it really hard for me to find paid work. The little businesses that are interested in my skill are interested in my skill only, but they do not want the baggage that goes with it. And I can respect that. I accept that. I don't like it, but I accept it, and have had to accept it.

I say have to because I found my spirits would be really down and I'd be really low in energy and just had this really sad face. Bit directionless. But in the back of my mind, always striving for direction, for a purpose with a method to it. It might seem like there's a method to the madness, and that's better than no method at all, sort of thing. I had to go through a little bit of a bump and curve period there, and it was really, really hard.

What do I make of benefit dependency? I believe the benefit is a safety net on the journey, not the destination. There's a generation growing up today who've become so used to the idea of welfare that working seems like not worth it. Sadly enough, some of them are my family members and my close friends' children.

I can say that Chris, for example, Chris definitely had that same thing himself. "If I got a job that pays $12 an hour after tax, that's not really worth it, I might as well stay on the dole at $5 an hour at half the pay, but I don't do any work. Free money."

The mindset of it all, it's laziness, it's hands out, "I expect and you bloody give it to me" is overall what I've experienced with Chris. In this generation today. "Mum, you're supposed to do this." My son, he tries it on me sometimes. "That's what a mother does."

"No no, it's my job to guide you and teach you how to become more independent as you grow older. And at this age, with your demands, you ought to be able to put out as much as you want. So if you want ten bucks, you show me ten bucks' worth of work or nah, don't even bother asking me." That's how it's been with Sean. He understands it. "A something for a something. Not you are just given whatever you want so you can sit there watching TV or whatever with expectancy on the tip of your tongue. Get that idea out of your head."

In saying that, Sean's only come back to live with me this year and I can honestly say I've only truly got this appreciation after all of this stuff that's happened with the twins. Because the whole experience of losing them and having to have to recall what happened to them has made me go back at the start. It made me do that because after the coroner's inquest I decided to engage in counselling. In fact, I remember telling you at the end of our first interview that I was telling you stuff I'd never been able to talk about, not even to the counsellor. You stirred up all that within me.

I soon realised that the first few counsellors I went to, they really were only looking at treating the symptoms. I learnt after about the third or fourth session, that it's not there that I needed to start. It is at the core or at the source of it – that's where I needed to start. Kind of where you'd taken me to. So I had to start with getting an understanding of how my thinking patterns had developed, what had triggered them in my life? What sort of things would make me engage certain feelings?

We looked at my reactions, why was I reacting badly? Somebody would talk to me in a certain way, I would react inwardly. Why? Because my recall of that was all associated with memories of negativity in my past, learned pathways in my brain that had a lot to do with my environment and took up a lot of my time. So in memory recall, naturally I was going to recall the first time I ever remembered pain. When I think of loss, for example, I think I've buried my own sons, I've lost my mum, I've lost my dad. And everybody who has been dead to me in some way or another, whether intentionally or not, I was not able to have a successful relationship with all these people. When I say successful, I mean successful where, even if there was a falling out, that after the harsh words or whatever I was able to go back there and say "You know what? That doesn't really matter. What matters to me is that you're ok. And are you ok? Are you ok with me? And if not, can we sort it?"

If I'd had the ability to know those simple tools, asking questions, not just any sort of questions, but the who, what, when, where or how questions that are specific, that would have let me drill down to the root causes of arguments or bad feelings. They made it easier for me to chop out the emotion, chop out the irrelevant stuff and start narrowing the list down, where I came to 'Oh, there we go. Right there is the source of it all'.

So in a sense I am bringing the fresh understanding that I have of myself, and where I went wrong, and I can share this with Sean in the way that I parent him. And I can see how his generation have these expectancies embedded into them, where if they don't get what they expect they react badly and the cycle begins – you can see it everywhere you look.

Sometimes we as parents sort of give up and say, "Well actually they spend more time at school, it's the school's fault." But that's just like saying "oh, my kid fell over and got hurt and I don't know why. So I'm not responsible."

Yes you are. You're responsible for your kids. To know how they think. You're responsible for engaging with them and asking questions, "What do you think about this?" If they don't want to answer you, too bad. You find a way to reach them until they do answer you. Why? Because that's you being responsible, finding out where their mindsets are, what their attitudes actually are. You're only going to find out that way, you can't just guess it.

Cause kids these days also know how to make it look good on the surface. They've watched us or they've watched others just display the 'right' things. You won't get looked at, don't be noisy and you won't be taken notice of. So in effect, noisy ones are always looked at. The quiet ones are not. Teacher doesn't worry too much about them. Got to watch the quiet ones because they aren't being heard.

The noisy ones, they're often part of this whole generation of hand outs, I call them, 'wanters and hand outers'. They stand there and want their hand out quickly. It's not on. It's not a healthy thing for us as parents or responsible people to allow our children to carry on doing.

Some of Sean's cousins, their parents are wealthy, good God-fearing folk, but their kids get $20 a day pocket money! And the kids – I love them to bits – are like "where's my money?" – that's the way they talk, they just expect it.

So sometimes I'll just randomly drop things into my conversation with my son, like when we discussed the pocket money, "So what do you think about doing no work but getting some money, do you agree with that?"

"Nah, nah I don't."

At least I know where his head is at. If there's a disagreement over something and harsh words are said, I'm like "Hold your tongue. This isn't the time to deal with it. We need mediation here, we need Nev (my partner). And we'll do it in a relaxed way. Right now you're pissed off, your language sucks and it's not cool. So you go and do the dishes or whatever. And we'll talk about this later."

When you look at infants, you need to constantly monitor them so they don't hurt themselves, and I don't think it stops just because they become teenagers. If we txt our son at 16, and he doesn't txt us back, he has a five minute window period and we're in the car looking for him and he knows. We're getting him into that routine. It's just so that he understands a send and receive of messages is important, and you respond immediately. "If you have questions that's ok, but at the end of the day, you're the child, I'm the parent, my job to guide you. Any problems, I'll take responsibility for that. And your job is to do as we ask you to do." And he gets it, but we're finding that it's a daily thing. We renegotiate our thinking and mind our language all the time, it's really important with teens. I don't know why, but it is.

"Sean, what's that on the ground?"

"Socks."

"Righty-o. Tomorrow you're going to take those to the lost bins so some more appreciative student that goes to your school can have them. Cause you don't want them."

"That's my last pair of socks out of five!"

"Well good, so you'll learn."

"Oh, well then I'm going to need a note for school."

"I'm not giving you a note for school, I'm sorry. You are going to have to wear the consequence yourself."

We did that with him. Of course we had to ring the high school and say "Please would you work with us on this? Rather than be harsh and nasty to Sean we're going to try this, will you work with us?"

She goes "Yep."

And it worked! He really values his things. But it's a learning curve for all of us, taking it a day at a time. Sean left my care at four years old. Eleven years after the fact, he came back to me. So I have to learn how to be his friend, be his mum, be his observer, be his growling person.

When he came here he didn't seem to have much confidence. He would not speak openly and would always just sit on the chair and not speak, not participate, and he would not look us in the eyes. Simple things. It was Nev who said "We just need to lift his spirit, pick the boy up."

Sean opens the door to the guy holding a Domino's pizza, and his eyes peer past my shoulder as if looking for the pizza delivery vehicle. You can see the gears whirring in his head, "what the heck is this middle-aged white dude in a tailored jacket doing delivering pizzas?" His face breaks into a welcoming smile when he realises who I am. Order is restored in the universe. He's just come in from rugby training, and there're still the lawns to mow, but a slice of pizza never goes amiss. "Would you like a strawberry tea?" he asks me…

He's well and truly come out of his shell. He's playing sports, has joined Kapa Haka. He wanted to be in the debating team but he talked too much!

It's a change from one to the other and the difference was that we had to apply ourselves to him. I had to give up my hopes of going back into study once we took him on board. We had to make decisions like that. They're important. You have to have your plan of attack or your plan of action in place. You have to have all these sorts of things in place, you really, really do. I notice the difference in him now, in such a short time. I don't attribute it to me going through this wonderful change. It's the kid, it's Nev, it's me in my willingness to change and understanding how to just be with him as a person. Not just relying on the fact that I'm his mum. All of it is relevant.

I don't do any of the things in my life any more that you've read about in this book. I don't drink alcohol, I've even given away tea and coffee as well. No drugs, no drugs whatsoever, no cigarettes. I don't go out to pubs and socialise, not even for social events. Nev still smokes cigarettes, but not around home, not around us, and he doesn't drink, and that's been a real positive influence for all of us.

So with all of these things removed from my life, I notice the blessings and I notice the changes, and they are healthy and helpful ones. My children like it, and I like that they like it.

Finally I've learned how to commit, I don't have commitment issues any more – I don't, it's fine. I realised that people were not committing to me because I was not committing to them. As I do to others, now they do to me. It's been a bloody hard learn, but I've learnt – what I do to others comes back to me.

When I got the chickenpox just after the Facebook thing, members of the church came over and dropped off half a cord of firewood for nothing, stacked it for me, and a cake. So good things do come to people, even as terrible and horrible as me. People are capable of change, but at the end of the day it's in the demonstration. Words can only go so far. I've made changes to my life that are worthwhile, and I would never ever have it any other way. If I was to go backwards again I think I would surely lose the plot and I don't think I'd be living on this earth for too much longer if I was to go back into the lifestyle I used to live.

As a mum it is pretty scary, every day, for me. I think about how I talk to my son. There's all these laws in place to help protect our children. Do I believe in it? Yep. Do I think they should be enforced on parents? Yep. If we want our children to be the best that they can be, we have to step up. We can't expect them to be the best if we ain't.

Bearing in mind how I was brought up, and everything I've lived through, I am scared, I am petrified, but I am vigilant and I am consistent. I do simple things with my son, I wake him up, I make his lunch, I make sure that he's OK. I make sure I know how he feels and who his friends are, and I make sure I know how his relationships are going at school, how he interacts with people. At the end of the day if someone goes, "where is your son?" I know where he is because I know what he likes to do and where he likes to hang out. Ten years ago I would not have even thought of half the things I do now.

I can't say it is all due to the trials and troubles – I've also grown up a lot too. But it's pretty hard to grow up when you have no one else to learn from. In my first 12 years of life I can say there was no one there as a positive role model whose guidance I could learn from and pass on to my children.

My daughter Narelle, she lives with Mum and Dad in Australia. She is very bright and a whole year above her level at school, very diligent.

Baby Shane, he's six now and in the custody of my relatives. I see him once a week on average.

My youngest daughter Katie, who I last held at the scene of the kidnapping in 2001 – I've caught up with her dad a couple of times. He shares photographs of our girl online. I know that Katie loves netball, as I do. She's a very well-raised girl. I don't have any physical contact with her or talk to her at all, but I have snuck looks and peeks of her when I've been on my travels. Katie's never ever known that I've been there. I've always been happy to know her from a distance.

I knew you would ask me why.

I really am still just coming to terms with what I did to her, I'm only just able to stop booting myself in the guts for failing to provide her with a mum. So it's me, really, and a lot of still actually getting over the things that happened with Gerald and I. I've apologised to him. He's apologised to me. But emotionally and making my memories forget it, so that when I recall it it's not all just a bad memory – getting to that stage is still in the works. Can't do it straight away and still find it hard.

One day I will have healed enough that I can face my youngest daughter. In the meantime, I am a work in progress.

Chris,
I write this letter to you so that you may
know from me, some of the things that I
feel. Not only is it important for me to tell you
how I feel, but it's important for me that you
acknowledge and take some accountability for the
things that happened leading up to the death of
my sons, who are also your sons.

I can't be sure if all the things I write about
will be in any sort of order or time-line but for
me they are all things I care about, they are all
things that affected me then as they do now.

First of all I would like to tell you how angry and
sad I feel about how you now "blame" and "accuse"
me of being responsible for the death of Chris & Cru.
How the heck do you justify your reasons for blaming
me? for the first time ever I heard evidence or statements
verbally spoken by your lawyer, who is instructed by YOU,
and I think your a coward. Your lawyer said things
like I never really went to my sister Em's, I doubled back
and killed Chris & Cru, got picked up by Em's and pretty
much framed you. You have no regard for how much
those allegations have affected me, my sister and her
family. Because of these things me & my sister have
had to basically defend ourselves. You are such a
low-life person to blame others because of your stupid
excuses. Em's has always, ALWAYS treated you well.
She helped us both with getting you a job. That job you
got only because of our relationship. Since the time
she met you, she has given food for YOU to feed
your family when none of you were getting any sort of
help from any of your other family members.
Em's has helped me care for your brothers & sisters
by taking them to doctors, family events and also
clothed them. You and your family were always made
to feel welcome at Em's house and this is how you
FINALLY thank her? This hurts me because she has

always been close to me and I feel as though you attack her only to hurt me. Emily is in no way responsible for what you & your lawyer accuse her, me or her husband of. What the heck are you blaming everyone for? Are you attacking us for any reason that is fact not just made up with your lawyers explanations as a guideline? Probability and all the big words aside, you Chris you know damned well that my sister would never ever allow a child hurt in front of her own eyes! You are shit, coward scum for accusing her. You accuse me of murdering ours sons and I am so deeply hurt. I still cry for them out of the blue, I have since taking them to the hospital only to learn they'd been severly hurt. I have never let anyone look, touch or verbally harm your younger brothers & sisters let alone my own sons! How the f*** can you accuse me? I have defended you and them against your dad, mum, uncles, aunty's even your sister Tracey. I did it many times, and now I think myself a fool, a stupid idiot because of what you now accuse me of. And then there's accusing Em's husband of not only being an accomplice to murder but also of threatening you with black power, you and me both know that you are a filthy liar on that count AGAIN! The only good thing that I have learnt from helping you, is that I realise I did help you for nothing else except to see you a little better off. Not for praises, but because you needed some goodness after being treated badly. What makes you do and and blame as you do?

Other things that I just can't seem to stop thinking about over and over again is what happened the night I left you and Shane, & Chris & Cru at home. First I want to know why you had lied to me about who'd visited you when I was gone? Shane, April and her grandson had been over home and arrived shortly after I had left. April's evidence was that she finished feeding Chris (baby chris) because you were a bit grumpy, what for?

April se2 she changed the boys after feeding.
Why did you keep that from me? Always it's important
to know who did what and when, this you knew but when
asked a few times you said then u didnt know. At coroners
inquest you could recall detail, time everything. I think
you are lying again! Chris suffered a broken leg which of
course you blame me for but evidence says it had been
broken at least 12 hours prior to me taking them to
hospital. The doctors explain that broken bones that do not
pierce the skin bleed internally. Internal bleeding can cause
many things in such a tiny body. So if you wonder what
am I getting at it is this: Chris ALWAYS ALWAYS
cried loud and oh time without fail since day one.
At feed times, nappy changes happen, why did you
not notice his broken leg? What made you not worry
for the boys after Cru held his breath and went blue?
What made you, your father AND your sister all lie to me
when you 3 said "your dad did the CPR"? But during trial it was
Why did the 3 of decide that driving from Mangere
to Papakura was better than taking Chris & Cru to the
friggin hospital? The hospital 5 mins away for ___ sake!.
Why did you decide to not come to the hospital with me
when we left doctor Nayars? Why would you not help me?
Why did you LIE about Shane getting into the nursery
and hurting the twins when you were washing out the
boys bottles when all along you knew you never even
fed them? Why had you lied to Police and say you'd
fed them? Why didn't you feed them?

How can you father more children after losing our sons?
What is it that you do to make you satisfied you are in
no way responsible? How does your consience regard your
actions and excuses? What accountability, responsibility
and ownership do you take for all that's happened with
the death of our sons? How do you even think that
you should now have custody of our only surviving son
Shane? Why do you think that you are a better choice
for full-time parenting of him? Why do you consider only
YOUR needs of him instead of his welfare?

Why do you continue to make public statements on
television regarding me, Chns, Cru and Shane?
Why have you done nothing, NOTHING to find out
what happened to our son's?
   My life has alot of painful memories assosiated
with our sons. Not a day goes by where I dont think of
them. I have nothing of there's left because the police
seized things left in their room and I can't be
sure I'll get everything back. I worked very hard
to keep them clean, at all times warm and most of
all healthy and LOVED. I can see their tiny faces if
I close my eyes. I remember some of their mouth
and hand expressions and I ache to hold them.
I shudder when I think of the physical pain their
little bodies must have gone through. I cry for them
for so many more reasons. I have some dreams of
them and they reocurr off and on. I cry for Shane
because he was a bouncy and bonny child and I
can't raise him as a result of what's happened to
our sons. Shane, now 5, has a stable family who
have some excellent principles that they live by.
Shane is respected, his well being is important to
his parents and I fear for him. I fear that you
will keep trying to gain custody of him.
I don't trust him in your care. Not no more
and not ever until he is a grown man. I worry
for Shane nearly everytime I hear from my lawyer.
There are so many questions that you refuse to
give any answer to, and I think of Shane and
how that may or may not affect him. I have had
visits with Shane and he has told me some of the
things you have told him while you have had visits
with him. I think you are dispicable!
You have fed him your version of "why he now lives away
from you". You cheating lying shit! You told him his parents
came to Auckland and took him away from YOU!...
not me his mum who did care and look after him
but YOU! That is not true and you know it.

I think he is a person in his own right.
I think you tell him only what serves you so that
he forms understanding based on "your story".
I think you do not value his trust when you tell
him things that are lies! His youthful innocence is not
respected and you dont care to be mindful at all!
How can you justify that? What makes you so selfish,
and so driven to meet your needs that you can't stop,
think and evaluate? From your actions, your lawyer,
your statements how the hell do expect me to let you
carry on as you are and take Shane from safety,
if the opportunity ever came your way?
  When do you ever think you will be honest and
answer at least some of my questions?
  What will it take to stop you from hurting me more?
I want you to leave Shane be, let him make a choice
to live with you WHEN he has the tools to make
solid decisions for himself. leave him with his parents
and take his better opportunities in life that they can give him.
You are only "1" of his parents. I dont agree in your favour.
You have 2 daughters younger than Shane, what of that?.
Still you are un-employed and you continue to take
refuge with your new partner and her family. Have
that life and leave Shane to his!

In regards to your "given" reasons that you say are what
make you "believe I hurt our sons", I think you
know well that YOU LIE AGAIN!! ... my question is why?.
At coroners inquest your lawyer put to me that I was
caught having affairs with your family members. What the
hell is that all about? You have seen and heard your
family making advances on me and I was pregnant!
Why now after all this time do you accuse? Is it all you
can come up with?. You think I held your family
members above my own sons so much so that I would
go to "hurt my sons" because you caught me? How
bloody rediculous are you getting with those
explanations? How do you think I could have gained
anything by hurting my sons because I was angry

with you? What makes you so important that you publicly make that accusation?
Why have you never confronted me PERSONALLY face to face. I did with you! I came to you and your family and hit you all up face to face!
Why have you chosen to give most of your additional information?. The media have made a full coverage of my life from College years from 1990 to 2010. How would you like to have your life exploited as mine has? You have had sexual relationships with your own _____ ! Your _____ did nothing to prosecute your uncle who raped them for two years. You knew about it from the first time and _____ told you about it, but you said and did nothing.

Sometimes I get so angry thinking about things that you "haven't said", that you "haven't done" but I dont want to strike out as you have!
Sometimes I feel so sad, so mournful with loss in mind that I dont bother to eat.
I have trouble not blaming myself for ever leaving me boys with you. I tell myself sometimes that this would never have happened if I'd taken them with me or stayed home with them.
I wonder what I could have done to change the whole situation. At other times I know that I must accept the boys, our sons have passed on and cant change what is.
I cry and have compassion for your family who have spoken against me and lied... for you!
I have faith that nature sends back what you send and karma will balance things somehow.
I cry because it's sad to hear and find out how willing people are to blame, deny and hurt others.
I cry because I understand that what's true for some is not so for others.

I cry in frustration and sometimes have thoughts to
return to you and yours what was given to me.
I cry because I don't want to think and act well towards
you and yours, I cry because I could not do what was
done to my sons, our sons. Everyone who lives has or
had parents and I could not bare to know I would
be the cause of some deeply hurtful pain for people/parents.
I would never wish that pain on others.
Losing loved one's is hard, children even harder.
Two sons Chris!. I grieve for them in nearly most of
the things I do in my life today. I have a fear of
being around people now. I fear they may attack me as
they have before. I've lost friends because their families
threatened to dis-own them if they remained friends with me.
I stayed away from my own family because I feared
media may interfere in their lives. My main place of
refuge has been with sister Em's and you have been
directly responsible for me leaving home because you
made statements to media, which inturn sent them on
a hunt for a reply from me!
I constantly wonder how you are okay with everything.
Most of your family including yourself have the
poor attitude of "oh I cant wait till inquest is done",
not, what about who did, what, when, where, how!
You, your new partner were on T.V in newspapers saying
that you wont stop till someone is prosecuted.
What the ___ is that crap about? Why do you think
aquittal was given? It does not make you innocent!
It means there is insufficient evidence to convict you
on murder. It means you cannot be charged twice.
Do you think that it means you shouldn't be held
accountable for not acting immediately when Cru
held his breath? Do you think you should not be
held accountable for them not feeding for 20+ hours?
Do you think you are honourable in blaming me,
my sister and her husband? Do your consider
yourself a person with renewed and honourable
integrity?

What about the boys unveilings?
How dare you do it without me?
Not only do you become selfish, but you do this
to strike out at me? I have for 3 years asked
Mona & Stu & you & your family to get in touch
with me regarding their un-veiting.
Only to have 1 days notice that you all intended
to do and did hold a ceremony without me!
I extracted from your sister that you all planned
it without a mention. TXT, phoned all family members
except me, and you allowed it, didn't care for me.
I can barely describe the outrage, anger, hurt, sad
feelings I have. My thoughts are disgusted, petty,
selfish, spiteful people you all are and I hope you
are satisfied with your decision to do that to me.
It was intended to hurt me, and it has, but not
as much a losing them, bua burying them.

If I were given the opportunity to confront you with
my questions, I would comply to communicating
well, not in violence. If I had to, I would
hold you to answer every question I had,
I would accept all your answers however
I dont know or I can't remember is not acceptable.
For far too long you have hidden in the safety of
your family, always looking to them to rescue you.
I dare you to challenge yourself and for once
in your life FRONT UP to some of your
responsibilities. STOP blaming everyone else and
hold yourself accountable even if it's just at
basic levels.

This is my letter to you, full of things I've
wanted to ask and say to you
One day, I aspire to make this possible so
I may have piece of mind.

May

Letter to Chris Kahui, written in October 2010,
never sent as it was sub-judice

If you need help or know someone who does, here are a list of organisations you can contact

Women's Refuge, www.womensrefuge.org.nz 0800 733 843

Jigsaw Child Protection, www.jigsaw.org.nz

Parents Inc, www.parentsinc.org.nz, 0800 53 56 59

If you are in an emergency situation, call Police on 111

Badlands
NZ: A LAND FIT FOR
CRIMINALS

David Fraser
with forewords by
Theodore Dalrymple
& Garth McVicar

THE NEW BOOK THAT EXPLAINS WHY NEW ZEALAND'S
CRIME RATE HAS BECOME SO BAD...
Get it at a bookseller near you
howlingatthemoon.com